Situating social theory

Situating social theory

Tim May

Open University Press
Buckingham · Philadelphia

Open University Press
Celtic Court
22 Ballmoor
Buckingham
MK18 1XW

and
1900 Frost Road, Suite 101
Bristol, PA 19007, USA

First Published 1996

A catalogue record of this book is available from the British Library

ISBN   0 335 19286 6 (pbk)   0 335 19287 4 (hbk)

Library of Congress Cataloging-in-Publication Data
May, Tim, 1957–
    Situating social theory / Tim May.
        p.   cm.
    Includes bibliographical references and index.
    ISBN 0-335-19287-4 (hb). — ISBN 0-335-19286-6 (pb)
    1. Sociology—Philosophy. I. Title.
HM24.M299   1996
301'.01—dc20   96-23676
                                                                CIP

Typeset by Type Study, Scarborough
Printed in Great Britain by Biddles Ltd, Guildford and King's Lynn

Dedicated to my parents, Roy and Sue May

Contents

Section 4   Modernity under the microscope

Acknowledgements

This book is part of a project that I began about five years ago. It entailed a deliberate strategy to read widely, thus being exposed to a variety of ways of looking at the social world. In environments where specialization, which is as much about detailed knowledge as narrowness of focus, is promoted, this was not always an easy task. In this sense I owe thanks to a number of people who have helped me on this journey which, of course, has no end.

First, my thanks to the referees of the proposal on which this book was based. They blended both constructive criticism and support for this project – a rare combination. I wrote this book because I believe that both social theory and social research are of central importance for understanding social life. In this sense, I should mention those who have supported and encouraged me in different ways.

My thanks go to Dee for her support and to Calum for destroying the drafts with a complete indifference to my efforts, as well as to Cian for appearing in our lives near its completion. Also, my thanks go to Lyn, Malcolm, Tracey, Ken, Jill, Mel, Bob, Carole and Danny for their friendship and support. There are also those friends and colleagues who have been kind enough to read various parts of the book. My thanks therefore go to Eric Harrison, Steve Fuller, Steph Lawler, Elaine Pullen and Tony Spybey for their supportive and helpful comments. Further, Justin, Jacinta, Pat, Joan, Sue and Janet at Open University Press have all been supportive and helpful in various ways, as was Christine Firth in her role as copy-editor.

Finally, my thanks to those persons whom I have met in academia in particular, as well as social life in general. In watching their behaviour they have taught me that in order not to become someone you once disliked, it is important to seek the company of those who will let you know when you slip from the path of your own aspirations.

| Introduction

I sat facing a lengthy computer index of publications, with books and articles spread across the floor. I had written a proposal detailing the rationale and contents of this book, which was refereed by those who made both supportive and constructive comments. I then signed a contract and negotiated what I thought was an appropriate time for producing the final manuscript. Despite this, I still had this overwhelming body of literature in front of me, all of which appeared relevant to my task. Where was I to start?

Writing the book: aims and motivations

Placing all the books and articles aside, I switched off the computer and sat down to remind myself why I was writing the book in the first place. My aims are twofold. First, how does one make sense of the complicated nature of social theory? If you will forgive the metaphor, a life-jacket is needed which enables a committed reader to swim through a conceptual pool, or swamp, depending upon their perspective! The life-jacket should provide buoyancy and provide its wearer with the confidence to continue on their journey. One of my aims is to attempt to provide such a life-jacket.

My second aim is to convey the central importance of social theory for the disciplined study of society and social relations. As part of this, I wish to demonstrate the vitality and diversity of social thought. However, when a reader is faced with different ways of looking at similar issues, a confusion arises. This often stems from eosteric theoretical debates which appear to have no immediate relevance to enhancing understanding. Despite my enthusiasm for the subject, I have some sympathy with this position. On the other hand, social life is both complicated and varied and social theory simply reflects this state of affairs. The result being that I must tread a fine line between enabling understanding, avoiding confusion and rendering justice to the range of ideas which I shall cover. For this reason, I shall assume that the reader has some familiarity with this subject.

Clouding my aims are three features of social theory which render its study difficult. First, all theories are not simply neutral mediums of interpretation. They contain a 'persuasive' power which seeks to render their accounts either superior over, or different from, those of others. Second, as will become apparent, social theory not only seeks to account for the dynamics of society, but also reflects upon how knowledge about the social world is possible, as well as the nature of 'social reality' (questions of epistemology and ontology, respectively). Third, social theories vary according to the cultural and intellectual traditions under which they are conceived and from which they draw their inspiration.

As a result of these characteristics, its study can appear to be inward-looking, frustrating, narrow, inapplicable and its ideas incommensurable and unduly 'philosophical'. Nevertheless, to theorize is a practice which either reflects upon, or assumes, the nature of knowledge and ideas of human action and consciousness. This means that there is a fine line between philosophy and social theory; which, it should be added, is a characteristic of sciences in general (Gjertsen 1992; M. Williams and May 1996). Therefore, in order to situate social theory, an understanding of the history and relationship between philosophy and social theory, as well as its cultural antecedents, is required.

Reading the book: structure and content

To meet my aims, in view of the above characteristics, requires me to compartmentalize and select social theories in order that they are intelligible and comparable. This tactic, however, does not always render justice to their richness and diversity. To take three examples. There are overlaps between the works of 'critical' theorists, which I shall cover in Chapter 2 and the writings of Michel Foucault, as discussed in Chapter 9. There are works which have discussed an encounter between symbolic interactionism, covered in Chapter 3 and poststructuralism and postmodernism, covered in Chapters 9 and 10. Similarly, feminisms, which are discussed in Chapters 1, 2 and 8, have engaged with social theories in general. It follows that whilst I incorporate an understanding of these issues throughout the book, the reader should be aware of how the text is structured according to my aims and motivations. For this reason, I have deliberately included extensive references for those who have the time and motivation to take their studies on a journey where it becomes less possible to compartmentalize in this fashion.

The book itself is divided into two parts. The first part has two chapters and the second has eight chapters. Part I is called 'situating social theory'. This is designed as a 'springboard' into the second part because it is necessary to know the history and issues within social theory before examining various schools of thought which currently exist on its terrain. Therefore, it differs from conventional accounts because it is explicitly designed to provide the historical antecedents of ideas in Part II.

Chapter 1 is a historical tour of the development of social theory from the Enlightenment to the turn of the twentieth century. Chapter 2 then focuses upon the issues which have been raised during the twentieth century by examining seven traditions within social and philosophical thought; all of which have a bearing on the form and content of contemporary social theory. There is no simple line which can be drawn between these two chapters, but they raise issues which the theories and theorists in Part II have sought to tackle in a novel and detailed fashion.

The purpose of Part II is to provide an exposition of a number of contemporary ideas. Each chapter is divided into two sections. First, the development of the respective theories are examined by situating them within the dicussions contained in Part I of the book. Second, there is an examination of some of the issues which their ideas raise in order that a greater insight into their strengths and weaknesses may be achieved. Now to the actual content of these chapters.

Chapters 3 and 4 focus upon 'micro' theories due to their concern with the creation of the social world by individuals interacting with each other in everyday life. In this section, I have chosen to concentrate on two schools of thought: ethnomethodology and symbolic interactionism. I shall examine the underlying assumptions of these theories, as well as the criticisms which have emanated from other schools of thought and social thinkers: in particular, the works of Erving Goffman.

Chapters 5 and 6 examine the ideas of two leading social theorists who seek to tackle the dualism between action and structure. The first of these considers the writings of Anthony Giddens and what is known as 'structuration theory'. Here we find not only an adherence to the creative capacities of people, but also a notion of social structure in terms of its ability to both enable and constrain their actions. We might also say, from a different point of view, that we habitually and not always 'consciously' act in our everyday lives. In terms of this consideration, Chapter 6 is devoted to the work of Pierre Bourdieu, who achieves theoretical insight via the utilization of an extensive body of empirical research.

Chapters 7 and 8 cover those schools of thought or theorists who view society as sustained by systems of domination in various forms. Again, this is a heuristic device which does not render justice to all theories. Indeed, there are those who would regard any questioning about social life, as opposed to just taking-it-for-granted, as a critical act in itself. What is distinctive about these theories, however, is their intent. In one sense or another, they share a concern to explain the ways in which modern societies control and subordinate people for the purposes of 'other' group interests which are then reflected in social, political and economic relations.

Given this broad aim, Chapter 7 examines the work of the social theorist Jürgen Habermas, who sits within the tradition of critical theory. As will become apparent, Habermas has modified this tradition in significant respects. Nevertheless, as with social theory in general, Habermas is said to lack an adequate consideration of the role of women in society. It is for this reason that Chapter 8 is devoted to an understanding of feminist theories which, as will be noted throughout the book, challenge so much of the taken-for-granted notions upon which ideas and practices routinely draw.

Finally, Chapters 9 and 10 seek to encapsulate those schools of thought which have challenged the assumptions of modernity and the Enlightenment project. For this reason, there is an examination of the works of Michel Foucault in Chapter 9, whilst Chapter 10 considers the broad school of thought known as postmodernism.

Social theory is a rich, diverse and complicated subject which attracts as much, if not more, misunderstanding, as it does controversy. It is hoped that this book will contribute, in some way, to moving beyond this to show social theory for what it can be: that is, an important means of enhancing our understanding of social relations and explanations of society which should be challenging and challenged.

PART I

The development of social theory

PART I

The development of social theory

1

The Enlightenment and the development of social theory

Chapters 1 and 2 offer an historical overview of the themes which emerged in the development of social theory in order to situate current social theory in terms of its past influences. At the same time, it is noted that an injustice will be committed if the reader simply concludes that the writings of past social theorists are not still of importance in understanding our modern times.

In order to achieve this aim, these chapters situate the development of social theories within the different intellectual, political and cultural contexts in which they were produced. Underlying this approach are two points requiring emphasis. First:

> No social study that does not come back to the problems of biography, of history, and of their intersections within a society, has completed its intellectual journey.
>
> (Mills 1970: 12)

It follows that in situating social theory according to the context of its production, theorists are not viewed as disembodied from their theories, but implicated in their production through addressing the problematics of their time. Second, the works of these thinkers have not only acted as catalysts for current thought, but also structured its agenda. Their works enable theoretical discourse by operating to 'fix' prior debates which then facilitates theoretical discussion without recourse to continual elaboration. One such example being works on capitalism. These will either explicitly refer to, or be compared with, Karl Marx's (1818–83) original analysis (Alexander 1990).

A note of qualification at this point. The reader will not find a comprehensive history of social theory in the following pages. In the opening sentence to his study *Enlightenment and Despair*, Geoffrey Hawthorn writes: 'The sociologist who begins a history of social theories is at once very tempted to stop' (1976: 1). The selection of particular thinkers is a choice which faces anyone who writes on this subject – whatever the space or time available to them. Given the aims of this book, I make no apologies for this. However, the sources that I have used are fully referenced in order that a more detailed study of the rich and fascinating history of social theory is then available to the reader.

The Enlightenment: cultural changes and philosophical ideas

The 'Enlightenment' may be characterized as a catalyst for the development of particular styles of social thought. It does not represent a set of ideas which can be clearly demarcated, extracted and presented as a list of essential definitions, but represents a general shift in thought:

> In its simplest sense the Enlightenment was the creation of a new framework of ideas about man, society and nature, which challenged existing conceptions rooted in a traditional world-view, dominated by Christianity.
>
> (Hamilton 1992: 23)

These ideas, when fused with governmental practice, produced some core themes. First, a concept of freedom based upon an autonomous human subject who is capable of acting in a conscious manner. Second, the pursuit of a universal and foundational 'truth' gained through a correspondence of ideas with social and physical reality. Third, a belief in the natural sciences as the correct model for thinking about the social and natural world over, for example, theology and metaphysics. Fourth, the accumulation of systematic knowledge with the progressive unfolding of history. Collectively, these changes acted as catalysts and/or informed the scientific study of human societies. It follows, therefore, that they need to be considered in more detail before moving on to examine the development of social theory in differing contexts. For this purpose, there follows a brief examination of these cultural transformations and philosophical ideas.

Cultural transformations: the emergence of modernity

The power and relevance of these cultural shifts cannot be underestimated:

> I believe that we are all to a greater or lesser extent children of the Enlightenment, and that it is from this standpoint that civilized

members of Western society – the heirs to a humane tradition more than two centuries old – almost necessarily judge the political and social movements of their own time.

(S. H. Hughes 1979: 27)

Even postmodernists, who challenge the dominance and assumptions of modernism, are forced to engage with it for it permeates our contemporary ideas and practices. To paraphrase Marshall Berman (1993), we cannot ignore or turn away from it, for it is the only world that we have. This is the world which became an object of inquiry for the social sciences. Emerging modes of political practice, however, contained within them both positive and negative elements.

In negative terms, the *Western Intellectual Tradition* (Bronowski and Mazlish 1970) may be characterized as one which invokes assumptions which are assumed to be applicable to all societies, or through which 'other' people may be evaluated according to its dominant intellectual, political, social and economic standards. William Du Bois (1868–1963), an American social theorist, recognized this 'double-edge' to its force and for this reason worked towards a multi-cultural social theory which would not exclude whole groups of people via its unexamined assumptions (Du Bois 1989). As Rattansi and Westwood put it:

> Issues around racism are crucially implicated in the question mark over Western modernity, for another side of this modernity has been its close involvement with, indeed its legitimation of, Western genocide against aboriginal peoples, slavery, colonial domination and exploitation, and the Holocaust, in all of which Western doctrines of 'racial' and cultural superiority have played a constitutive role.
>
> (Rattansi and Westwood 1994: 3)

In general terms, battle lines have now been drawn between the defenders of the project of 'modernity' or 'enlightenment' (Habermas 1992a), its detractors (Baudrillard 1983; Lyotard 1984) and those thinkers who, through their historical and philosophical excavations, have questioned the comfortable certitudes upon which modern practices and ideas have based themselves (Derrida 1978; Foucault 1992). In the following history of social theory, we will also find those thinkers who regarded modernity as an opportunity (Comte, Marx and Durkheim) and those who were more ambivalent in their evaluations (Montesquieu, Weber and Simmel).

When did these changes start? We cannot state a time at which the Enlightenment and what has been called 'the modern age' or 'modernity' began:

> How old is modernity? is a contentious question. There is no agreement on dating. There is no consensus on what is to be dated. And

once the effort of dating starts in earnest, the object itself begins to disappear.

(Bauman 1991: 3)

We still need some idea of its genesis. These broad changes have been examined in two ways. First, through the history of ideas, and second, through examining transformations in social practices. In terms of the former, Kroker and Cook (1988) have travelled back to the work of the theologian Augustine (354–430) whom they describe as 'the Columbus of modern experience' (1988: 37). They argue that modernity is characterized as the search for a 'theory of representation' whereby it becomes possible to explain a variety of human experiences in different contexts. Augustine placed this in question:

> To suggest a historical thesis, it is our position that Augustine was the first postmodern thinker. . . . Refusing the alternatives of rationalism and materialism, or tragic idealism and dogmatic scepticism, Augustine demonstrated the fatal flaw in enlightenment modernism: its absence of a directly experienced creative principle which could serve to unify the warring tendencies in Western experience. . . . When enlightenment returns in the seventeenth century, it reawakens the fatal flaw in Western metaphysics, and thus experience, which Augustine had laid to rest for a period of eleven centuries.

(Kroker and Cook 1988: 28)

In terms of social practices Toynbee (1954) saw the emergence of a 'modern age' in the ways of life of European people on the Atlantic coast in the fifteenth century, whilst Marshall Berman (1988) argues that there are three historical periods to modernity. The first being from the sixteenth to eighteenth centuries, the second being with the French Revolution and the accompanying rapid changes in social and political life, and the third giving rise to a 'world culture of modernism' with its growing turmoil and uncertainty.

Shifting this emphasis towards the experiential aspects of modernity has witnessed one nineteenth-century writer describing it as: 'ephemeral, fugitive, contingent' (Baudelaire quoted in D. Sayer 1991: 9). This continues into the twentieth century with Michel Foucault (1926–84) describing it as more of an 'attitude' which informs practices, rather than any actual period of history:

> And by 'attitude', I mean a mode of relating to contemporary reality; a voluntary choice made by certain people; in the end, a way of thinking and feeling; a way, too, of acting and behaving that at one and the same time marks a relation of belonging and presents itself as a task.

(Foucault 1984: 39)

This experiential focus also permits a comparison between 'discontinuities' in contemporary social institutions and their effects on daily lives, with traditional social orders which are seen to have represented both stability and continuity (Giddens 1990).

In these attempts to pinpoint a meaning for and genesis of modernity, one of the central characteristics of the debate appears to be 'the extent to which key terms have evaded clarification' (Smart 1990: 16). Nevertheless, there remains a relationship between emerging ideas in this period and the development of social thought.

Philosophical ideas: catalyst to the Enlightenment project

The journey begins with Immanuel Kant (1724–1804). Kant added power to the search for a universal truth through his inheritance of two philosophical traditions: rationalism and empiricism. Rationalism was represented by the work of Descartes (1596–1650).

Using a method of doubt, Descartes asked how it is that people 'know' that the knowledge they possess is true? After all, people disagree over experiencing the same thing: to one person a plate may be hot, to another only warm. Further, it is often difficult to tell the difference between dreams and reality – a recurring dream can eventually come to seem like reality itself. As such, the senses distort reality. Therefore, how can social or physical reality be known with any degree of certainty? The basis for knowledge is *reason*. As experiences play tricks on the mind, they cannot be considered a satisfactory foundation for knowledge. However, as long as the individual believes that they are 'something', then an 'I' can be said to exist. This is a basic 'truth' and the foundation for knowledge (see Doney 1967). To put it into its famous phrase, only one statement can be made with any degree of certainty: 'I think, therefore I am' ('*cogito, ergo sum*').

Kant was also influenced by the idea that knowledge of the social and physical worlds is gained through experience. One of the most famous thinkers in this school of thought (known as *empiricism*) was the Scottish philosopher David Hume (1711–76). Hume drew a distinction between 'impressions' and 'ideas'. The former, he argued, have more influence upon understanding. Whilst complex ideas do not necessarily resemble impressions – a mermaid may be imagined without necessarily having seen one – the parts that make up complex ideas are themselves derived from impressions and impressions, in their turn, from experience. It is from a multitude of experiences in social life that ideas are then derived (see Chappell 1968).

Kant's resultant fusion of reason and empiricism is highly complex. For the purposes of this journey, what is of importance is that his work contains a *focus imaginarius* as a 'built in feature of the human mind'. This is concerned with '*absolute* truth, *pure* art and humanity *as such*' (Rorty 1989: 195–196, original italics). Freedom is derived from an individualism which regards human subjects as autonomous and transcendental through the exercise of reason. In this way, a link is established between scientific knowledge and moral rules (each governed by 'laws'):

> Everything in nature works according to laws. Only a rational being has the capacity of acting according to the conception of laws, i.e. according to principles. This capacity is will. Since reason is required for the derivations of actions from laws, will is nothing else than practical reason.
>
> (Kant quoted in Albrow 1987: 167–168)

Kant concluded that the material world causes sensations, but mental apparatuses order these and provide the concepts through which people understand their experiences in the 'phenomenal' world (the 'noumenal' world being beyond experience). Out of this fusion of ideas comes an ability to reflect upon nature and society in a rational manner:

> Rational mastery of nature and society presupposed knowledge of the truth, and the truth was a universal, as contrasted to the multi-fold appearance of things or to their immediate form in the perception of individuals. This principle was already alive in the earliest attempts of Greek epistemology: the truth is universal and necessary and thus contradicts the ordinary experiences of change and accident.
>
> (Marcuse 1969: 17)

Reason is the guarantor of universal knowledge. Add to this the Cartesian claim of a universal standard against which truth could be objectively measured, independent of the objects of scientific inquiry, then the Enlightenment comes to represent an ascending history of the scientific colonization over 'valid' knowledge. This requires that 'other' forms of knowledge are supplanted in the quest for objectivity, defined as

> the basic conviction that there is or must be some permanent, ahistorical matrix or framework to which we can ultimately appeal in determining the nature of rationality, knowledge, truth, reality, goodness, or rightness.
>
> (Bernstein 1983: 8)

Equipped with reason, scientists could emerge as the legislators, not simply the interpreters of knowledge concerning the social and physical worlds (Bauman 1987). Science could establish the difference between 'truth' and 'falsity'. Via Kant's *a priori* categories of thought, the individual could make sense of their empirical world and the worlds of culture and nature become distinguishable:

> As a result, the individual (not only the Cartesian mind) emerged as the subject, as subject of the world. Experiencing the world, the individual

could claim to have a transcendental source of certainty within himself. He could set out to realize himself by realizing the world within himself.

(Luhmann 1986: 317)

We now have a combination of influences with which to contextualize social theory. However, these were interpreted according to different political and intellectual cultures. These diluted, modified and challenged these insights. It is to an understanding of this process to which I now turn.

The development of social theory

Society: an object of study

In Italy, there was a social theorist who was already anticipating three trends that were to emerge in the nineteenth century. First, an interest in the nature of social development and social origins. Second, the merging of history and philosophy into a 'science of society'. Third, the attempt to discover rational-empirical causes for social phenomena in place of metaphysical or theological ones (Bottomore and Nisbet 1979a: 563).

Giambattista Vico (1668–1744) was no friend of the dominant ideas of his time, particularly Cartesianism. Perhaps for this reason he was little understood or read in his own time. Nevertheless, Vico had an influence on later thinkers such as Auguste Comte (1798–1857), Robert Michels (1876–1936) and Georges Sorel (1847–1922). His argument was that social theory should be centred around a human subject whose actions could be understood only in relation to the whole of society. In other words, the individual could not be abstracted from their social context. People were social creatures whose feelings came from their socio-cultural environment. These feelings were 'sensory topics' which

provide the 'roots' of a 'civil society'; they constitute the shared sense (*sensus communis*) which arises among a social group who already share a set of circumstances – and it is against the background of such feelings as these that any conceptualization of what we take our human nature to be can be judged for its adequacy.

(Shotter 1993: xiii–xiv, original italics)

In England at this time, an inspiration for feminist ideas was apparent in the writings of Mary Astell (1668–1731) and later, Mary Wollstonecraft (1759–97). In 1694 Astell wrote *A Serious Proposal to the Ladies* (Rogers 1979). Differences between the sexes were not attributed to some un-examined idea of 'nature' or 'reason', upon which so many thinkers had drawn from the Greeks onwards (Griffiths and Whitford 1988; P. Johnson 1993; Okin 1980), but to the power that men held over women in society. If

Descartes has proclaimed reason in all, then it must also be available to women:

> It was this notion that the feminists seized upon so avidly. Mary Astell boldly proclaimed the radical thesis that God had given all mankind the same intellectual potential – whether ancient or modern, rich or poor, male or female. Circumstances determine the extent to which men and women may exercise their rational faculties, but the faculties are present in all.
>
> (Kinnaird 1983: 34)

Nearly one hundred years later, in 1792, Wollstonecraft (1989) called for women to enjoy the changes occurring within society. In the spirit of modernity she argued that women should aspire to the realm of reason over that of pleasing men's desires; a relationship which serves to reinforce their subordination. These tensions between reason and emotion forms, as we shall see in chapter 2, a central part of the feminist critique of social theory.

In Scotland the so-called 'Scottish School' of Adam Ferguson (1723–1816), John Millar (1735–1801), David Hume and Adam Smith (1723–90), centred around Edinburgh, contributed to the 'Scottish Enlightenment'. This group added to the idea that society was an object of study, with its own underlying properties, which should be examined through observation. Like Vico, they saw a link between social context and human actions. Hume characterized society in terms of customs and between social customs and ideas a link may be discovered. Overall, Hume's work may be seen in terms of the dissection of human nature in order that he might advance the understanding of history: 'In this sense, Hume's thinking was totally secular and empirical' (Heilbron 1995: 102).

In the case of Ferguson, it was the study of groups which formed the basis of his ideas. Indeed, he regarded conflict as a characteristic of society long before later 'conflict' theorists such as Max Weber (1864–1920) and Georg Simmel (1858–1918). Further, his ideas on the division of labour predated those of Marx and Emile Durkheim (1858–1917). In Ferguson's view, the increased division of labour which came with modernity possessed the potential for progress, as well as to threaten social stability.

Although more rationalist in orientation than England or Scotland, French social theorists incorporated the challenge to rationalist epistemology from empiricism. However, the individualism of Descartes and Kant, when fused with the experiences of the French Revolution, were not a sufficient basis for a cohesive social order. Diverse as the ideas of French Scholars became, these influences led to the emergence of some core themes:

> Instead of a God-ordained society they spoke of reason; instead of regarding sin as inherent in man, they pinned their faith to human perfectibility and believed that education could remould the human

personality; instead of the privileges of the different orders, they insisted upon egalitarianism.

(Beloff 1954: 176)

One of the main representatives of this tradition was Montesquieu (1689–1755). His main concern was with human freedom and how government could be most efficiently organized to secure it. As with Vico, he was interested in the connections between people's opinions and the nature and structure of society. In the process, people were viewed

> not as a multitude of individuals under one government, but as a community distinguishable from others by their manners and institutions. All institutions, political, religious, domestic, economic, and artistic, are, in his eyes, intricately related to one another, so that any considerable change in one is bound to affect the others.
>
> (Plamenatz 1963: 256)

Through systematic study, Montesquieu wished to see how, in ways previously unsuspected, society forms people as 'social creatures'. At the same time, he did not view society in terms of progressive development, but one of advances and set-backs in the path to liberty and all that was 'good'. This distinguishes his thought from the Enlightenment idea of progress found in the work of Comte. Where Comte emphasized unity, Montesquieu remained aware of diversity.

In Comte's time the climate of opinion was more favourable to new ideas than it was for Montesquieu (Bierstedt 1979). Indeed, Comte is a central figure in the intellectual lineage of structuralism. This may be characterized in terms of: 'the relation is more important than the parts' (Bottomore and Nisbet 1979a: 558). This places structuralism at odds with the individualistic emphasis of other socio-theoretical traditions; in particular, those in nineteenth-century England.

Comte was to embrace the positive-rationalist idea of social progress, together with a belief in the scientific method for the purposes of studying and reconstructing the social, political and economic spheres of human life. Such was his faith in Positive Philosophy, which he learnt through his work with Saint-Simon (1760–1825), that he refused to read newspapers or books which had a bearing on his work; all part of his system of 'cerebral hygiene' (Bosanquet 1967). He was, therefore, a pioneer of positivism which

> in its classical nineteenth-Century form is an empiricist interpretation and systematisation of the sciences combined with a general theory of history and society which can be understood as theoretical articulation of a definite set of political problems.
>
> (Benton 1977: 28)

In this way Comte added power to one of the central pillars of the Enlightenment: that is, the superseding of metaphysical and theological thought by science. This rejection of speculative thought placed sociology, as the highest science, firmly within the natural scientific paradigm. His view of 'social physics', with its theme of social statics (the science of order) and social dynamics (the science of progress), rejected the idea that social elements existed in separation from one another. As such, the individual subject could not exist separately from the society of which they were a part:

> there must always be a spontaneous harmony between the whole and the parts of the social system, the elements of which must inevitably be, sooner or later, combined in a mode entirely comfortable to their nature.
>
> (Comte in Parsons *et al.* 1965: 126–127)

This torch of positivism was taken up and held in different ways in the works of the English utilitarian philosopher John Stuart Mill (1807–73) and the social theorist Herbert Spencer (1820–1903), both of whom were influenced by the political culture of English individualism. Mill developed his positivism based on the idea that although society was constantly changing, human nature was itself fixed. The task of social science became to explain observations and construct social laws as deduced from a constant human nature. In the case of Spencer, he held an evolutionary view of society through combining a radical individualism with a collectivist organicism – as derived from biology – of society's social structures and institutions. Contrast the following with the quote from Comte above:

> Society is made up of individuals; all that is done in society is done by the combined actions of individuals; and therefore, in individual actions only can be found in solutions of social phenomena.
>
> (Spencer 1969: 49)

Spencer was widely read in Victorian England, probably due to the support his ideas gave to the individualism of *laissez-faire* capitalism. This system of economic exchange was then provided with an intellectual legitimacy for its functioning, promises and effects. The same could hardly be said of a contemporary of Spencer's: Karl Marx.

Modernity: from historical consciousness to capitalism

In Comte's positivism and structuralism there is a 'philosophy of history' (P. Burke 1980). Each of the aspects in his work – the unfolding of history, the condemnation of individualism, a belief in science and progress towards more enlightened times – are also characteristics of Marx. Here, however, the parallels end. Marx's ideas were formed through the influences of Saint-Simon, but also in his encounters with the German idealist philosopher Georg Hegel (1770–1831) and with what are known as the 'English political economists' (see Barber 1981).

In terms of tracing the twists and turns of the Enlightenment, it is the influence of Hegel which forms an important part of the background to Marx's work:

> His belief in history . . . more than anything else, distinguishes him from his predecessors and above all from Kant . . . Reality is to be understood in becoming and therefore in history. For Hegel the dialectical process, in which truth came from the coming together of opposing views, was only the mirror of a dialectical process in reality.
>
> (Lindsay 1967: 58)

People become viewed as historical beings, not philosophical abstractions. Nevertheless, where Hegel was to emphasize consciousness, Marx was to emphasize actual human existence in given social situations. For Marx it was not ideas which formed society but, on the contrary, the actual material conditions under which people lived. Marx came to consider the 'dialectic of history' in opposing terms to Hegel. To understand this it is first necessary to consider Hegel's work in some more depth. It is not easy, but here we go!

For Hegel reason could become manifest in history. History unfolds in a dialectic from thesis and antithesis to a synthesis. Two Enlightenment ideals are worth noting here: progress and freedom from an external world. Human 'being' must be defined, not in terms of something external to people, but in ways which depend upon an internal relation within and between each other. This is where his concept of 'mind' and its historical unfolding towards self-consciousness enters.

The Phenomenology of Mind (Hegel 1967a) is a study of how minds appear to themselves (phenomenology being the study of how things appear to people). Kant had argued that reality could never be known as it was, but only comprehended through the *a priori* categories of thought (space, time and causation). These are not part of reality, but the means through which it is grasped. Kant thus started with the idea of a 'reality' and 'that knowledge is some kind of instrument or medium by which we grasp reality' (Singer 1983: 50). This presupposes a difference between human beings and the reality they inhabit. Despite this, knowledge is still regarded as being part of reality. The question remains, however, as to how reality can be known by people, given their separation from it?

The Kantian answer to this question is that the instruments through which people seek to gain a knowledge of reality must be known. It is this which forms the basis of Hegel's critique of Kant's epistemology:

> We ought, says Kant, to become acquainted with the instrument, before we undertake the work for which it is to be employed; for if the instrument be insufficient, all our trouble will be spent in vain . . . But the examination of knowledge can only be carried out by an act of knowledge. To examine this so-called instrument is the same thing as to know it. But to seek to know before we know is as absurd as the wise

resolution of Scholasticus, not to venture into the water until he had learned to swim.

(Hegel quoted in Singer 1983: 51)

The starting-point for knowing reality is now consciousness of that reality. Upon examination, the limitations of consciousness may be discovered. This will enable the development of a more sophisticated form of consciousness and so on . . . until 'absolute knowledge' is reached. Therefore, it is not necessary to be content with a Kantian 'appearance of reality'. Instead, knowledge can be gained of reality itself, for Hegel regards knowledge as historically constituted. 'Being' is linked with history and the 'Real' is the 'Rational':

> History is the substance of society, since the substance of society is nothing more than continuity. Humanity's being therefore lies in its historicity.

(Heller 1984: 28)

Hegel then links this with politics (Hegel 1967b). For clarity of exposition, we can say that the 'idea' or 'ideal' is to realize our potential in reality. This is freedom from a bond with nature through the development of self-consciousness. However, as people are socially constituted (the development of our personalities is a societal, not individual matter for Hegel), there must be a relation between our internal consciousness and the external sphere of the society which we inhabit. In other words, there must be a social means through which we are recognized as 'free agents'. The means is 'possession' and its social manifestation is 'property' (see Ryan 1986). Yet there must be some regulatory relation between the seeking of individual ends and the wider society in order that it is maintained and reasonably stable. Aside from property, an answer to how this relationship is achieved is found in Hegel's writings on the State.

The State is seen as a fusion between self-consciousness and the manner in which it is objectively manifested in social, political and economic relations. The rights of the individual and universal reason can thereby be united and the social problems created by a competitive society tempered. What Hegel termed 'civil society' can be moderated by this higher unity. Its absence would exacerbate a tendency towards what he called an 'alienation of the spirit': that is, the duality within people to regard their freedom as freedom from the constraints of the material world and to strive to be purely spiritual whilst, at the same time, recognizing that they are part of that world and thus cannot escape from it, nor transcend it.

To finally link Hegel to Marx we must do so via the work of Ludwig Feuerbach (1804–72). Feuerbach was a 'Young Hegelian' who examined 'religion' and 'God', but in so doing adopted a position opposed to Hegel. Broadly speaking, he argued that God was a creation of human beings and not the other way round. Marx also reversed Hegel's idealism, but as applied to the State. As people had created God, so they had created the State. Hegel argued that social relations were dependent upon the 'Idea of the State' manifested in reason. Marx, on the other hand, argued that consciousness did not create institutions, but the material conditions under which people actually lived: 'With me . . . the ideal is nothing else than the material world reflected by the human mind, and translated into forms of thought' (Marx 1983: 29):

> Marx reached the conclusion that it was not spiritual attitudes, but external conditions, the wealth men enjoyed or lacked, the ways they had to labour, which shaped society. Epochs were controlled not by conceptions of man but by material ends and means. The ruling interests and difficulty of men was relating to the *world*, not to the *self*.
> (G. A. Cohen 1984: 22, original italics)

The explanation for civil society is now found in the material conditions of social life. History was not the unfolding of a 'dialectic of spirit', but a dialectic resulting from changes in the means of production. This is the guiding thread of Marx's social theory:

> In the social production of their life, men enter into definite relations that are indispensable and independent of their will, relations of production which correspond to a definite stage of development of their material productive forces. The sum total of these relations of production constitutes the economic structure of society, the real foundation, on which rises a legal and political superstructure and to which correspond definite forms of social consciousness.
> (Marx 1980: 181)

Given this, Marx was critical of philosophy in terms of both Hegel's idealism and Feuerbach's materialism (Marx 1961; 1964). Social theory now needs to explain the context of people's actions so that thought and practice can fuse in what he termed *praxis*. The scientific validity of this theory rests upon its capacity not only to explain social life, but also to change it.

To achieve these aims Marx had to embark upon an empirical examination of capitalism, as well as a critique of the economic theory which provided for its legitimacy. Political economy, which assumed the existence of private property, did so without explaining the cause of the division between labour and capital in the first instance. Economic exchange is not some 'accidental fact': 'The only wheels which political economy sets in motion are *greed* and the *war amongst the greedy* – competition' (Marx 1981: 62, original italics). In a similar way, society, the state and social relations are not manifestations of some 'spirit', but of the ways in which people organize their societies on the basis of the means of production (the 'base'). This, in turn, structures all other relations within society (the superstructure). Labour and the need to sell labour to capital, for the extraction of surplus value, in order to survive, oils the capitalist machine to the benefit of the few, not the many. Although Hegel was correct to connect 'being' to social relations and to restore history and meaning to the human realm, he was wrong to view this in terms of something called 'will'. For Marx, the implications of this position were clear:

> What is society, whatever its form may be? The product of men's reciprocal action. Are men free to choose this or that form of society? By no means. Assume a particular state of development in the production faculties of man and you will get a particular form of commerce and consumption. Assume particular stages of development in production, commerce and consumption and you will have a corresponding social constitution.
>
> (Marx to Annenkov 28 December 1846, in
> Marx and Engels 1953: 40)

Alienation also has a different origin. Hegel's outstanding achievement was to see the connection between self and social environment, but he was wrong to see labour only in terms of 'mental' labour. People are distinguished from all other living things through their ability to produce, but in a manner which takes account of their needs. They create through their labour, but capitalism, as a system of production, is dehumanizing. People become alienated from each other and the world in which they live through the use of their labour by a system which expropriates and abstracts it from their daily lives. Nor is private property the affirmation of self-development, but its very denial. The link between 'being in society' and the system under which people live is now established in a material, not idealist sense:

> What Marx saw as capitalism's most basic contradiction, between its increasingly social productive forces and its enduringly privatized mode of appropriation, reaches deep: into our selves. Modernity constitutes individuals as subjects not through but in opposition to the real sociality which concretely defines and differentiates them.
>
> (D. Sayer 1991: 72)

Capitalism now defines the character of modernity and capital becomes: 'the demiurge of the modern world' (D. Sayer 1991: 12). Marx noted how the division of labour 'seizes upon, not only the economic, but every other sphere of society'. It provides, at the expense of everything else, an 'all engrossing system of specialising and sorting men' (Marx 1983: 334). In this analysis, there was the potential for change. The end point of history is not self-consciousness, but communism. Here, co-operation and freedom from alienation would exist.

Despite the power of Marx's argument two questions, in particular, remain. First, how is capitalist society to be condemned, if it also contains within it the seeds for a better future? As Alisdair MacIntyre puts it: 'if the moral impoverishment of advanced capitalism is what so many Marxists agree that it is, whence are these resources for the future to be derived' (1985: 262)? This has led to a number of debates over the relationship between Marxism and morality (see Lukes 1985; McLellan and Sayers 1990). Second, does Marx's work inevitably imply the need for revolution, or could a better society be obtained through revisionism?

Attempts to answer these questions have moved through a myriad of ideas, which include the work of critical analysis to help the demise of capitalism on its way (Lukács 1971). In the case of the 'revisionist-controversy', this was sparked by the writings of Bernstein, leading to a debate involving key Marxist figures at the turn of the twentieth century: for example, Kautsky, Luxemburg and Hilferding (see Laclau and Mouffe 1990). Four schools of thought then emerged within Marxist thought: the orthodox school; the revisionist school; the Austro-Marxists and Lenin and the Bolsheviks (Bottomore 1979). All of which leads to a rich history of Marxist thought (see Kolakowski 1978a; 1978b).

The use of Marx's work to come to terms with the nature of modernity and its propensity for change is a continual feature of social and political thought. In terms of our immediate journey, when it comes to an absence of a consideration of the ethical realm in social life, over the predominance of the economic realm, we find one social theorist who, like many European social thinkers at the turn of the twentieth century, was looking for new sources of inspiration. As S. H. Hughes puts it regarding this phenomenon:

> in asking themselves whether Marxism could properly be considered a science, they were inevitably led to pose the further question of what one meant by a science of society and the extent to which such a body of scientific knowledge was attainable at all.
>
> (S. H. Hughes 1979: 73–74)

Modernity: ethics and social integration

As we have seen, for Comte, societal development was governed by social laws. With Hegel, history was conceived of in terms of the progress of the mind, with an ultimate dialectical progression towards self-consciousness. For Marx, history was seen in terms of progress but, in an inversion of Hegel's idealism, then theorized in terms of the actions of people in concrete social situations. When it comes to the work of Emile Durkheim, however, he was to emphasize the ethical aspects of social life. In Durkheim's hands, morality was to become a defining characteristic of modern society that expresses its collectively held needs.

Durkheim's intellectual legacy was Montesquieu, Comte and Spencer, not Hegel and English political economy. There is also the political context in which he lived. As with Comte before him, this was a time of considerable change in France. Whereas for Comte it was the legacy of the French Revolution, for Durkheim it was events such as the Dreyfus Affair, defeat in the Franco-Prussian War (1870–1) and the German annexation of Alsace-Lorraine. Here is a writer who has been characterized as an idealist, a materialist, a social realist and a neo-Kantian (Lukes 1981). His social theory has been seen as a link between French conservatism and systematic sociology (Nisbet 1970: 13), as well as there now being critical' and 'radical' interpretations of his work (Gane 1992; Pearce 1989). Despite these contradictory interpretations, there is one thing that can be said about Durkheim's work with certainty: in his hands, social theory and in particular, sociology, were to receive major boosts.

Durkheim's work was organized around three goals. First, the establishment of sociology as a scientific discipline. Second, the foundation of a basis for the unity and unification of the social sciences. Third, the provision of an empirical, rational and systematic basis for modern society's civil religion (Tiryakian 1979). Together with French intellectual figures such as Le Play, Proudhon and Comte, Durkheim contributed to the development of a normative social theory which sought to integrate morality and economic life for the purpose of social stability. This was a key feature of the liberal left in French social thought, translating into the political question as to how the traditional structures of society were to be incorporated and adapted to fit these new emergent forms? In terms of his third goal, his work may thus be characterized as contributing to the moral integration of the Third Republic. Aside from those already mentioned, what were the influences on his work towards this end?

First there were the rigorous historical methods of Gabriel Monod and Fustel de Coulanges (Lukes 1981: 58–65). To this can be added the influence of the German social thinker Albert Schäffle and his idea of society as an 'organism'. However, whilst defending Schäffle's socialism against the charge that it was collectivist and authoritarian, the idea of an organism was a metaphorical, not literal device. On this Durkheim was clear. Society is not a set of material relations in the sense in which an organism is governed 'mechanically', but it is a set of relationships of ideas which neither are reducible to the persons who make up that society, nor can be separated from them.

In his encounters with socialism, Durkheim was always to emphasize morality over economics. This stemmed from the need to find

> a substitute for traditional Christian teachings, so as to legitimate itself and win the broader support of new generations of schoolchildren, wrestling them away from the moral authority of the Catholic church.
>
> (Tiryakian 1979: 195)

Without a moral basis for society, France would represent, as it had in the First and Second Republics, the exercise of power in the hands of one person, with the alternative being anarchy as manifested in a proletarian uprising. The solution to this problem lay in a rational and systematic inquiry into the causes, consequences and conditions for social order.

In this quest, Kant was to be an important inspiration, but this was Kant mediated not through the works of Hegel, but through the writings of Renouvier. Renouvier was a thinker from whose philosophy, it has been claimed, no less than the political culture of the Third Republic was derived (Lukes 1981: 55). His concerns were then reflected in Durkheim's writings:

> his uncompromising rationalism; his central concern with morality and his determination to study it 'scientifically'; his neo-Kantianism emphasising the compatibility of the determinism of nature with the freedom presupposed by morality; his Kantian concern with the dignity and autonomy of the individual together with his theory of social cohesion based on the individual's sense of unity with and dependence on others; his preference for justice over utility and denial that the first can be derived from the second; his notion of existing society being in a state of war and his view of the State's role being to establish 'social justice' in the economic sphere.
>
> (Lukes 1981: 55)

Renouvier was critical of Kant's idea that experience was given via the *a priori* categories of thought. Instead, as in the works of Vico, Montesquieu and Marx, what if reason and categories of thought are not given *a priori*, but produced socially? From a structuralist vantage point, a change in the structures of society would then mean an alteration in experiences. This emphasis was to form a central pillar of Durkheim's social theory whereby the philosophical, sociological and political fuse.

Durkheim's 'sociological epistemology' would allow him to derive a new approach to ethics that would be capable of providing a basis for stability in times of change. Accepting that people are rational and 'free', rationality would be exercised through the construction of laws applicable to all. Society would then be the transcendental source and not universal reason as such. Society would possess an authority not only because it transcended each individual, but also because it was also contained within them. It therefore possessed a two-fold source of morality:

> It was a set of facts-in-the-world from which correct moral inferences could be made and it was the authority for moral judgements.
>
> (Hawthorn 1976: 121)

Together with his nephew Marcel Mauss (1872–1950), Durkheim saw sociology as the correct means for deriving moral forms within society. From a political point of view he argued for a harmony between the individual and the State and against the utilitarian individualism of Spencer and others. For Durkheim, this would result in what the philosopher Thomas Hobbes (1588–1679) referred to as the 'war of all against all'. At the same time, he defended the individual against large impersonal institutions. For instance, in a review of Merlino's *Formes et essences du socialisme* he argued that the State, if it is to remain 'normal', should be moderated by autonomous, restricted groups: for example, professional associations. He takes up Merlino's assertion that the individual and the State are necessarily antagonistic to each other:

> Nothing could be more contrived than this so-called antagonism, the idea of which Merlino is quite wrong to borrow from orthodox economics. The truth is that the State has been quite the opposite – the liberator of the individual. It is the State which, as it grew stronger, freed the individual from private and local groups which tended to absorb him: the family, the city, the corporation, etc.
>
> (Durkheim 1992: 57)

A series of sociological questions were then generated on the relationship between the individual and society. For instance, in the Preface to the first edition of *The Division of Labour in Society* Durkheim writes:

> This work has its origins in the question of the relation of the individual to social solidarity. Why does the individual, while becoming more autonomous, depend more upon society? How can he be at once more individual and more solidary?
>
> (Durkheim 1964: 37)

The moral dimension to social life continually returns in his work. For instance, in the increasing division of labour, as represented in the transition from mechanical to organic solidarity, we find that the emergence of modernity leads to a greater recognition of a need for each other. This 'togetherness' 'was the coming thing, rather than something which we were losing' (Gellner 1988: 30). The *laissez-faire* ideal would not bring peace to people and Durkheim viewed Marx as sharing this economistic approach to social life which ignored the moral dimension and the 'fact' that the division of labour not only limits people's activity, but also increases it (Durkheim 1964: 305). Indeed, in comparing their writings on anomie and alienation we can say that: 'Social constraint is for Marx a denial and for Durkheim a condition of human freedom and self-realization' (Lukes 1967: 142). Through employing Darwin's (1809–82) ideas, he reconciles a greater population density without an exacerbation of social conflict. An increased specialization of labour is argued to counteract the tendency towards conflict, as it enables coexistence in the performance of different services, yet in parallel to each other (Durkheim 1964: 266–267).

The balance between autonomy and togetherness is actuated through 'moral individualism'. The source of this is Christianity; Protestantism to be more exact:

> Since for the Christian, virtue and piety do not consist in material procedures, but interior states of the soul, he is compelled to exercise a perpetual watch over himself . . . Thus of the two possible poles of thought, nature on the one hand, and man on the other, it is necessarily

around the second that the thought of Christian societies has come to gravitate.

(Durkheim quoted in Giddens 1971: 115–116)

Comte was thus criticized for calling for a return to traditional times. The march of individualism could not be stopped and a new bridging system was required between the individual and society. Durkheim was clearly aware of the tensions which existed between pre-modern and modern forms of society. His belief in the *potential* harmonic position between the individual and society has frequently been stressed over the tensions he saw within society: for example, he has been characterized as a consensus theorist, in contrast to the conflict ideas of Marx, Weber and Simmel. Yet a motor of societal progress is expressed in terms of anomie, whilst he notes the role of desire and feeling in human relations, in contrast to the usual neo-Kantian readings of his work.

This emphasis on desire and feeling leads into the writings of the German philosopher Schopenhauer (1788–1860), who wrote on the 'will' and 'irrationalism' in social thought. Progress is seen in his work not as the triumph of reason, but as the furtherance of the power of the 'will'. After all, myths, habits and rituals should not, as both Veblen (1857–1929) and Freud (1856–1939) recognized, be simply dismissed as irrelevant or uninteresting in the study of social life. If this reading of Durkheim is accepted, he recognized the tensions in modernity between will and reason. Is it this which gave rise to his desire to find a new basis for social solidarity in the France of his day, without recourse to the egoistic tendencies in modern Western societies. A socially-derived reason might just then be triumphant over the increasing 'barbarism' which characterizes the modern world (Meštrović 1993).

At this point we can make a link here from Durkheim to another leading social theorist: Max Weber. Schopenhauer influenced Friedrich Nietzsche (1844–1900) who refused the Hegelian revision of a philosophy of history. In so doing: 'He renounces a renewed revision of the concept of reason and *bids farewell* to the dialectic of enlightenment' (Habermas 1992a: 86, original italics). The influence of Nietzsche is to be found in the writings of Weber.

Modernity: the forward march of rationalization

For Weber there are no historical laws, or any resolution of history through revolution. This has given rise to wide-ranging debates over his ideas, their meaning and applicability to contemporary times (Lash and Whimster 1987; Ray and Reed 1994). At the same time, he became an inspiration for a number of scholars (Dahrendorf 1959; Goldthorpe and Marshall 1992; Rex 1961). We may be distinguish him, in part, from either Marx or Durkheim because of his unwillingness to see science as a means for prescribing ends:

Science today is a 'vocation' organized in special disciplines in the service of self-clarification and knowledge of interrelated facts. It is not the gift of grace of seers and prophets dispensing sacred values and revelations, nor does it partake of the contemplation of sages and philosophers about the meaning of the universe. This, to be sure, is the inescapable condition of our historical situation. We cannot evade it as long as we remain true to ourselves.

(Weber in Gerth and Mills 1970: 152)

We are led away from history as resolved by the 'mind' (Hegel), or the actions of people with common interests (Marx), or by the laws of historical evolution (Saint-Simon, Comte and Durkheim). Instead, history is resolved by 'will' (Hawthorn 1976). The link between modernity, rationality and progress is now cast into the realm of uncertainty. Weber becomes a theorist of 'fate' (B. S. Turner 1981) for whom modernity came to represent the forward march of rationalization. This can stifle the individual, but is a condition from which they cannot escape:

Weber saw historical change as the unintended effect of endless social processes and contingent circumstances . . . this world-view is a social liberalism which asks us, given the complexity and uncertainty of knowledge, to behave responsibly – that is, as agents with 'personality' who are forced to make choices in conditions of unreliable knowledge.

(Holton and Turner 1990: 9)

These tensions are also apparent in the writings of two of Weber's contemporaries: Georg Simmel and Ferdinand Tönnies (1855–1936). The nature of Simmel's work has made for a myriad of interpretations. It has been characterized as 'fragmentary' and 'unsystematic' (Frisby 1992a; 1992b), whilst he is said to be the first sociologist of modernity (Frisby 1991), as well as the first sociologist of postmodernity (Weinstein and Weinstein 1991)! As for Tönnies, he employed the ideas of 'community' (*Gemeinschaft*) and 'society' (*Gesellschaft*) to consider the changes from a rural to an industrial Germany in the forward march of modernity. The former is characterized by a 'natural will' of habit and instinct, whilst the latter is characterized by a 'rational will' which is instrumental in terms of its selection of means for ends. For Tönnies, there were ramifications for the ways in which individuals then related to one another. Parallels become evident in both of their works with Weber in terms of a concern for the fate of the individual in modern society.

It is the sheer range of intellectual influences which informed German social theory at this time which leads to this range of interpretations. When it comes to Weber, to the neo-Kantians and Nietzsche, we may add Marx, or more accurately those Marxists who were busy interpreting his work. In addition, Freund (1979) notes two other influences. The first of these derives from the distinction which Hegel made between the state and civil society (which Marx had criticized). This is basic to an understanding of German intellectual culture at this time. Broadly speaking, the institution of the State is seen as 'the source of all liberty, while society is the field of economic activity, which is the source of dependence and servitude' (Freund 1979: 151).

The second influence was that of psychologism and historicism. According to the former, society could be studied in terms of a collective psychology. The focus here is upon, for example, languages, myths, habits, customs etc., which permits one to speak of a 'spirit' in Hegelian terms. Wilhelm Dilthey (1833–1911), for instance, sought to discover an epistemological basis for the human sciences through their being rooted in 'inner' experience, rather than a natural-scientific 'outer' experience. This concentration on under-standing social life and the meanings for the individuals who comprise it, led him to develop a 'descriptive psychology'. Historicism is then of importance due to a focus on the 'lived experience' of people. As such, history could not be ignored in the process of social inquiry.

It was in economics that an influential historical school emerged and from this discipline Weber had emerged. Together with the work of Windelband and Rickert on the role and meaning of history in knowledge, this fusion of intellectual cultures – psychologism, historicism, neo-Kantianism, Nietzsche and Marx – led him to reject all attempts at finding an 'inner meaning' or objective social laws in history. His methodological writings exhibit a combination of Dilthey's idea of the meaningful 'inner' experiences of people (understanding), *together with* an analysis of the observed regularities of human behaviour in terms of the natural scientific idea of cause and effect (Weber 1949).

To the above we must add the changing political and economic culture of Germany in order to fully situate Weber's work. As with Durkheim, Weber's writings took place against the background of political problems. In particular, Weber was concerned to analyse the conditions of industrial expansion in Germany in the post-Bismarckian era. This led to an emphasis in his political sociology on two aspects. First, the furtherance of the German nation state and second, that all politics is, in the last analysis, a struggle for power (*Macht*):

As a witness of Bismarck's unification of Germany and the virtual elimination of the liberal, middle-class movements from positions of political influence, Weber became convinced that great goals could be achieved only by power politics. For the rest of his life he set a premium upon examining political life without illusions, looking at it as a struggle between individuals and groups with conflicting beliefs and interests, always decided in the end by the reservoir of power available to the winning side and by its greater ability to use that power effectively

(Bendix 1977: 7)

In charting these reactions to modernity, clear differences emerge between Weber and the other thinkers considered so far. His emphasis on the never ending nature of power struggles and his unwillingness to reduce the political sphere to the economic, separates him from both Durkheim and Marx. In addition, although a defender of the objectivity of social science, he acknowledged the 'extra-scientific' dimension to its practice: for example, the cultural values which exist within particular societies and the ways in which they affect the reception of particular ideas.

The above noted, we also find a common reaction in the work of Weber and Durkheim, for both

> have their origin in an attempt to defend – or rather re-interpret – the claims of political liberalism within the twin pressures of Romantic hypernationalistic conservatism on the one side, and revolutionary socialism on the other.
>
> (Giddens 1971: 244)

This shared quest was one of generating a liberal political consciousness in the face of the forward march of modernity. Here, we also find similarities with Marx who, after all, took aim at Romantic conservatism and utilitarian ideas. This emphasis not only allows for a modification of Marx and Durkheim's insights, but also provides for a re-examination of the relationship between Marx and Weber (Löwith 1993; D. Sayer 1991).

Although differences do exist between Marx and Weber, Weber told one of his students in the later years of his life:

> One can measure the integrity of a modern scholar, and especially of a modern philosopher, by how he sees his own relationship to Nietzsche and Marx. Whoever does not admit that he could not accomplish very important aspects of his work without the work that these two have performed deceives both himself and others. The world in which we ourselves exist intellectually is largely a world stamped by Marx and Nietzsche.
>
> (Weber quoted in Mommsen 1992: 54)

This fusion proved to be a 'massive, but brittle, intellectual synthesis' (Giddens 1972a: 58). Yet it is a dynamic which permits two outcomes. First, it renders Weber's work of contemporary importance to understanding social life. Second, it allows a questioning of the simple distinction which can be made between Marx and Weber on the grounds that the former was a materialist and the latter an idealist critic of Marx. Weber, for example, refers not just to the importance of ideas in examining social relations, but also of material interests – as is manifest in his observations on the Russian Revolution (Beetham 1974).

This situation is compounded through a failure to locate their works in terms of the social content in which they wrote. Weber read of Marx through the lenses of Friedrich Engels (1820–95) and Karl Kautsky (1854–1938); both of whom tended to perpetuate a view of Marx as somewhat mechanistic in his conceptions of society and social relations. What was lost in this interpretation was the element of *praxis*. After all, Marx provided 'a theory for practical orientation, requiring human action to become reality' (Mommsen 1992: 56). On this basis, Weber and Marx share an anthropological concern with the whole question of the relationship between the individual, modernity and social reality. For one, this reality was characterized as self-alienation, for the other, by a process of rationalization in which the individual found themselves increasingly trampled by vast impersonal forces.

As capitalism was the main characteristic of modernity for Marx, so rationalization was for Weber. In particular, what he referred to as formal rationality: that is, the application of rational calculable principles to everyday action. In contrast to the usual preoccupations of the Marx versus Weber debate,

> a more appropriate approach to Weber's sociology may be located in the problems of modernization and modernity, and that we should regard rationalization as the process which produced modernism.
>
> (B. Turner in Holton and Turner 1990: 69)

This theme was given special emphasis in Weber's writings on religion and the emergence of capitalism (Weber 1985). In the 'last analysis', it was rationalization which gave rise to capitalism and under which all else is subsumed, including those elements prioritized by Marx:

> Weber did not regard capitalism as a power made up of 'relations' of the forces and means of production which had become autonomous, so that everything else could be understood therefrom in terms of ideology. According to Weber, capitalism could only become the 'most fateful' power in human life because it had itself already developed within the framework of a 'rational way of life'.
>
> (Löwith 1993: 63)

Here are echoes of Kant and Hegel, fused with a Nietzschean fatalism. Human meaning and values were declining in the modern world. This was a situation which might be rectified by powerful leadership. To re-cap, it was Hegel who historicized Kant, leaving his abstract considerations on transcendental reason to became rooted in the unfolding of human history. Brunkhorst (1992) argues that in Weber's social history of religion we find a Hegelian objective 'spirit' (in this case, of capitalism) as a correlate of Kant's abstract concept of a 'categorical imperative' (simply put, the duty to act according to a universal moral law regardless of the consequences of one's actions). However, we should note that Weber would not guarantee an outcome for this process through his refusal to employ Enlightenment principles without qualification:

> 'Scientific' pleading is meaningless in principle because the various value spheres of the world stand in irreconcilable conflict with each

other . . . I do not know how one might wish to decide 'scientifically' the value of French and German culture; for here, too, different gods struggle with one another, now *and for all times to come.*
(Weber in Gerth and Mills 1970: 147–148, emphasis added)

Modernity now appears tinged with disenchantment, not absolute progress. Formal rationality increasingly undermines substantive rationality which involves

a conscious belief in the absolute value of some ethical, aesthetic, religious, or other form of behaviour, entirely for its own sake and independently of any prospects of external success.
(Weber in Parsons *et al.* 1965: 1063)

The Protestant ethic is the key element in the rise of capitalism for Weber. This leads to the unintended consequence of an increased rationalization of social life. Weber's social theory can thus be read as preoccupied with the everyday world of human culture (Schroeder 1992). History moves from the personal to the impersonal, leaving human meanings and values in its wake. Ironically, what starts as an irrational quest for salvation, ends up as the 'iron cage of rationality':

The premiums were placed on 'proving' oneself before God . . . and 'proving' oneself before men in the sense of socially holding one's own within the Puritan sects.
(Weber in Gerth and Mills 1970: 321)

This drive towards self-perfection has a high cost:

No one knows who will live in this cage in the future, or whether at the end of this tremendous development entirely new prophets will arise, or there will be a great rebirth of old ideas and ideals, or, if neither, mechanized petrification, embellished with a sort of convulsive self-importance. For of the last stage of this cultural development, it might well be truly said: Specialists without spirit, sensualists without heart; this nullity imagines that it has attained a level of civilization never before achieved.
(Weber 1985: 182)

Summary: the legacy for social theory

The Enlightenment formed a backdrop against which the development of social theory could be evaluated. It would be incorrect, however, to characterize this as a determining relationship. This was a relationship which was modified according to the cultural and political circumstances and intellectual traditions in which social theorists worked. It is these very aspects of social theory which provide it with the power of insight, relevance and critique.

Writers such as Vico, Montesquieu, Hume, Smith and Ferguson, in their different ways, viewed people as 'social creatures', not metaphysical entities capable of floating freely over their social universes. This affected the nature of the relationship between the individual and society which witnessed a journey from Montesquieu, through Comte's structuralism, to Spencer's methodological individualism. In the process, ideas on how history unfolded, what the future might be, how it might best be secured, what constituted valid knowledge and what it was to be human, were illuminated.

Marx considered the relationship between the individual and society in dialectical terms. For this purpose, he drew upon the work of Hegel, whose achievement was

> to link a philosophical idea of rationality, couched in the broadest possible terms to comprehend mind, consciousness, the following of rules, the essence of what it was to be human, with everyday understanding of people about their practical business of learning skills, trading goods, getting married or engaging in state activities.
>
> (Albrow 1990: 112)

Hegel challenged the idea of absolute truth and error characteristic of 'the traditional, foundational picture of knowledge' (Sayers 1989: 34). Marx took this on board, but applied a more materialist than idealist reading, ultimately viewing capitalism as the defining characteristic of modernity. For Marx, walking in the shadows of the Enlightenment, history would still unfold, but towards communism, not the idealist concept of self-consciousness.

Durkheim, like Marx, was concerned with the fate of the individual in modern life. However, he was concerned with the future of social solidarity in the France of his time. Changes in society required new modes of social integration which would respect individual autonomy, but without recourse to egoism. This moved him away from an economic, to an ethical focus in human affairs. Indeed, Durkheim's greatest influence on the development of social science was probably the idea of society as an 'actively moralizing force' (Bauman 1989: 172).

In Weber's work neo-Kantianism became fused with Nietzsche. Although committed to the idea that social science should start with the subjective meanings that people attach to their social lives, Weber was concerned with the fate of individuals in the forward march of modernity. Therefore, can this journey be characterized as one which travelled from the optimism of the early Enlightenment to one of pessimism? Put in these terms, this might not be unreasonable. However, if Weber appeared as a pessimist, he was not a full-blown fatalist. He drew the boundaries of science far tighter than had many of his predecessors. Science could not enter into the realm of value judgements. At best, it might help to decide upon the best means for the achievement of preselected ends.

We might now observe that at the end of this journey there appears a common thread amongst thinkers at the end of the nineteenth century. This *fin de siècle* spirit parallels that of recent times:

> a deliberate breaking away from the seriousness of tradition . . . and a seemingly liberal concern with what might still be termed socialist, democratic, humanistic ideals of justice and equality.
>
> (Meštrović 1992: ix)

This characterization it not without its problems. Yet it does serve to question the idea that past social theorists simply built their ideas upon the comfortable certitudes of something called the 'Enlightenment' and that their ideas therefore no longer speak to contemporary concerns. In continuing this history of social theory, we will find that revisions and critiques are plentiful. In the process, ideas regarding the promise of modernity and the relationship between the individual and society were to be viewed in new and illuminating ways.

2

Seven traditions: renewal, modification and critique in the Enlightenment project

Together with the intellectual legacies considered so far, the traditions of thought examined in this chapter had profound implications for the future direction of social theory. This is not an easy history to document and for this reason the chapter is divided into two main sections.

In the first section of the chapter I shall examine three traditions of thought: hermeneutics, phenomenology and pragmatism. For ease of understanding the first two are examined in one section. Although there are clear differences between and within these three traditions, they all contributed to a shift in theoretical focus towards understanding the role of history, human actions and meanings in everyday life. In the second section four traditions of social thought are then considered: critical, structuralist, systems and feminist theories. Each of these have also added to and informed the direction of modern social theory. In order to specify how these traditions are connected to ideas in Part II of the book, each section will conclude with a summary discussion.

The Enlightenment: modification and critique in three traditions

Hermeneutics and phenomenology: history, consciousness and being

Although there were differences amongst the neo-Kantians, they did share a scepticism regarding the possibility of utilizing a model of the natural sciences for the development of a 'science of society'. In so doing, they placed Enlightenment 'scientism' in question:

> 'Scientism' means science's belief in itself: that is, the conviction that we can no longer understand science as one form of possible knowledge, but rather must identify knowledge with science.
>
> (Habermas 1989a: 4)

The challenge to scientism, in terms of a separation between the realm of nature and human activity, informed the writings of Dilthey. This, however, leaves two questions. First, if the social sciences could no longer march in the shadow of the natural sciences, what was the alternative? Second, what implications does this have for the direction of social theory?

Dilthey's answer to the first question was to turn to an assessment of the scientific validity of historical writings. In the process, he sought nothing less than to provide new epistemological foundations for the human sciences. In this attempt, the influences so characteristic of German thought at this time emerged in his ideas:

> Kantian memories, strict historical training, a nostalgia for the spiritual world of the Enlightenment, a respect for the aims of positivist investigation, and, still hovering in the background, the misty pantheism of Romantic theology.
>
> (S. H. Hughes 1979: 193)

This latter influence came from Schleiermacher (1768–1834) in whose writings the seeds of hermeneutics, defined as the theory and practice of interpretation, were laid. The question was how to produce a scientifically based hermeneutics? For this purpose texts had to be situated and interpreted in the social context in which they were produced. It would then be possible to replicate a central characteristic of science: to move beyond 'particularity' to the 'general'. To achieve that

> it is necessary to rise above, not only the particularity of texts, but also the particularity of the rules and recipes into which the art of understanding is dispersed. Hermeneutics was born with the attempt to raise exegesis and philology to the level of a *Kunstlehre*, that is, a 'technology' which is not restricted to a mere collection of unconnected operations.
>
> (Ricoeur 1982: 45, original italics)

From a methodological point of view, the analyst must then start with a text and seek to understand it through an act of interpretation which connects them with the author and what was known by them when they constructed the text. What is often referred to as the *hermeneutic circle* involves a relationship between the part and the whole or, to put it another way: 'the relation between an isolated expression or work and the pre-given totality of language or literature' (Thompson 1981: 37).

This move also paved the way for a general inquiry into the nature of human understanding. Therefore, in seeking to fulfil his aims, Dilthey moved from the perspective of individualistic psychology, to an historicist view based on Hegel's objective 'mind' or 'spirit' as indicative of a given age:

> Every single human expression represents something which is common to many and therefore part of the realm of objective mind . . . the individual always experiences, thinks, acts, and also understands, in this common sphere.
>
> (Dilthey quoted in Outhwaite 1975: 26–27)

Dilthey could now argue that the human sciences could respect both individuality and universality through their ability to locate the 'inner' experiences of people in terms of their history. This contrasts with positivism, whose scientific aim is to explain the 'outer' observable patterns of human behaviour in terms of the relations of cause and effect. Nevertheless, how are these 'understandings' to be validated?

A solution to this problem was the adoption of *verstehen* (interpretative understanding). This allows the social sciences to possess something *in addition to* the natural sciences through their ability to understand the social meaning of an event for social actors. After all, the natural sciences explain an event by considering it as *'the effect of a cause'* (Strasser 1985: 2, original italics). To study human relations, on the other hand, must involve 'understanding what makes someone tick' or how they 'feel or act as a human being' (Taylor 1981: 30). A precondition of theoretical development then becomes an understanding of the consciousness which informs human actions.

Adding a voice to this breakdown of the unity of the human and natural sciences was the philosopher Edmund Husserl (1859–1938), whose concerns were, once again, a defence of the 'legitimacy and dignity of the human sciences' (Nuyen 1990). Husserl's route was to seek to establish 'truth' in the realm of human consciousness. This led him to a concern with perception in the attempt to grasp something called 'true understanding'. The method he advocated for this purpose was to question, or suspend, any presuppositions regarding society by adopting the strategy of 'bracketing'. People would then be freed from their historical context and enabled to uncover a 'true understanding' which is pre-theoretical and free from prejudice. Given this:

> Phenomenology asks us *not* to take received notions for granted. It asks us to *question* them – to question nothing less than our culture, that is, our way of looking at and being in the world in which we have been brought up.
>
> (Wolff 1979: 500, original italics)

Without bracketing experiences in this way the result would be, in what Husserl called the 'natural attitude' of everyday life, people simply taking-for-granted the world around them.

Husserl's teacher, Franz Brentano (1838–1916), stressed the idea of 'intentionality' in human psychology whereby consciousness is always directed towards 'something'. Husserl then took Descartes's act of perception and added an important dimension: the 'thing' which is perceived. As such, objects of thought, including society and social relations, are viewed as being constituted in and through consciousness. In contrast to positivism, there is no separation of the social world from the act of perception, for it is an object of 'consciousness'. Husserl thereby transforms Descartes's famous statement into *ego cogito cogitata*, translated as 'I think, and what I am thinking are the objects of my thoughts' (Strasser 1985: 124).

Knowing' is now reduced to a perceiving subject. For this reason, a phenomenologically informed social theory is required to focus upon a description and understanding of subjective perceptions, not an explanation of objective conditions. Questions such as 'What is social reality?' are then replaced by two different questions. First, 'How does reality come to be constituted by mental operations as a known object?' Second, 'How do we go about constructing our ideas of what reality is?' (T. Johnson, Dandeker and Ashworth 1984: 78).

Although discussions of phenomenology are found under the broad heading of 'interpretivist social theory', there are important variations in its unfolding history. After all, in their different ways, Husserl and Dilthey were still pursuing an Enlightenment ideal: that is, the search for 'true' knowledge. Their approach was to be challenged and modified in the writings of Martin Heidegger (1889–1976) who moved the focus of phenomenology from epistemology to ontology. In the process he was critical of Kant. He argued that we are not just observers of an external world mediated through our consciousness (Husserl), but are members of a world who exist as 'beings-in-time'. This moves away from Dilthey's neo-Kantian preoccupations with method, to the study of what Heidegger called *Dasein*. This is best described as 'pre-understanding':

> the *place* where the question of being arises, the place of manifestation; the centrality of *Dasein* is simply that of a being which understands being.
>
> (Ricoeur 1982: 54, original italics)

This is not an easy notion to grasp. For our purposes, however, what Heidegger is criticizing is the concept of a 'transcendental ego'. He does not attempt to 'solve' the subject–object dichotomy by prioritizing human consciousness, as had Husserl and Dilthey, because understanding is seen as part of a 'mode of being'. It emerges, for example, from the gap which exists between where people are located in time and the possibilities which are available to them for the future. These possibilities are then 're-projected' into the present which can become 'an object of potential questioning, challenge, and change' (Bauman 1978: 166). The implication being that social theory should cast its gaze upon historically given subjects who exist in a 'lifeworld' in which a series of possibilities for social action are then contained. The practices within the lifeworld contain interpretations of, as well as methods of coping with, social relations. Hermeneutics is now the act of interpreting people's everyday interpretations.

Making connections with Part II

Hans Georg Gadamer (1975) is largely responsible for the contemporary interest in hermeneutics. Following Heidegger, Gadamer does not see hermeneutics as a method for study, but part of the condition of human existence. These arguments have had an effect on the development of the social sciences. For instance, Jürgen Habermas seeks to develop a 'depth hermeneutics' which draws upon but is also critical of, Gadamer. Heidegger's ideas appear in the work of Jacques Derrida, Michel Foucault and Norbert Elias (1897–1990), whose 'process' theory represents a critique of the subject–object dualism in social thought (see Elias 1991; Mennell 1992). Additionally, structuration theory will be shown to be ontologically based in terms of an emphasis upon human 'being' and 'doing', whilst Pierre Bourdieu considers the sociological implications of Heidegger's philosophy for generating a theory of human practice.

A more general phenomenological input into social theory is apparent in the work of Alfred Schutz (1899–1959). Schutz was a central figure in the development of phenomenological sociology, from which ethnomethodology derives part of its inspiration. Schutz rejected positivism as a model for the human sciences and was critical of the concept of *verstehen*. He did not view this as a method for 'doing' social science, but social science should study how people interpret the social world. In other words, *how* it is that people produce social life in a meaningful way. As Berger and Luckmann put it:

> Commonsense contains innumerable pre- and quasi-scientific interpretations about everyday reality, which it takes for granted. If we are to describe the reality of commonsense we must refer to those interpretations, just as we must take account of its taken-for-granted character – but we do so within phenomenological brackets.
>
> (Berger and Luckmann 1967: 20)

Together with Winch, who imported the insights of the philosopher Ludwig Wittgenstein (1889–1951) into social science, Schutz added to the focus of social theory on the rule-following and meaningful nature of human actions in everyday life.

The pragmatists: action, consciousness and the self

Little in the way of American social thought was noted in chapter 1, aside, that is, from a reference to Veblen. North America was left to be 'imported' into European social theory via Alexis de Tocqueville's (1805–59) interests in democracy. All of this was to change in the nineteenth century with the work of those such as William Sumner (1840–1910) and Edward Ross (1866–1951). Nevertheless, this did not involve travelling down a Hegelian-historicist road; one reason being that they regarded their own revolution, in contrast to that of the French, as a success (Ross 1991). This was to change with events such as the American Civil War and the process of industrialization.

Towards the end of his life Durkheim devoted a set of lectures to pragmatism for two main reasons. First, he saw in pragmatism an attack on rationalism which had informed so much of French intellectual life and was thus a threat to French culture in general (Joas 1993). Second, he viewed pragmatism as undermining the idea that 'true' knowledge was possible (Durkheim 1983: 1). Contained with these lectures was a veiled attack on his contemporary Georges Sorel, who distrusted intellectualist formulations and insisted: 'on the origin in *practical action* of all valid social theory' (S. H. Hughes 1979: 176, original italics). Given this we must ask what are the main elements of pragmatism which provoked such reactions? One approach to this question allows us to compare pragmatism with German-idealist attempts to ground epistemology in human consciousness:

> the basic idea of pragmatism, namely that it is actions rather than consciousness which are the foundations of thought, was developed in the 1870s by a group of young thinkers in Cambridge, Massachusetts, and was first publicly voiced by Charles Peirce in 1878.
>
> (Joas 1993: 95)

Charles Peirce (1839–1914) began his studies with the prejudices that people actually possess in everyday life, not with Descartes's abstract method of 'doubting'. The Cartesian solitary ego then became replaced by a 'cooperative search for truth for the purpose of coping with real problems encountered in the course of action' (Joas 1993: 19). A similar argument also evolved in the work of John Dewey (1859–1952). For Dewey, ideas and actions should be judged according to the social situations which give rise to them. In contrast to the 'top-down' approach of metaphysical speculation, the social sciences should now concern themselves with the concrete social conditions under which actions take place. To add to this, William James (1842–1910) sought to critique the idea of consciousness as a resolution to the subject–object dilemma:

> Consciousness, he says, 'is the name of a nonentity, and has no right to a place among first principles' . . . he is not denying that our thoughts perform a function which is that of knowing . . . What he is denying might be put crudely as the view that consciousness is a 'thing'.
>
> (Russell 1955: 840)

The consequences of these positions are far-reaching. Pragmatism displaces the relationship between thought and reality in terms of how truthfully one may be represented by the other. Thinking is now seen as a social, not solitary act, which takes place within a 'community of others'. Over time, however, this insight became distorted such that knowledge was to be judged in terms of its 'use-value'. The implication being that social practice is the means through which social theory becomes judged and validated.

Here we may detect a link between pragmatism and Marx's concept of *praxis*. That said, Marx would not have accepted the 'instrumentalism' of this position such that: 'knowledge should be judged as more or less "useful" rather than as true or false' (A. Sayer 1992: 70). The parallels with Heidegger's reflections, on the other hand, are more readily apparent:

> At the center of the first section of *Being and Time* stands the analysis of the concept of world. From the perspective of manipulation, and in general of nonobjectifying, practical dealings with physical components of the lifeworld, Heidegger explicates a concept of world as a network of involvements reminiscent of Pragmatism.
> (Habermas 1992a: 148, original italics)

Heidegger and the pragmatists may be seen to be calling upon social theory to shift its attention away from consciousness towards people's adaptions and methods of coping with the world in their everyday lives.

Making connections with Part II

The clearest way in which the influence of pragmatism may be traced in social theory is via the work of George Herbert Mead (1863–1931), the Chicago School of sociology and the symbolic interactionists. These are the subjects of chapter 3. Mead's work, in particular, represents the desire to overcome the subject–object dualism in social thought. To recall the discussion so far. Following Kant, the individual had been considered as both 'a *world-generating* and *autonomously acting subject*' (Habermas 1992b: 158, original italics). As Habermas goes on to suggest, the conceptualization of the subject then 'fell between the cracks' of a transcendental ego, apparently capable of surveying the world around it through the exercise of reason and an empirical ego, who simply exists as one among many in the social world.

In Mead's work we will find neither an interest in utility-oriented action (towards a desired end) or a Kantian style moral-individual action (transcendental ego), but an examination of the relationship between consciousness and action. Social action is not conceptualized in terms of an orientation to a predetermined end, for the very consciousness which formulates an individual's ends cannot take place outside of the context of the action itself:

> Rather, the setting of an end can only be a result of reflection on resistances encountered by the variously orientated behaviour of a life

form whose world is always already schematized in a practical manner prior to all reflection.

(Joas 1993: 248)

Social 'selves' are viewed as being formed through a process of confronting the world of which the individual is a part in dialectic relation between subject and object. Only by encountering objective conditions are people able to gain a sense of 'who' they are.

There are a further six ways in which connections between pragmatism and modern social theory can be drawn. First, in Peirce's work on semiology (the study of signs and their systems) the idea of 'indexicality' appeared. This suggests that we may understand an utterance only in the context in which it is made. As we shall see, this is part of the theoretical armoury of ethnomethodology. Second, is Habermas's theory of communicative action. Whilst his critical theory has foundationalist aspirations, the linguistic aspects of his work contain a pragmatist theory of meaning which revolves around the assertion 'that to understand an utterance is to understand the claim it raises' (Cooke 1994: 95). Third, pragmatism forms an essential part of the ideas of the contemporary 'anti-foundationalist' American philosopher Richard Rorty (1982). Despite his own reservations on this trend in social thought (Rorty 1993), his works have added to the 'postmodern turn' in social theory. Fourth, Alfred Schutz used James's ideas in order to develop his phenomenological social theory. Fifth, pragmatism existed in the critical thought of Charles Wright Mills (1916–62) who called for a fusion of the practical and intellectual within social science (Mills 1970). Finally, alongside the ideas of Durkheim, phenomenology, linguistics and ethology, we shall uncover its influence in the works of Erving Goffman (1922–82).

Having examined these philosophical schools in terms of their implications for the development of social theory, attention is now turned to four traditions of social thought which represent the journey of renewal, modification and critique in the Enlightenment project.

Four traditions in social thought

Critical theory: for (and against) modernity

Under the auspices of its second director, Max Horkheimer (1895–1973), the Institute for Social Research at Frankfurt came to centre its interests around six broad areas. First, the seeking of explanations for the absence of a unified working-class movement in Europe. Second, an examination of the nature and consequences of capitalist crises. Third, a consideration of the relationship which existed between the political and the economic spheres in modern societies. Fourth, to provide an account for the rise of Fascism and Nazism as political movements. Fifth, to study socialization in families in terms of ego development. Finally, to undertake a sustained critique of the link between positivism and science (adapted from Held 1990: 35; Habermas 1987: 378–379).

In order to adequately examine these questions a new theoretical approach was required which involved a 'refusal to champion vulgar idealism as an antidote to vulgar materialism' (Jay 1973: 294). This involved a return to the Hegelian strand in Marxism in order that the concept of human *praxis* might be recovered from overly materialist readings of Marx. Yet between Hegel and the Frankfurt School stood such figures as Schopenhauer and Nietzsche, both of whom had questioned the Enlightenment project. Therefore, it was necessary to engage with these ideas in order to recover the promise of Marxism.

To these intellectual antecedents and aims we must add the political context in which these scholars wrote in order to fully situate their work. In Nazi Germany, the Institute found itself under threat with the result that its leading members, including Theodor Adorno (1903–69), Max Horkheimer and Herbert Marcuse (1898–1979), emigrated to the United States (Adorno and Horkheimer returned after the Second World War). Here they found the self-confidence of bourgeois liberal-capitalism with its apparent ability to absorb and neutralize proletarian consciousness. To analyse how this occurred necessitated a consideration of culture which, up to this point in time, had been largely devalued in Marxist circles (see Raymond Williams 1961).

The work of these scholars was inter-disciplinary, accompanied, as noted, by a rejection of 'scientific Marxism', together with critiques of positivism and interpretivism. As Horkheimer said of the relationship between social philosophy and positivism:

> Contemporary social philosophy, as we have seen, is in the main polemically disposed toward positivism. If the latter sees only the particular, in the realm of society it sees only the individual and the relations between individuals; for positivism, everything is exhausted in mere facts [*Tatsächlichkeiten*]. These facts, demonstrable with the means of analytic science, are not questioned by philosophy.
>
> (Horkheimer 1993: 7)

Positivism turns human relationships into nothing more than abstract categories through a failure to examine the conditions under which they develop and are sustained. In this sense it represents part of the increasing desire to control the social and natural worlds in the name of profit (Adorno *et al.* 1976). What makes critical theory 'critical' is precisely this recognition of the connection which exists between knowledge and human interests.

Interpretivist social theories were also inadequate due to an exclusive concentration upon the process of self-understanding and self-consciousness. The result being that they exhibit an uncritical acceptance of dominant forms of consciousness within given societies and fail to consider the structural determinants of human actions, as well as the role of the unconscious and power and control in human relations. Indeed, in another direction, critiques of this type led to attempts to fuse phenomenology and Marxism (Paci 1972) and an emphasis upon ideological mechanisms of control as apparent in the works of Georg Lukács (1885–1971) and Antonio Gramsci (1891–1937). It was Gramsci who employed the concept of *hegemony* whereby it is held that the bourgeoisie exercises its social control through both coercion *and* consensus within institutions. What presents itself as common sense is actually symptomatic of ideological distortion (Gramsci 1971). This notion still inspires cultural studies (Nelson and Grossberg 1988), as well as leading to a framework for 'post-Marxist' politics (Laclau and Mouffe 1990).

The 'critical theorists' themselves focused upon the concept of ideological incorporation. Herbert Marcuse (1968a) spoke of the 'technical-administrative control' of society and took aim at a growing corpus of social theory which claimed to have witnessed a vindication of capitalism through what was known as the 'end of ideology' thesis (Bell 1960):

> The capabilities (intellectual and material) of contemporary society are immeasurably greater than ever before – which means that the scope of society's domination over the individual is immeasurably greater than ever before. Our society distinguishes itself by conquering the centrifugal social forces with Technology rather than Terror, on the dual basis of an overwhelming efficiency and an increasing standard of living.
>
> (Marcuse 1968a: 9)

It follows that the rationality of 'the system' itself had to be subjected to critique. One way in which this took place was through an investigation into the Enlightenment project. Here we find history interpreted as a journey towards a 'new kind of barbarism' whereby:

> The individual is wholly devalued in relation to the economic powers, which at the same time press the control of society over nature to hitherto unsuspected heights . . . The flood of detailed information and candy-floss entertainment simultaneously instructs and stultifies mankind.
>
> (Adorno and Horkheimer 1979: xiv–xv)

On this basis Weber was criticized for confusing capitalism as a process of rationalization with reason itself (Marcuse 1968b). Instead of liberating the subject, the Enlightenment had witnessed a growing disjuncture between reason and rationality: 'The unleashed market economy was both the actual form of reason and the power which destroyed reason' (Adorno and Horkheimer 1979: 90). The result being a 'fractured' subject through self-alienation perpetuated by positivism with its fetish for collecting social facts. Modernity now represents a loss of meaning:

> For the Enlightenment, whatever does not conform to the rule of computation and utility is suspect. So long as it can develop undisturbed by any outward repression, there is no holding it . . . Every spiritual resistance it encounters serves merely to increase its strength . . . *Enlightenment is totalitarian.*
>
> (Adorno and Horkheimer 1979: 6, emphasis added)

This meta-critique noted, the question remains that having rejected inter-pretivist social theory how can the important analysis of mental states be achieved? This is where Sigmund Freud enters as part of the whole history of the relationship between psychoanalysis and social theory (see Elliott 1992).

Freud sought to supplant the idea of the conscious process of human thought with a theory of the unconscious. Whilst he acknowledged that an unconscious process could be inferred only from observing patients, he believed it to play a dominant role in the determination of behaviour. He thus placed the idea of the 'conscious subject' into question, but for different reasons that any we have noted so far:

> According to Freud . . . we are not who or what we think we are: we do not know our own centers; in fact, we probably do not have a center at all. Psychoanalysis undermines notions about autonomy, individual choice, will, responsibility, and rationality, showing that we do not control our own lives in the most fundamental sense.
>
> (Chodorow 1986)

This focus moves away from an understanding of the solitary ego in the social world, to the *self-misunderstanding* person who fails to see the causes of their own symptoms. Indeed, Freud's whole metapsychological project can be read as one which sought to show 'who we are', whilst psychoanalysis is a practice for the development of autonomy and control in the 'self' (Chodorow 1986).

More specifically, Freud viewed all behaviour as being motivated or caused – whether it be 'neurotic' or 'normal'. This could be attributed to earlier determinants which appeared as symptoms whose purpose was to avoid painful memories. In the self there exists a continuous struggle between 'internality' and 'externality' or, to express it another way, between mental structures (id, ego and superego) and life-experiences. This, however, does not simply take place 'within' the individual, but is a response to their physical and social environments. These may be manifest in a whole series of 'slips' (Freud 1938) and the idea of civilization itself (Freud 1969).

A Freudian approach to the unconscious and self-misunderstanding permitted the Frankfurt theorists to concentrate on the process of ideological distortion under capitalism, without resorting to some notion of conscious-ness as an explanatory framework: 'it is only through the process of interpretation that subjects can come to know the conditions and complexities of their own existence' (Thompson 1981: 212). An emphasis of this type has given rise to a school of thought known as 'crisis theory' (O'Connor 1987).

Despite this utilization of Freud, we are still left with problems. Up to the time of the Frankfurt theorists Marxists had dismissed psychoanalysis as unworthy of attention (see Osborn 1937). After all, the problematic fusion of Marx and Freud is apparent at different levels:

> On the practical level, psychoanalysis is carried on by rich doctors on richer patients. Conceptually, it starts from the individual's problems and tends to play down social conditions and constraints.
>
> (Ollman 1979: 177)

Therefore, if Freud's work was to serve the needs of critical theory, it required modification (Marcuse 1966). At this point, Leo Lowenthal and Eric Fromm enter the scene as central to this process. Fromm, for example, examined the relationship between the individual and totalitarianism (Fromm 1969). He also held throughout his life that our capacity for love and freedom: 'depends almost entirely on the given socio-economic conditions' (quoted in Jay 1973: 100). The interest in Freud was also apparent in socio-psychological studies on the structure of modern personality types (Adorno et al. 1950), as well as in the writings of Willhelm Reich on the relationship between sexuality and capitalism (see Ollman 1979). Fromm also examined politics from a psychoanalytic point of view:

> It has shown that this irrational acting and feeling are the result of certain instinctual impulses, of which the actor is often unconscious, but which compulsively condition him or her. It therefore seems to follow that psychoanalysis could also provide the key to an understanding of similarly conditioned *social* action, of similarly irrational *political* events.
>
> (Fromm in Bronner and Kellner 1989: 213, original italics)

Making connections with Part II

The critical theorists left a legacy which is still the subject of new interpretations and understandings (Bronner 1994; Hoy and McCarthy 1994; Wiggershaus 1995). Of all contemporary scholars, it is Jürgen Habermas who sits most firmly within this tradition but who, as we shall see, has submitted it to extensive modification. However, if we broaden our horizons to trace a critical 'intent' in the development of social theory, the picture becomes less restrictive. For instance, Pierre Bourdieu sits within a tradition which runs from Marx to the Frankfurt School (Calhoun 1995). There are also the ideas of Michel Foucault, whose own words suffice here:

> As far as I'm concerned, I think that the Frankfurt School set problems

that are still being worked on. Among others, the effects of power that are connected to a rationality that has been historically and geographically defined in the West, starting from the sixteenth century on. The West could never have attained the economic and cultural effects that are unique to it without the exercise of that specific form of rationality.

(Foucault 1991a: 117)

Whilst the Frankfurt scholars were writing, another tradition was active in French intellectual life. Starting with an examination of language and working through to anthropology, it culminated in the works of a Marxist thinker who, unlike the above, sought to expunge any Hegelian trace in Marxism to provide it with a 'scientific' status.

Structuralism: farewell to the subject?

The French intellectual climate was undergoing rapid change in the post-Second World War period. Existentialism and phenomenology were vying for intellectual ascendancy with mixtures of Marxism, the psychoanalysis of Freud and Jacques Lacan (1901–83) and interpretations of the structuralist writer Ferdinand de Saussure (1857–1913).

Structuralism may be distinguished from other traditions by noting its contention that knowledge cannot be grounded in individuals nor their historically given situations. Structuralism also rejects empiricism for its failure to distinguish between the appearance of a phenomena and its underlying 'reality'. It is a 'science of relationships' with the emphasis of holistic structuralism being upon the interconnections or interdependencies between different social relations within society (Runciman 1973). This position holds that we cannot understand the dynamics of a society by studying each of its parts in isolation. Instead, we can explain its parts only through their relationship with other constituent elements in a given system. To give an everyday example. We stop at a set of traffic lights because we contrast the signs with each other. Red signifies that we should 'stop' because it is contrasted with green which means 'go': 'When we see red we see red-and-not-green' (Keat and Urry 1975: 124).

Saussure, the founder of modern structural linguistics, separated the regularities or codes of language (*la langue*) from its usage by an individual who externalizes the underlying system (*la parole*). Saussure argued that there is no consciousness before language. He considered the relationship between thought and language via a comparison with a sheet of paper:

thought is the front and the sound the back; one cannot cut the front without cutting the back at the same time; likewise in language, one can neither divide sound from thought nor thought from sound ...

Linguistics then works in the borderland where elements of sound and thought combine; *their combination produces a form, not a substance.*
(Saussure in Easthope and McGowan 1992: 7, original italics)

Language itself is grasped through an ability to assimilate and order a system of signs which are its basic units. Signs are divided into two parts: the signifier (the sound) and the signified (the idea or concept to which the sound refers). The latter does not refer to an actual object in the material world, but the way in which the system of language, through its signs, organizes the world, with signs becoming defined by their differences within the language system itself. In this way, the conscious individual is supplanted by a system of language which is prioritized over its manifest utterances in individual speech-acts. Given that the relationship of signs depends upon a network internal to the language system itself, they are seen to possess value before signification. Thus, within language, there are no absolutes, only relations of mutual dependence (as with our traffic light example):

The idea or phonic substance that a sign contains is of less importance than the other signs that surround it. Proof of this is that the value of a term may be modified without either its meaning or its sound being affected, solely because a neighboring term has been modified.
(Saussure in Easthope and McGowan 1992: 13)

As language is self-referential, it can be studied as an internal system through which both subjectivity and the social world are produced. Saussure envisaged that this may be applied to the non-linguistic realm as part of the science of semiology. It is the development of this insight that explains much of the history of twentieth-century structuralist thought. Consider, for example, observing a game of chess. It may be concluded that people adhere to common rules. An analysis of those rules would then indicate the strategies of the players, with a direct involvement in the game not being necessary for explanatory purposes. The same can be said of an analysis of food:

The *menu*, for instance, illustrates very well this relationship between language and speech: any menu is concocted with reference to a structure (which is both national – or regional – and social); but this structure is filled differently according to the days and the users, just as a linguistic 'form' is filled by free variation and combinations which a speaker needs for a particular message.
(Barthes in Lemert 1993: 343, original italics)

This focus upon language without reference to a speaking subject, uncovers an affinity with Freudian psychoanalysis. Whereas Freud prioritized the unconscious processes of human behaviour over consciousness, Saussure prioritized the system of language over the intentions and meanings for an individual speaker. Ricoeur refers to this joint combination of attacks on the theory of the subject as the 'semiological challenge' (1982: 35). It is evident in the work of the anthropologist Claude Lévi-Strauss.

Lévi-Strauss (1963) starts his study of 'myths' with a dilemma: that is, their content is contingent but why, given this, are they so similar throughout the world? This is explained through the prioritization of form over content. In using the methods of Freud, he seeks to account for diverse social phenomena in the logic of the human mind itself. He argues that myths are not reducible to individual consciousness, but are themselves a product of a 'collective unconsciousness' (the influence of Durkheim being mediated here via Mauss). This exists prior to individuals and is constraining upon their actions and thoughts. Myths then work to organize social relations and they have a cognitive function.

In the study of myths Lévi-Strauss argues that he has uncovered the universal structures of the human mind. These structures are derived from binary oppositions. The very ability of people to think is governed by dualisms: for example, between raw and cooked; us and them; ideal and material, etc. Whilst there may be cultural variations in the content of these oppositions, their underlying form is universal. Here we can detect a neo-Kantianism. Although not rooted in consciousness, verbal categories are considered as the mechanisms which link the *universal* structures of the human mind to the *universal* structures of culture. However, in this process the subject is displaced by structures beyond their conscious apprehension. This position is also found in the work of Louis Althusser (1918–90).

In contrast to Sartre's (1905–80) existential interpretation (1960), the structuralist reading of Marx enjoyed an enormous resurgence in Althusser's arguments (1969). His aim was to recover the scientific element of Marxism from the tradition of existentialism, without succumbing to the problems of a materialist philosophy of history. To achieve this he employed a 'symptomatic reading' of Marx (a term borrowed from Freud). Broadly speaking, he argued that there was an 'epistemological break' in Marx's writings – between the early (pre-1845) and 'mature' Marx. The latter provided the scientific basis for an explanation of history thereby constituting a dismissal of the Hegelian legacy.

Whilst Engels had added to the one-sided materialist interpretations of Marx, he also wrote:

> According to the materialist conception of history, the *ultimately* determining element in history is the production and reproduction of real life. More than this neither Marx nor I have ever asserted. Hence if someone twists this into saying that the economic element is the *only* determining one, he transforms this proposition into a meaningless, abstract, senseless phrase.
>
> (Engels to Block in Marx and Engels 1953: 498, original italics)

Althusser took this qualification as indicative of the 'relative autonomy' of the ideological and political spheres from that of the economic. How does this translate into structuralist language?

The answer to this question may be seen in the relationship between the system (society) and its constituent parts (people). Society pre-exists the individual and ideological practices provide the means through which people relate to the world around them. What Althusser calls 'Ideological State Apparatuses' (ISAs) – the family, media, educational and religious institutions – constitute who we are, how we think of ourselves and may even be the origin of our individual traits. In other words, they both work through us and yet enable us to recognize ourselves. We even learn the idea of the autonomous bourgeois subject from families and therapists. Speaking of which, Althusser used concepts from the writings of the psychoanalyst Jacques Lacan. Where Althusser sought to conceive of Marxism without Hegel's absolute subject, so Lacan thought of psychoanalysis without Freud's ego (Sarup 1993). Now, in the works of Althusser and his contemporary Nicos Poulantzas (1936–79), who sought to employ Althusserian concepts (Poulantzas 1978), structures do not come from the universal categories of the human mind (Lévi-Strauss) or from language (Saussure), but from the history of class societies.

Making connections with Part II

Whether through critique, revision or contrast, structuralism has generated extensive interest. In terms of contrasts, we can compare Lévi-Strauss's with the utilitarian-based exchange theories of those such as Homans (1961) and the 'rational-choice' model of human behaviour which has enjoyed a well-argued defence in the work of James Coleman (1990). Revisions include the neo-structuralist Mary Douglas (1970; 1978), but her intellectual debt is more to Durkheim given an emphasis on ritual and symbol in social life.

By the mid-1970s, Althusser's legacy had withered and the critiques were numerous. These included the French Marxists Henri Lefebvre (1901–91) and Cornelius Castoriadis, as well as the English historian E. P. Thompson (1924–93). Yet it can be argued that his legacy is apparent in the most productive area of contemporary Marxism: the analytic Marxism of Cohen, Elster and Erik Olin Wright, amongst others (see Mayer 1994). It is argued that the questions they pursue are only possible when Hegelianism is abandoned. In this sense, this school could be termed 'post-Althusserian Marxism' (Callinicos 1993).

As for critical contrast, the structuralist 'dissolving' of the subject has informed ideas on the social 'self' and the agency–structure debate. Anthony Giddens, for example, accepts the problems of prioritizing a 'philosophy of consciousness' in social theory, but does not accept the idea of a 'subject-less history'. As a thinker steeped in the traditions of French social thought, Pierre Bourdieu is clearly influenced by structuralism. Nevertheless, he aims to return agents, rather than subjects, back into the terrain of social theory.

Structuralist connotations will also be found in Habermas's ideas via his use of the work of structural psychologist Jean Piaget (1896–1980), whilst Michel Foucault is often interpreted as working within this tradition.

Structuralism also appeals in the realms of literary criticism, cultural studies and history; the latter being exemplified in the work of the 'Annales' historians (see Clark 1991) who have influenced the 'world-systems analysis' of Immanuel Wallerstein (1990). In terms of literary criticism, Jacques Derrida's engagement with and critique of structuralism in terms of the arbitrary character of signs, has provided the catalyst for an enormous growth of interest in textual analysis (Kamuf 1991; Norris 1987). For one writer, Derrida has been responsible for starting an 'anti-humanism in the humanities' of almost epidemic proportions (Schwartz 1990). Finally, Jean Baudrillard treats commodities as systems of signs which have a reference only to each other. Hence, as will be noted in Chapter 10, he criticizes Marxism for concentrating on production and exchange, rather than consumption and style in contemporary mass society.

Lévi-Strauss developed his methods against the idea that society was essentially stable. He also prioritized structure over function. Yet the inspiration for normative functionalism, which we shall consider in examining the work of Talcott Parsons (1902–79), also stemmed from the structuralist writings of Comte and Durkheim. This found its twentieth-century expression in the work of the social anthropologists Bronislaw Malinowski (1884–1942) and A. R. Radcliffe-Brown (1881–1955).

Systems theory: Talcott Parsons and the celebration of modernity

The emphasis of functionalism, as with structuralism, tends towards the synchronic and holistic. On the other hand, normative functionalist explanations downplay the search for origins or causes of social phenomena in favour of seeing cultures as total systems of functionally interrelated parts. Teleological explanation is then employed whereby the statement: 'the function of X is to maintain Y, implies that X has some kind of causal influence on Y' (Dore 1973: 66). This may be illustrated through the Durkheimian argument that religion exists to provide the moral foundations of society. In order to see how this develops in one particular direction, attention will be focused on the writings of Talcott Parsons.

Parsons perceived a convergence in social and economic theory around the turn of the twentieth century. This centred upon a concern with the subjective experiences and actions of individuals combined with the Hobbesian problem of social order expressed in terms of the question: how are diverse interests in a society possible? Parsons then embarked upon the building of bridges between dualisms in social thought; in particular, between positivism, which ultimately regards human action as a passive adaption to the social world and utilitarianism, where only an actor's orientation to an end is required to understand their actions. According to this idea, social order results from the egoistic pursuit of ends from which is supposed to emerge the 'public good'. Parsons, as Durkheim before him, found this theory to be fundamentally flawed. After all, the pursuit of private ends would be best achieved by 'force and fraud' from which social chaos, not order, would emerge. He thus sought an explanation which moved away from the simplistic notion that action was motivated by self-interest. What form did this take?

Parsons's (1937) theory of action contained four parts. First, the actor. Second, the desired state of affairs towards which their action is oriented (this is the teleological aspect of the act). Third, the social situation in which the action takes place. Here, those social situations over which they have control are called 'means', whilst those over which they have no control, he calls 'conditions', including not only the physical environment, but also biological potential and limitations. Fourth, a 'normative orientation'. This normative orientation he regards as the 'motor' of social action (Parsons in Hamilton 1985: 73–78). Social action is thus conceptualized in terms of the use of means to reach desired ends in a process infused with societal norms. The Hobbesian problem is then resolved via a process in which the actor is seen to possess a sensitivity to the meanings in their environment which they then take account of in acting:

> These normative rules both define what immediate ends should and should not be sought, and limit the choice of means to them in terms other than those of efficiency. Finally, they also define standards of socially acceptable effort. This system of rules, fundamental to any society . . . is what I call institutions. They are *moral* norms, not norms of efficiency.
>
> (Parsons in Hamilton 1985: 62, original italics)

In Parsons's 'second phase' (Hamilton 1983), in which he published *The Social System* (Parsons, 1951), the emphasis of his thought then shifts towards 'social structure', meaning

> a system of patterned expectations of the behavior of individuals who occupy particular statuses in the social system . . . Such a system of patterned legitimate expectations is called by sociologists a system of roles. In so far as a cluster of such roles is of strategic significance to the social system, the complex of patterns which define expected behaviour in them may be referred to as an institution.
>
> (Parsons in Hamilton 1985: 126–127)

Analysis focus is now less upon the actor's rationality and more a specification of what is meant by 'normative orientation' in the choice of actions. Parsons is now more concerned with the means through which social organization may be explained in functionalist terms. Social stability is conceptualized in terms of social institutions which provide 'behavioural forces' which act as linking mechanisms between actions and systems. These institutions ensure 'that action can be sufficiently regularized so as to be compatible with the functional requirements of a society' (Parsons in Hamilton 1985: 127).

In these terms cultural patterns provide the framework for choices between courses of action. These options were reduced by Parsons to four dilemmas, each containing two responses with a definite meaning for the actor concerned. They are: affectivity versus affective neutrality; universalism versus particularism; achievement versus ascription and specificity versus diffuseness (a fifth, self-orientation versus collectivity-orientation, was later dropped). These may be manifest in the following way: the choice to set aside feelings or become more involved in a relationship; to judge an object according to general or specific criteria; to judge an object either in terms of its use, or in terms of a quality independent of its benefit and finally, to come into contact with others only in specific contexts or in many contexts, in which case relationships are more diffuse.

For Parsons the above could be used to categorize modes of action at increasing levels of abstraction: from the personality system, to the normative requirements of the social system and the value-patterns of the cultural system. These formulations involve a movement away from his Weberian and Paretian preoccupations with the rationality of action, towards a Durkheimian emphasis on the internalization of moral order for the purpose of social solidarity. In order to specify these mechanisms of internalization, Parsons employed Freudian psychoanalytic insights. Yet the insights of Durkheim and Freud appear contradictory. After all, in Freud's work cultural patterns were understood in terms of the structure of personalities, whereas Durkheim sought these in society itself through the *conscience collective* as an expression of the aggregate of individual minds. How was this tension addressed?

Within his overall convergence thesis, Parsons viewed Freud and Durkheim as working on the same problem. What was needed was a fusion of the internalization–externalization process which linked the needs-dispositions of personality with those of the social system. However, this did not mean that there exists a simple correspondence between the structure of personalities and social institutions because 'persons occupying the same well-defined status in the social system will be found to cover a wide range of personality types' (Parsons in Hamilton 1985: 127). The need exists, therefore, for 'motivating mechanisms' which take account of such diversity.

Although his preoccupation with social integration is still apparent, following the influence of the Harvard physiologist Henderson, he now begins to see societies more as organisms. For Parsons all theories involved two elements: the static and the dynamic. The static aspect is, as with structuralism, the *structure* of the social system. Its dynamic elements are the means through which the static categories are linked; this is the concept of *function*. The relationship between subsystems of action and the social system as a whole is now of interest where functions provide the links between the dynamic and structural aspects of a social system. An emphasis upon cybernetics, defined as the study of communication between different elements in a social system, now becomes evident in his work.

Drawing on the work of Robert Bales and together with Edward Shils, Parsons then argued that each system, from the *unit-act* to the social system as a whole, had four functional problems. These were listed in order of significance as: pattern maintenance; goal attainment; adaption and integration (AGIL). Pattern-maintenance is concerned with socialization and its focus is upon the structural category of social values. Stability is the key here, involving 'tension-management' due to the potential of 'strain' between personality and the needs of the social system. Goal-attainment is accomplished by the state and polity for the purposes of establishing goals and the motivating elements in the system towards their achievement. Meeting the needs of the system in terms of the acquisition and distribution of resources is required to ensure equilibrium. In a situation of a plurality of goals, however, the question of their 'cost' relative to others will arise. Therefore, a need exists for the economic system to maximize: 'generalized disposability in the process of allocation between alternative uses' (Parsons 1965: 40). Lastly, as systems are differentiated and segmented into more or less independent units, there is the question of their adjustment and contribution to the effective functioning of the social system as a whole. Norms are then required to establish coherence and control between subsystems. As Parsons notes:

> In a highly differentiated society, the primary focus of the integrative function is found in its system of legal norms and the agencies associated with its management, notably the courts and the legal profession.
>
> (Parsons 1965: 40)

In sum, the functional maintenance of the social system is achieved through four functional prerequisites. For the purpose of social stability, values then link the need-dispositions of personality with that of the social system which, in turn, is linked via role-expectations to cultural consensus. Husserl's 'transcendental subject' is now replaced by a 'transcendental actor' given that Parsons sees society and culture as the transcendental conditions for human action (Bauman 1978). By starting with meaningful action and then moving on to consider the cultural and social systems as coordinating mechanisms for that action, neither the individual nor society are prioritized. Therefore, contrary to popular interpretations, he does not simply abandon the individual for the social system over the course of his work. It is more productive for the development of understanding social relations, to see his work as moving from an analysis of action to social interaction within social systems as a whole.

Making connections with Part II

Perhaps the first point to note in reflecting upon Parsons's work was his optimism:

> industrial society is the end of a long road, the culmination of a slow process of maturation. It is the most finished form of society because social organization and human rationality find their finest expression within it.
>
> (Rocher 1974: 158)

We do not discover a longing for a bygone age of community in the face of the forward march of industrialism. On the contrary, the focus on values in modern society was undertaken without a nostalgia for the pre-modern. Yet Parsons was also aware of the major shifts within modern societies towards the expressive and symbolic. In that sense he anticipated some of the modern versus postmodern debates in contemporary social theory (B. S. Turner and Robertson 1991).

In terms of his more direct influences, Habermas, whilst subjecting his work to extensive critique, also utilizes the AGIL schema and systems' ideas (Habermas 1975). Habermas writes: 'no theory of society can be taken seriously today if it does not at least situate itself with respect to Parsons' (1987: 199). Part of this is explained by Parsons's conceptual bridge building between continental and Anglo-American social theory (Sciulli 1985) and we find the systems theorist, Niklas Luhmann, interpreting Parsons in a way which owes more to Heidegger than Husserl. The social system is then seen to require increased mechanisms of control as society becomes more complex and existential anxiety is exacerbated. For the neo-fuctionalist Jeffrey Alexander, however, the system is then over-determined for, in Luhmann's conservative emphasis, no conflict is considered outside of the demands of the system (Alexander 1984). Therefore, we should note that for the more liberal-minded Parsons: 'culture is always a system analytically separated from society' (Alexander 1984: 402).

In the United States Robert Merton (1968) was to modify the functionalist tradition. In particular, his preference for a 'middle-range theory', more amenable to empirical testing, was in tune with American intellectual culture (Bershady 1991). Further, one of Parsons's graduate students, Harold Garfinkel, went on to consider the gaps in his action theory and became the founder of ethnomethodology. Whether in terms of continental or Anglo-American social theory, or as a theorist against which to sharpen theoretical axes, his legacy cannot therefore be ignored.

Embodied in Homans's (1973) article, 'Bringing Men Back In', is the criticism that Parsons gives us an over-determined view of social relations. Whilst a more productive reading has been suggested, its acknowledgement permits me to employ some licence for the purpose of continuity in this unfolding history. Homans may or may not be correct, but what of 'bringing back in' the other half of the population: women?

Feminisms: social theory and social practice in question

The potential for Enlightenment thought to marginalize whole groups of people was noted at the beginning of Chapter 1. Indeed, within feminist thought there exists a consensus that the intellectual and political cultures which have evolved over time have been invented by and for men. For some, the entire social universe of women's lives, including language and meanings, are viewed as saturated with male power (Spender 1980).

This section aims to bring attention to the ways in which theorists, in general, draw upon their 'background assumptions' (Gouldner 1971) to reproduce dominant ideas of men and women and from there, particular images of social relations. Biography and autobiography become important topics for this focus. For instance, in her study of housework, Ann Oakley takes Marx to task for the contradictions between the way in which he lived his life and the generation of his theoretical and political ideas (Oakley 1974). By not reflecting in this manner, social theorists and scientists in general are found to produce partial accounts and explanations which then masquerade as generalizations (Haraway 1991; Harding 1991). In the social sciences this has resulted in a lack of consideration of a whole range of core social activities fundamental to an understanding of social relations: 'areas like domestic work, or reproduction, or intimate relationships' (Oakley in Mullan 1987: 194).

One aim of feminist theory is therefore to focus upon an explanation for the exclusion of women from the considerations of social theory and social life in general. In the twentieth century this scholarship was inspired by those such as Virginia Woolf (1882–1941) and Simone de Beauvoir (1908–86) and then in what is known as a 'second-wave' feminism. Writers within this genre include: Eva Figes (1978), Shulamith Firestone (1988), Betty Friedan (1965), Germaine Greer (1970), Kate Millett (1969) and Juliet Mitchell (1966).

From an historical viewpoint, there exist feminist ideas born out of the daily struggles of women in their everyday lives. These are then mobilized for the purpose of critically investigating the prevailing social order. Take, for example, the history of North American feminism. In the nineteenth century the women's movement aligned itself with the slavery abolition movement (Hole and Levine 1979). Sojourner Truth, once a slave herself, then illustrated the 'double jeopardy' that Black women faced when she spoke at a Women's Rights Convention in 1851:

I think that between the Negroes of the South and the women of the North all talking about rights, the white men will be in a fix pretty soon. . . . That man over there says that women need to be helped into carriages and lifted over ditches, and to have the best place everywhere. Nobody ever helped me into carriages, or over mud puddles, or gives me any best place . . . and ain't I a woman? . . . I have borne thirteen children and seen most all sold off into slavery, and when I cried out with my mother's grief, none but Jesus heard – and ain't I a woman?

(quoted in Almquist 1979: 433)

Feminism takes particular aim at the alleged separation of theoretical justifications and social practices for the purpose of contributing to political change. This separation is often maintained for the purpose of enabling a 'distance' to be achieved in the analysis of society and social relations. From this arises notions of objectivity. Yet upon examination, the basis of this strategy is seen to rest upon unexamined assumptions concerning differences between the sexes. For instance, consider the culture–nature divide. In terms of the Enlightenment quest to differentiate ourselves from nature, women have been reflected in social and political thought via the view that culture is symptomatic of the 'rational man' and nature is closer to the 'emotional woman'.

Distinctions of this type are a topic for feminist theory. It is not suggested that biological differences do not exist between the sexes, but that these gain significance: 'within the framework of culturally defined value systems' (Ortner 1992: 489). Fused with their institutional reproduction within society, these ideas produce both social situations and images of women's place within society:

the organisation of work, the division of labour, the ways in which political and social stability were envisaged, and the respective roles of husband and wife in childrearing . . . The divisions between male and female, science and nature, did not remain at the level of theorising but set the terms for a whole range of concrete struggles which are still being enacted today in the Western World.

(Brown and Jordanova 1981: 239)

In these terms, the masculine becomes the sign of reason and is contrasted with the feminine as the sign of emotion. One is then a standard against which the 'other' is measured. As Lois McNay argues:

A masculinist cultural hegemony is maintained through a process which involves the constantly practised differentiation of itself from what it believes it is not – the feminine.

(McNay 1994: 37)

After all, we have found that a central way in which humanity has been considered is through the ability to exercise reason. In subtle ways, however, the 'knowers' of the Cartesian subject have been assumed to be men:

> Thus it would seem, if this assumption were right, that being emotional, or close to one's body and feelings, would mean being less rational, and therefore less free, and therefore less able to fully participate in all aspects of human life as a mature adult – less than fully human.
>
> (Griffiths 1988: 132)

In subjecting such ideas and practices to critical scrutiny, feminists seek to show that the ideas of 'men' and 'women' are social, political and historical constructs and not based upon so-called 'natural' differences. In applying this form of analysis to the ideas of Marx, Weber, Durkheim and Freud, all are found to be implicitly drawing upon the nature/culture and reason/emotion divides. Durkheim, as opposed to examining the role and place of women in society, simply asserted that they should seek a role commensurate with their 'nature' (Sydie 1987). This view was not based on 'science', but an 'alliance of sociological acumen with strict Victorian morality' (Lukes 1981: 533). 'Society' in Durkheim's work becomes 'a code word for the interests and needs of men as opposed to those of women' (Sydie 1987: 46).

Max Weber, on the other hand, did provide an analysis of patriarchy as a form of traditional power. This was seen to be characteristic of the clan or household group, organized on kinship and economic terms. The patriarch then exercises power based on the interests of the other members of the household. If their actions violate this tradition, then opposition will be directed at the person holding the power, but not the form of the domination as such. Given this: 'Incompetent or wicked patriarchs may be overthrown, but they are usually replaced' (Sydie 1987: 57). Despite this recognition, Weber considered only the father–child, not the mother–child, relationship. In this way the 'private' domestic sphere is analysed in terms of the 'public' sphere:

> In Weber's view the natural (biologically based) relations between mother and child may provide a basis for subsequent social relations but it cannot by itself be considered a social relation. Like other theorists, Weber did not distinguish between the biological capacity of women to reproduce and the social arrangements which surround that action and the subsequent care of the offspring.
>
> (Sydie 1987: 63)

A comparative analysis of these relationships, beyond the confines of Western systems, would have thrown light on its social, as opposed to natural, origins (Oakley 1972).

The focus on the social aspects of *reproduction* produces images of another important notion in the development of social theory: the sphere of *production* in the work of Marx and Engels. However, Marxist-inspired class analysis prioritizes class belonging over other social identities (see Miliband 1990). The operation of patriarchy, defined broadly as the exercise of male power which serves to oppress women, is thereby reduced to the dynamics of capitalist relations. Yet feminist scholarship has shown that capitalism has particular effects not only upon women as a whole, but upon working class women in particular (Rowbotham 1973). This stands in contrast to the idea that the working class form a homogeneous group in relation to the means of production. From a historical viewpoint, it has been argued that the sexual division of labour actually predates capitalism (Barrett 1988). Findings of this type thus throw doubt upon the ability of Marxism to explain the roles and positions of women in society.

Those feminists who seek to use Marxism for the purpose of explanation have reacted to this state of affairs in differing ways. Some, whilst finding analytic mileage in Marx's writings, find it difficult to 'stick to the letter' of his works because the oppression of women, as a distinct class, did not concern him (Delphy and Leonard 1992). Overall, the necessity of modification renders the marriage between Marxism and feminism somewhat 'unhappy' (Weinbaum 1978). Either it should become 'healthier' or it will result in 'divorce':

> The struggle against capital and patriarchy cannot be successful if the study and practice of the issues of feminism is abandoned. A struggle aimed only at capitalist relations of oppression will fail, since their underlying supports in patriarchal relations of oppression will be overlooked.
>
> (Hartmann in Humm 1992: 109)

Whatever the ways in which feminist theories manifest themselves, it is clear that in meeting mainstream theory there is general agreement over the necessity for critique, modification or abandonment, depending upon the perspective from which the relationship is viewed. Therefore, in the encounter between Marxism and feminism new ideas have emerged. Take, for example, socialist feminisms which comprise:

> a set of interventions by feminists into socialist and especially Marxist theory, which aims to analyse and end the oppression of women in capitalist society. As such Socialist Feminism is built upon key texts, writers, political events, and organizations which comprise the Marxist tradition. It is these which have helped shape the agenda for Socialist Feminist debates and reformulations of Marxism.
>
> (L. C. Johnson 1990: 304)

Similarly, out of a confrontation with Freud's work, psychoanalytic feminisms have developed whilst within the writings of radical feminists two themes, in particular, become apparent. First, women as a distinct social group are oppressed by men, where patriarchy is taken to be *the* structure of oppression. Second, given the problems of incorporating male theories for the purposes of developing feminist ideas, radical feminism is seen to be created by women for the purposes of their liberation: 'So reproduction, marriage, compulsory heterosexuality, and motherhood are primary sites of attack and envisaged positive change' (Rowland and Klein 1990: 273). Given this, differences between Marxist, Socialist, radical and psychoanalytic theories frequently centre upon whether ideas generated by men can be used to explain the position of women in society. This, in turn, clearly relates to the political question of what is required in order to achieve women's equality. The theoretical and political are thereby fused.

Making connections with Part II

The development of feminist ideas has necessitated a recovery of women's ideas from their historical marginality (Spender 1983). Further, there exists a continual need to maintain a link between theory and practice for the purposes of social, political and economic change. In its historical unfolding over several hundred years, feminist ideas have worked towards this end in a variety of ways.

In the first instance, there was the call for an incorporation of women into the changes taking place with the rise of modernity. In the works of both Wollstonecraft and de Beauvoir, for example, reason and liberalism combined in order that women may gain equality with men. However, on whose terms? If this is to utilize existing legislation, then are laws to be seen as neutral instruments? This is a highly problematic assumption given the nature of patriarchal relations. Here we witness another direction being formulated within the broad feminist agenda. A stress upon a more gendered view of social relations also appears which

> glorified differences between men and women . . . Emphasis was placed on what is essential to women; by seeing the world through a woman's eyes, by allowing for a women's standpoint, we see not only a new perspective but one that is significantly better, more inclusive, and more life affirming. The celebration of women's traits, when linked to the idea that the marginalized and oppressed have an interpretive edge, gives women an epistemological or epistemic privilege.
>
> (Farganis 1994: 23)

The aim of this new generation of ideas was to erode 'the old distinctions between men and women' (Mitchell 1986: 45). This, as discussed, took place via a critique of the very grounds upon which dominant modes of thought and practice had based themselves. For some, this necessitated concentrating on patriarchy as *the* oppressive mechanism to the exclusion, for example, of the economic sphere. For others, as will become apparent in chapter 8, this emphasis was too one-dimensional.

What we now find is a terrain of feminist social theory which has been influenced by a rich history of ideas. In some cases, paralleling a current trend in social theory, the recognition of differences and diversities between women has led to the abandonment of any explanatory 'meta-narratives' which seek to account for the experiences of *all* women. The essential category 'women' as a social class and their relationship with men then gives way to an examination of the differences between women. Once the coherence of women's identities are questioned in this way, it has ramifications for any political movement which assumes a degree of homogenous characteristics amongst a group which may act as a unifying catalyst for change. Many of the contributors to one feminist reader thus question the use of Enlightenment rationality for the development of feminist theories in general (Barrett and Phillips 1992).

To the contemporary theoretical landscape of socialist, radical, Marxist, liberal and psychoanalytic feminisms, we must now add both postmodern and poststructuralist feminisms. Given this, it is accurate to talk of 'feminisms', not feminism (Humm 1992). Therefore, in chapter 8 I shall outline the development and modification of feminist ideas since the mid to late 1960s. This history will then be continued in chapters 9 and 10 where the issues raised by poststructuralist and postmodernist social theories are examined.

Summary: the legacy for contemporary social theory

In the beginning of this journey we found Dilthey's hermeneutics as a neo-Kantian defence of the dignity of the human sciences. Dilthey, combined with Hegel, placed history firmly within the realm of social-theoretical development. This was a 'turn' in the Enlightenment project because it focused social theory on human understanding and away from a more positivist orientation on the externally observed regularities of human behaviour.

Phenomenology then entered our intellectual terrain and found us travelling from Husserl's transcendentalism to Heidegger's existentialism. Husserl, along with Dilthey, worked on an Enlightenment-based epistemological problematic. The result was that he prioritized 'consciousness' and added to the more subjectivist and action-oriented approach to social theory. This views society as

> the creation of its members; the product of their construction of meaning, and of the action and relationships through which they attempt to impose that meaning on their historical situations
>
> (Dawe 1970: 214)

Heidegger then subjected the divorce of knowledge (epistemology) from 'being' (ontology) to critique. In following the implications of this position social theory could no longer assume a unitary 'subject' who stands at the centre of the social universe. This is manifested in social theory in a number of ways. The combination of Heidegger and Nietzsche can be argued to have provided for the postmodern turn in social theory (Habermas 1992a), whilst Heidegger provides for a more ontologically focused social theory. This also affects how the 'subject' is conceptualized which, up to this point in time, had largely been assumed as something 'fixed':

> From Descartes's *cogito*, to Kant's and Husserl's transcendental ego, to the Enlightenment concept of reason, identity is conceived as something essential, substantial, unitary, fixed, and fundamentally unchanging. Yet other modern theorists of identity postulate a non substantiality of the self (Hume), or conceive of the self and identity as an existential project, as the creation of the authentic individual (Nietzsche, Heidegger, Sartre).
>
> (Kellner 1993: 142, original italics)

This challenge to the subject, combined with cultural and economic changes and critiques from other traditions of thought, has led social 'identity' to become a core topic in modern social theory (Calhoun 1994). Heidegger's critique of subject-centred consciousness also questions the mind–body duality which, since Descartes's time, had often been taken-for-granted. Together with the insights of feminist theory on the nature–culture divide, this has added to an interest in the 'body' within social theory (see Featherstone and Turner 1995; Shilling 1993). Nevertheless, this does not imply the acceptance of biology as a focal point for its development.

Moving away from the German-idealism that informed Husserl and Dewey's writings, the pragmatists tackled the subject–object dualism through concentrating on the inextricable link between consciousness and action in everyday life. Therefore, although developed in the United States, the potential existed for an alliance with both Nietzsche and Heidegger in a critique of the Enlightenment. This inspiration, from variants of pragmatism in our age of uncertainty, have moved the focus away from a search for foundations for social theory and ideas of 'absolute truth', to the notion that truth is dependent on what is 'useful' for action.

In another direction, phenomenology was found to stress a humanism through viewing the human subject as the source of knowledge (humanism also denotes secular atheism: see Blackman 1967; 1968). In Chapter 1 we found Marx stressing a dialectic between human agency and material circumstances. At one level this gave rise to a humanist-Marxism, whilst the issue of structural or system determination versus a more action-oriented social theory, informed the work of the critical theorists who sought to recover the Hegelian and emancipatory aspects of Marx's work. In so doing, they had to encounter thinkers who had challenged Enlightenment thought. In seeking to illuminate a number of central problematics, they needed to overcome the materialist–idealist dichotomy in social thought and take account of both objective and subjective factors in social life. This was achieved without a resort to consciousness by utilizing Freud's work. This also represented a critique of Cartesianism. In the resulting synthesis of ideas, an increased scepticism over the potential for emancipation within the Enlightenment project became evident via the argument that reason and rationalization were at increasing odds with each other.

Marx has also been read as a structuralist. As a general tradition of thought this travelled in two directions. First, there were the works of Saussure and Lévi-Strauss, both of whom worked outside of the Marxist tradition. Their ideas had implications for the study of social life through, in particular, a dissolving of the 'subject'. At the same time a neo-Kantian theme could be traced in the ideas of Lévi-Strauss. Second, there was Althusser who, in returning to Marx's work, argued that there was an 'epistemological break' in his writings which provided for a 'scientific' Marxism.

A neo-Kantianism was also found in the work of Parsons. He perceived a convergence in social thought at the turn of the century and sought to overcome a dichotomy between positivism and utilitarianism in order to develop an action-oriented social theory. Whilst the subject of sustained criticism, Parsons brought the Anglo-American and continental traditions of social thought together. His ideas were then traced in the work of Luhmann, Habermas, Merton and Alexander. More generally, they have acted as an intellectual grinding wheel against which other social theories have sharpened their insights.

Feminism then entered this journey of ideas. Here was a body of thought whose beginnings reach far back into history. Yet these are the very voices that have been eclipsed through a series of unexamined presuppositions, replicated in everyday discourse, which are assumed to exist between the sexes. The implications of feminist critiques are wide-ranging. In particular, scientific thought and practice both reflect and justify a view of society which often excludes from consideration half of the population. This also opens up questions concerning the whole relationship between social theory and masculinity (Hearn and Morgan 1990), as well as the ways in which women and non-white peoples are excluded from dominant modes of thought and practice.

Collectively, these are a heady brew of ideas with which to travel into the terrain of contemporary social thought. Nevertheless, some clear themes have emerged. There is the question of the focus of social theory. Should it explain society without recourse to understanding the subjective interpretations of individuals, or should it seek to understand these everyday meanings, or can it achieve both? This opens up the general question of the nature of the relationship between the individual and society.

With this general theme in mind, my aim is now to examine the terrain of contemporary social thought. Each chapter will start by tracing the antecedents of the theories covered, with a view to the above discussions, whilst considering how they have developed in distinct and illuminating ways. I shall then consider some critiques and modifications to the ideas examined in order that a greater overall understanding is achieved in relation to both their strengths and weaknesses.

PART II

Contemporary theories on society and social life

Section I

Producing society in everyday life

3
Symbolism and performance in everyday life

Chapters 3 and 4 consider the intellectual histories of two action-oriented social theories. This chapter will consider symbolic interactionism and the next, ethnomethodology. As with all the chapters in Part II, this exposition is not intended, nor can it be, exhaustive. The purpose is to examine the development of their ideas on social relations by situating them within the discussions contained in Part I.

In Chapter 2 it was suggested that there were a number of different ways in which the influence of pragmatism may be found in modern social theory. Most of that section was devoted to a discussion of the work of Mead. This was a deliberate strategy. Mead's work represents a bridge between pragmatism as a philosophy and its translation into a social psychology which may be found in the symbolic interactionism of Herbert Blumer (1900–86). It is to the intellectual antecedents and subsequent development of this school of thought to which attention is now turned.

The intellectual development of symbolic interactionism

They are a number of influences on the development of symbolic interactionism. Norman Denzin (1992) 'arbitrarily' dates its beginnings in four publications: Cooley (1902), Dewey (1896), James (1890) and Mead (1910). John Petras (1968) adds to these the psychology of Baldwin, whilst John Lincourt and Peter Hare (1973) talk of the neglected theory of meaning in the work of one of Mead's teachers, Josiah Royce. Paul Rock suggests that interactionism may be viewed as 'an amalgam of Simmel's formal sociology and a pragmatist epistemology' (1979: 28). Here we find the influence of Simmel being mediated through the works of Robert Park (1864–1944), and William Thomas (1863–1947). Sheldon Stryker adds to this list Weber, anthropology and the 'Scottish School' of Hume, Smith and Ferguson who emphasized:

> the relevance of the natural (including the social) world for the emergence of the individual, the organized and internally dynamic character of the human mind, the susceptibility of the human psyche to study within the framework of science . . . and the mind as an instrument for adaption or adjustment.
>
> (Stryker 1980: 20–21)

In terms of enabling some coherence to this intellectual lineage, the works of Mead, Park and Thomas form the basis of a history which develops in different directions. A 'second generation' of interactionists then emerged, most notable Herbert Blumer and Everett Hughes. Differences in theoretical interpretation and empirical direction then arose between Blumer's 'Chicago' and the so-called 'Iowa School' of interactionism, as represented by Morris Kuhn (Meltzer and Petras 1973). 'Third generation' interactionists then arose who took their work in varying directions, thus modifying the tradition. These scholars include Erving Goffman, Howard Becker, Anselm Strauss and Barney Glaser. The modification also continues in the writings, for example, of Denzin (1992), Lofland (1976), Lyman (1991), Shott (1987) and Stryker (1980).

   Given these divergences, the elements of pragmatism will be emphasized in this unfolding history. It begins by considering how Mead provided the basis for symbolic interactionist theory. To complete this intellectual lineage, however, also requires an examination of the work of Thomas and Park. Collectively, their works were to be utilized by Herbert Blumer whose ideas on social life are examined below. In the second section of the chapter, attention will then be devoted to the modification of interactionist ideas with reference to the studies of Erving Goffman.

Mead: the dialectical formation of self in society

Under the influences of James and Cooley, Mead incorporated the subjective states of individuals into the ongoing flow of social action. This resultant link between consciousness and action then became evident in his ideas on the social self; an elaboration of which will assist in understanding the relationship between the individual and society in his work.

   For Mead, the social self was divided between an 'I' and a 'me'. What Mead calls the 'I' is the 'conversational character of inner experience' and is not assumed to be 'an object in consciousness'. As he goes on to suggest, the 'I' is

Kant's transcendental self or 'the soul that James conceived behind the scene' (Mead in Reck 1964: 141). The 'me', on the other hand, becomes the reply to an individual's own talk and represents:

> an importation from the field of social objects into an amorphous, unorganized field of what we call inner experience. Through the organization of this object, the self, this material is itself organized and brought under the control of the individual.
>
> (Mead in Reck 1964: 140)

The result is that the 'self' is no longer considered a Cartesian subject rooted in consciousness (Mead 1930). Whilst Mead conceptualized the mind as a tool which seeks an 'adjustive relationship' (Meltzer, Petras and Reynolds 1975: 30) between the individual and their social environment, there is potential for misunderstanding here. Mead does not conceive of the mind in a crude behaviourist fashion such that it becomes a simple mirror of the social environment. For this purpose, he had to reject not only the mentalism of Cooley, encapsulated in the notion of the 'looking-glass self', but also the individualism apparent in the work of James (Faberman 1985). How did Mead achieve this?

To overcome both these objectivist and subjectivist tendencies, Mead argued that 'subjects' become 'objects' to themselves via symbolic communication. More specifically, language becomes seen as the medium through which people speak, hear themselves speak and thus evaluate their utterances according to the responses of others. The 'I' becomes a 'conversation' within the person and language the medium of reflexivity. This process permits a person to think of themselves as a 'whole'. The 'me', on the other hand, 'is the organized set of others' attitudes which the person assumes through communicative interchange' (Coser 1979: 310). Individuals are therefore engaged in a constant process of monitoring their actions and social selves. This produces a 'self-consciousness' in the individual, thereby overcoming any objectivist tendencies in Mead's thought:

> The self acts with reference to others and is immediately conscious of the objects about it. In memory it also redintegrates the self acting as well as the others acted upon. But besides these contents, their action with reference to the others calls out responses in the individual himself – there is then another 'me' criticising, approving, and suggesting, and consciously planning, i.e., the reflective self.
>
> (Mead in Reck 1964: 145)

Individuals gain the ability to shape who they are by 'taking the role of others'. They conceive of themselves through the responses, attitudes and expectations of both 'significant' and 'generalized others' via symbolic communication. In the normal course of events, social interaction occurs through the ability to attribute appropriate meanings to words, gestures and actions. Young children, as the self develops, relate to a range of significant others: for example, parents and sisters and brothers. Here we see an emphasis (shared with Dewey) on the creativity of the individual through 'the conscious "playing through" in imagination of alternative performances of action' (Joas 1993: 249).

From this 'play' stage, the child develops through to the 'game' stage which involves regulated procedures and rules. This enables the process of self-formation to gain a stability within differing social contexts. A notion of the 'generalized other' develops which controls conduct via an expectation of the reaction of others which occurs within the self. This becomes the means through which the individual and society are inextricably interwoven. Even 'thought' itself becomes 'the conversation of this generalized other with the self' (Mead in Reck 1964: 246). However, as with Weber, Marx and Durkheim, a concern is apparent in Mead's work for the fate of the individual in the face of increasing impersonal forces. On this occasion, it is manifest in what Mead calls 'unaesthetic toil':

> The isolated man is the one who belongs to a whole that he yet fails to realize. We have become bound up in a vast society, all of which is essential to the existence of each one, but we are without the shared experience which this should entail.
>
> (Mead in Reck 1964: 301)

Thomas and Park: the self, society and social change

In order to complete an understanding of the intellectual antecedents of symbolic interactionism, it is necessary to consider the ideas of Thomas and Park who came to their work via the humanities and periods of study in Germany. We find in Thomas's work the first important link between pragmatism and social research. Park's main legacy, on the other hand, was the provision of a macro-sociological frame of reference for future empirical studies of everyday life in American cities (Joas 1993).

As with Mead, Thomas and Park displayed an interest in the creative individual. For Park, such individuals were leaders who could: 'grasp basic human nature and human processes in order to know the potential and limits of change' (Fisher and Strauss 1979: 462). Although sharing these similarities, in part derived from intellectual roots in nineteenth-century European evolutionary theory, there were differences between them when it came to the conceptualization of social progress:

> For Thomas, progress was the history of social groups mounting a ladder which had problematic rungs, at different rates, and with different degrees of opposition or help from other groups. For Park, progress itself was problematic. One could be sure only of ceaseless change – the clash and accommodation of groups – but it was always

possible that groups would become more democratic in spirit, more rational in direction, and more functional in organization.

(Fisher and Strauss 1978: 75)

Chicago, with its changing population, was to be a rich ground upon which to explore the dynamics of social change. The result was an enormous range of empirical studies (Bulmer 1984; Kurtz 1984). Here, I shall concentrate upon the relationship between the individual and society and the nature of social change in their work. In the case of Thomas, this is enabled via a consideration of the relationship between consciousness, action, culture and social change. In Park's work, this is manifest in the relationship between social change, communication and awareness, which themselves give rise to the potential for consensus and understanding.

In Thomas's pioneering work with Znaniecki on Polish peasants in Europe and North America (Thomas and Znaniecki 1918–19), the key themes of his work emerged. In the evolution of history, from the traditional to modern periods, the relationship between the individual and society, or what Thomas calls 'life-organization' and 'social organization', becomes of central importance. Under normal circumstances, people act under habit and continue in this way on a day-to-day basis; until, that is, they are confronted by 'crisis'. At this point in time there is need for a 'conscious operation' (Joas 1993: 30) on the part of the individual where new habits of behaviour are formed. However, as the individual is bound up with the collectivity, a resulting cultural ambivalence arises within them which leads to a pragmatic need to refashion the self. More generally, this necessitates that groups redefine their social situations and in so doing regain control over them – hence Thomas's idea of progress as a 'ladder with problematic rungs'.

The actual resources which are mobilized for reasserting control over social situations are derived from the society of which an individual is a part. At the same time, the social self is bounded by both space and time. The relation between subject and object is then manifest in terms of the values of a society to which an individual belongs (objective conditions) and the attitudes which an individual then adopts in response to them (subjective 'definitions of the situation'). Therefore, whilst social 'facts' are given and transmitted from the past, they must be understood in terms of how they are interpreted by people in given social situations. From this is derived Thomas's famous methodological maxim: 'If men define situations as real, they are real in their consequences' (Thomas and Thomas 1928: 572). It follows that if social theory is to further its understanding of social life, it must study both the objective and subjective features of social life via the relationship between social conditions and group development.

As the earlier quote indicated, progress is conceptualized in Robert Park's work as the 'clash and accommodation of groups'. At an empirical level, this is manifest as a struggle for space in urban settings. A pragmatic emphasis on the social self may then be detected in the idea that people are 'always changing' and 'never self-consistent' (Park 1972: 29). In parallel to Thomas, therefore, the basis-unit of society cannot be the isolated individual, but is

> understood to be the volitional attitudes (willattitudes) [*Willenshaltungen*] of individuals interacting in a group situation. These attitudes can either be expressed as feelings (wishes and beliefs) or as conscious ideas.
>
> (Park 1972: 31)

In this way society becomes a source not only of obligation, but also of inspiration. For Park, even an individual's ability to think is regarded as an expansion of the ideas of those who have gone before them (Park 1972: 125).

Park takes Dewey's idea of communication as the basis for maintaining a social group's unity and integrity during times of social change. As he says: 'Culture includes all that is communicable . . . the essence of culture is understanding' (Park 1972: 102). What he calls 'collective representations', via communication, form the basis of collective actions out of which arise social forms which underlie symbols and social processes (the influence of Simmel is apparent here). This concern with communication and change took him in particular directions. On the one hand, he recognized that only a Durkheimian-style 'moral order' was regulated by the meanings and values extant within a social grouping. However, another form existed which was controlled by competition, or what Darwin called the 'struggle for existence' (quoted in Park 1972: 118). This form is not 'social', as defined in Deweyian terms (as exhibiting meaningful communication), but is maintained by a symbiosis which comes from the division of labour amongst competing groups. This is what Park termed the 'ecological order' (Park 1936).

Having identified these two forms of social order, a central question then preoccupied Park: that is, how do people overcome barriers to communication, which is the precondition of democratic communities, given the competition that existed between groups? The preoccupations of his continental predecessors are apparent at this stage for the question is framed in terms of individual creativity versus the pressure to conform in an increasingly impersonal society. In seeking a solution to this tendency, he merges knowledge and feelings within his ideas (Schopenhauer does appear in his work). Modernity is then seen to require a combination of the knowledge of other group's customs and histories, together with the exercise of compassion which comes from such understanding. This fusion, Park believed, might then permit social change by building bridges between conflict and communities (Fisher and Strauss 1979).

We now have a very rich mixture of social thought upon which to draw that still yields valuable insights on contemporary social, political and economic conditions. Having considered the main themes in the works of these three authors, attention is now turned to the development of symbolic interactionism in the work of Herbert Blumer.

The social theory of Herbert Blumer: society as symbolic interaction

In terms of this unfolding history, it is Mead's work on 'role performance' that is of interest (Mead also used this concept to derive a general theory of the social constitution of intelligence, as well as ethical development: see Joas 1985). Whilst emphasizing the creative aspects of individual performance, the concept of the 'generalized other' permits an individual to anticipate the conduct of person's occupying particular roles. However, this forms a dualism in Mead's thought. On the one hand, creativity is emphasized and on the other, the existence of social roles is posited which create expectations upon their incumbents as to their appropriate behaviour. This dualism permitted Talcott Parsons to draw upon Mead's ideas in linking norms and values to system needs in his action, rather than interaction, theory (J. H. Turner 1974). As will be evident, this is a very different emphasis from that found in Herbert Blumer's work.

Blumer was to emphasize the aspects of creativity in role performance; the result being that he was open to the charge of selectively interpreting Mead (McPhail and Rexroat 1979). Actually, Blumer coined the term 'symbolic interactionism' in order to contrast it with stimulus–response models of human behaviour which were so popular at the time (Blumer 1937). He argued that the responses of human beings to their environments are mediated by meaningful interpretations. Mead's intellectual legacy thus becomes apparent through its ability to conceptualize what such acts of interpretation mean for a general understanding of human being, human action and human association (Blumer 1972).

The following quote encapsulates not only Blumer's interpretation of Mead, but also how he distinguishes it from either a structuralist or systems approach to social life. For Blumer, Mead's whole approach

> sees human society not as an established structure but as people meeting their conditions of life; it sees social action not as an emanation of societal structure but as a formation made by human actors . . . it sees group life not as a release or expression of established structure but as a process of building up joint actions . . . it sees the so-called interaction between parts of a society not as a direct exercising influence by one part on another but as mediated throughout by interpretations made by people; accordingly, it sees society not as a system . . . but as a vast number of occurring joint actions . . . all being pursued to serve the purpose of the participants and not the requirements of a system.
>
> (Blumer 1969: 74–75)

It is not suggested that social structures do not exist: 'Such a position would be ridiculous' (Blumer 1969: 75). However, they become admissible only in so far as they enter the interpretations and definitions of social actors who pursue 'purposes'.

Given the above, we can detect three distinctive features to Blumer's interactionist social theory. First, symbolic interactionism may be contrasted with psychological and sociological concepts – from personalities and attitudes to social roles and structural constraints – because the interpretations of ongoing actions involve a constant process of reorganization or adjustment in intentions and attitudes, as well as judgements as to the suitability of norms and values to given social situations. Both pre-existing psychological and social factors are then of interest: 'only in terms of how they are handled in the interpretative process' (Blumer 1969: 66).

Second, whilst social life is both fluid and dynamic, forms of conduct must be 'fitted together' to enable both the establishment and transformation of patterns of group life. Here we can see the influence of Park on Blumer's work:

> Established patterns of group life exist and persist only through the continued use of the same schemes of interpretation; and such schemes of interpretation are maintained only through their continued confirmation by the defining acts of others. It is highly important to recognize that the established patterns of group life just do not carry on by themselves but are dependent for their continuity on *recurrent affirmative definition*.
>
> (Blumer 1969: 67, emphasis added)

As such, the very ability to interpret the acts of others requires communication and the social fixing of definitions in order that interpretations can take place in the first instance. Only then is it possible to engage in the redefinition of acts in the continual flux of social life. This, in turn, enables the formative aspects of human interaction which gives rise to new relations, behaviours, conceptions, etc. Additionally, this process allows groups to deal with the problems that they encounter in social life (Blumer 1969: 67).

Third, given the focus upon interpretation and definition in human interaction, Blumer argues that symbolic interactionism 'is able to cover the full range of the generic forms of human association' (Blumer 1969: 67); examples he gives include domination, exploitation, consensus, conflict and co-operation. This is contrasted with Parsonian systems theory with its assumption of the 'complementarity of expectations' (Blumer 1969: 68). As a result, the question of the relationship between the individual and society is not given through the inculcation of values and norms, or any structural forms which pre-exist or underlie individual actions and utterances.

Instead, Blumer offers a pragmatist conception of negotiation, communication, interpretation and definition. For this reason, Lewis and Smith (1980) argue that Blumer took a 'nominalist' reading of Mead (this states that there is no independent social reality which exists separately from the 'mind'), whereas Mead can be interpreted as a 'realist' (reality exists, to some degree, independently of the mind).

In replying to this contention, Blumer (1983) seeks to further clarify the relationship between what he calls 'social' or 'joint acts' and 'individual acts'. In these terms, society is viewed as 'the fitting together of acts to form joint action' (Blumer 1969: 76). To return to an earlier point, the individual motivations which give rise to these alignments take a myriad of forms and are therefore viewed as 'the formation of workable relations' (Blumer 1969: 76). Joint actions, which range from collaborative acts between two individuals, to the acts of large corporations, fit together through the acts of interpretation and definition in pragmatic mode. By identifying the social acts which they are about to join, an individual is then able to orientate themselves. These acts of interpretation thereby guide actions, as well as serve as orientating mechanisms towards the actions of others.

The relationship between individual and joint acts involves the continual process of interpretation and definition, built up over time. This introduction of history, or what Blumer (1969) calls a 'career', is ordered through the employment of common definitions. However, lest this be seen as habitual, as with the earlier pragmatist emphasis, Blumer always sees uncertainty constantly looming in the background – no emphasis on modernity as continuity here. These uncertainties can be manifested in a number of ways. For instance, joint acts may not be initiated; they may be abandoned or transformed; the participants to such acts may not create a common definition and hence they rest on unstable premises or, even if they possess common definitions, wide discrepancies are exhibited in the course of joint actions and new situations may then arise which call for exploratory work in order that acts can, once again, be 'fitted together'. Blumer also notes that individuals who are party to joint actions may come to rely on 'other considerations' for the purposes of interpretation and definition, aside from those commonly defined by the participants.

This latter point is somewhat ambiguous. Do these 'other considerations' include the resources that people bring to interactions? If so, do these then enable them to determine the definitions which are employed in their social encounters? Once again, the question of the dualism in Mead's thought, with which this section began, arises; albeit in a different form. Quite simply, if there are 'other considerations', how does this leave the relationship between the individual and society in terms of the notions of creativity and constraint? This is where Erving Goffman enters our theoretical stage.

Modification and critique: exploring the interaction order

Erving Goffman was influenced by the work not only of Blumer, but also of Everett Hughes (1971). However, to these we must add no less than the ideas of Durkheim, Simmel, James, Schutz, Kenneth Burke (1969), social anthropologists, linguistic philosophers and ethologists! They are all mobilized to illuminate a key feature to his work: 'the explanation for action in its meaning for others rather than in its causal origins' (Burns 1992: 3). This is organized around three themes: social order, social interaction and the self. With these in mind, the purpose in this section is to examine the connections between everyday interactions (micro) and society (macro) in Goffman's work. In so doing, it will become clear that he cannot be situated within the symbolic interactionist tradition as presented so far.

In *The Presentation of Self in Everyday Life* (1984), Goffman quotes from a book by William Sansom. It is an account of the ways in which Preedy, a vacationing Englishman, projects certain impressions of himself when making his appearance on a Spanish beach for the first time. In discussing this, Goffman argues that such impressions are symptomatic of an act of calculation by an individual which is oriented towards significant others. These acts of calculation are both intentional and conscious. In addition, as Blumer noted, whilst significant others may be impressed, they may also 'misunderstand the situation', thereby reaching conclusions which bear no relation to the person's original intent in their performance (Goffman 1984: 18). At the same time, the traditions of a group will require particular expressions of an individual in a given role (Goffman 1984: 18). Therefore, although impressions are 'well-designed', the individual who enacts them may do so either consciously or unconsciously. Yet, despite this latter possibility, Goffman argues:

> in so far as the others act *as if* the individual had conveyed a particular impression, we may take a functional or pragmatic view and say that the individual has 'effectively' projected a given definition of the situation and 'effectively' fostered the understanding that a given state of affairs obtains.
>
> (Goffman 1984: 18, original italics)

Although Goffman admits of the potential for actions to be unconsciously motivated or historically informed, his focus is directed upon the meanings of individual actions for significant others. In *The Presentation of Self* this even extends to the abilities of individuals to check upon the validity of a person's utterances by, for example, observing their non-verbal behaviour and interactions with others. Hidden motivations can lurk behind every appearance. Even an attention to the detail of one's dress, in order to project a particular impression of oneself to others, may have to be disguised as it is not assumed to be material to conversations in general. The intent, in other words, which underlies impression management, must remain 'hidden' (Goffman 1971: 23). Hence, Goffman prioritizes 'intentionality' in everyday conduct, over other forms of explanation, in the social arena he calls the 'interaction order':

> Social interaction can be identified narrowly as that which uniquely transpires in social situations, that is, environments in which two or more individuals are physically in one another's presence.
>
> (Goffman 1983: 4)

This is the micro-analytic arena in which Goffman's observations are so acute. It is a 'space' which comprises not 'personal' space but, more generally, the regions or social situations in which the interaction takes place. Therefore, these arenas are also defined as physical areas 'within which two or more persons find themselves in visual and aural range of one another' (Goffman 1981: 84). Meanings are then attributed to both verbal and non-verbal behaviour. The body, for example, may be mobilized to create an impression to significant others, whilst also enabling a space, or what Goffman (1971) calls an 'egocentric territoriality', to be produced by an individual who draws upon the cultural resources at their disposal.

Intriguing as this is, the question still arises as to whether Goffman's emphasis on intentionality still provides us with a subjectivist social theory? Like Blumer, when Goffman is faced with the choice between individual creativity and constraining influences in the analysis of human action, does he always opt for creativity? Or is this a false dichotomy? If he admits of the former then, in terms of role performance, the pre-existence of roles would exercise a constraint upon the scope for impression management and definitions of the situation; the idea of which, it has been argued, was present in Mead's work.

In illuminating the nature of this relationship, Goffman takes a very different line from Blumer. His earlier work on social interaction can actually be characterized as one which examines how the gap between the macro and micro social worlds can be closed (Burns 1992). In the interaction order, the conduct of individuals is viewed as being part of society and social order. Yet, is this not a structuralist answer in terms of the subject simply becoming a conduit through which pre-existing societal forms flow?

Goffman's is neither structuralist, nor individualist. The former would assume that the interaction order is determined from 'above', whilst the latter would assume that it is determined from 'below' via, for example, the calculative procedures of individual actors. Both of these approaches would neglect the fact 'that we not only take other people into consideration when we act, but that we also give consideration to others' (Robin Williams 1988: 67). What Goffman does is to conceptualize this in terms of 'ritual', which he uses in two senses. First, in terms of the moral character of interaction and second, in terms of its 'standardized' or 'ritualized' character (Robin Williams 1988). Habit is apparent in the second sense with a pragmatist focus upon creativity being evident within the first. A working relationship is then established within interactions which themselves vary from setting to setting. Thus, within the interaction order there evolves a

> definition of the situation which involves not so much a real agreement as to what exists but rather a real agreement as to whose claims concerning what issues will be temporarily honoured.
>
> (Goffman 1984: 21)

In this way Goffman admits of the general properties which people possess in order to creatively contribute to the interaction order in the first place. He notes that a psychology is involved, but it is: 'one stripped and cramped to suit the sociological study of conversations, track meets, banquets, jury trials, and street loitering' (1972: 3). The result is a circumscribed interaction order: 'Not, then, men and their moments. Rather moments and their men' (Goffman 1972: 3). As such, the social order provides the interaction order with the resources which it needs to sustain and reproduce itself. Ritual is the bridge between the macro and the micro or, more particularly, the Blumerian concepts of role creativity and history as manifest in the notion of 'career' (Manning 1992).

Exactly how the idea of role provides a macro–micro bridge is illuminated in Goffman's essay on 'role distance'. To paraphrase him, a 'role' is defined as those activities a person would engage in if they acted in accordance with the normative demands made upon someone in that position (Goffman 1961: 75). On the other hand, 'role performance' is the actual conduct of the person in that role. However, the issue still revolves around the notion of role as obligation and expectation. In being obliged and expected to act in certain ways, creativity, in terms of role performance, is clearly circumscribed. To emphasize the normative constraints on a particular role would clearly tend towards a Parsonian interpretation which omits the details of action in favour of theorising it in terms of functionally related system needs.

In considering this tension, Goffman suggests that it is necessary to focus upon both role systems *and* the manner in which individuals manage their roles. Roles then become defined as 'the *typical* response of individuals in a particular position' (Goffman 1961: 82, original italics). What sits between the typical and actual response of an individual in a given role depends upon perceptions and definitions of the situation (Goffman 1961: 82). The researcher may then proceed to create an *analytical category* which allows them to 'bracket off' people whose 'common life situation' is of interest. The normative aspects of a role are then the means through which the individual is enabled to perform their role in accordance with, for example, their life chances and biography. It follows from this that the precise relationship between a person and their role in a given social situation is deliberately held open to empirical investigation: 'Individuals are almost always free to modulate what they are required to do' (Goffman 1961: 133). At the same time, the role, the place and others present will affect that performance, whilst 'other affiliations' will be given credit in that performance.

Two points, in particular, follow from the above. First, in terms of social identity there is no Cartesian ego. Instead, there is a focus upon the social construction and management of the self. Second, Durkheim's world of the sacred and profane, or Park's world of the moral and ecological, are not distinct. One is seen as a resource for the other. This is enacted by the individual through 'role distance', where the role may be prescribed, but the manner of its performance is variable. It is then open to the analyst to study the flux of everyday life: 'One can never expect complete freedom between individual and role and never complete constraint' (Goffman 1974: 269). Thus, whilst the desire to perform the role of mother, for example, may come from a number of sources, these could include the 'political doctrine of destiny' which serves 'to keep women in their subordinate place' (Goffman 1974: 270). On the other hand, what Goffman calls 'situated roles' (1961: 85), do enable agents to produce an impression before others, whilst also taking account of their activities and actions. In that sense, the very presentation of the self in everyday life becomes a constraint upon actions (Rawls 1987).

This approach to the study of roles is a clear modification to the Blumerian tradition of symbolic interactionism. Methodologically, we find a different emphasis as employed in his studies of 'total institutions' (Goffman 1968) and the analysis of everyday talk (Goffman 1981). In his most theoretical work on 'frames', Goffman (1974) argues that the reason for their use rests upon the fact that there is no 'single reality' or 'definition of the situation' which is constructed out of the interaction order. This also places him at odds, as will be noted in the next chapter, with ethnomethodology. Instead, the analyst examines 'frames' in order to understand the 'general properties' that people draw upon in their daily interactions:

> I assume that definitions of a situation are built up in accordance with principles of organization which govern events – at least social ones – and our subjective involvement in them; frame is the word I use to refer to such of these basic elements as I am able to identify. That is my definition of frame. My phrase 'frame analysis' is a slogan to refer to the examination in these terms of the organization of experience.
>
> (Goffman 1974: 10–11)

To return to the discussions in Part I, this move allows Goffman to side-step the epistemological problematic upon which so much social theory came unstuck: that is, the prioritization of subject over object and vice versa. Following James, Goffman does not ask 'what is reality'? Instead, he asks:

'*Under what circumstances do we think things are real?*' (Goffman 1974: 2, original italics). In this way, he can then move on to examine

> under what conditions such a feeling is generated, and this question speaks to a small manageable problem having to do with the camera and not what it is the camera takes pictures of.
>
> (Goffman 1974: 2)

Essentially, in suggesting that the social analyst bracket types of role, or view frames as the means through which people organize their meanings and involvements in everyday life, Goffman sits within the neo-Kantian tradition (Robin Williams 1980; 1988).

We can now say that in terms of the mobilization of particular resources that parties bring to their interactions, their representations of reality can affect reality itself. Thus, when it came to representations of gender in advertising, for example, the male norm of dominance and the female norm of submission were apparent in his analysis (Goffman 1979). At another level, non-verbal gestures, through bodily posture, can also be implicated in meaning production and power relations which then act as tactics of control and exclusion (Bourdieu 1992a).

Having briefly considered the potential for power to govern the interaction order, I just wish to finish this section by noting what will not be found in Goffman's work: that is, an explicit analysis of social structure as manifest, for example, in race and class relations. As he puts in *Frame Analysis*:

> I am not addressing the structure of social life but the structure of experience individuals have at any moment of their social lives. *I personally hold society to be first in every way and any individual's current involvement to be second.*
>
> (Goffman 1974: 13, emphasis added)

To some commentators, this means that Goffman trivializes social life and ends up producing a somewhat conservative view of social relations (Gouldner 1971). On this aspect of his writings, it is best left to Goffman to say how his legacy should be interpreted. When it comes to the sleep of false consciousness in everyday life and to what is often called the awakening of people to their 'true' interests, his overall intention was not to 'provide a lullaby but merely to sneak in and watch the way people snore' (Goffman 1974: 14).

Summary

In terms of Mead's work, we now have new interpretations which are producing rich insights into social life. As Blumer wrote of Mead, his thought will continue to attract interest 'because of the distinctive way in which it ties together individual action and group life' (Blumer 1983: 143). This is the continuing essence to Mead's legacy for contemporary social theory and one which, as we shall see, has been utilized by Jürgen Habermas amongst others.

As for Blumer, his translation of the Meadian legacy was manifest in his call to situate people within the context of their actions in order that the production of meanings and definitions of the social world could be understood in their 'natural settings'. For this reason, he advocated the use of naturalistic research which was taken up and modified in various ways. However, it has been suggested that Blumer selectively interpreted Mead which led to the production of a subjectivist version of the dynamics of social life. Whereas Mead rooted 'perception and meaning in a common praxis of subjects', Blumer focused upon 'verbal communications about definitions which is unrelated to praxis' (Joas 1985: 166). Therefore, it became a point of contention in the development of symbolic interactionism that in this interpretation and his subsequent methodological maxims, Blumer reintroduced the dichotomy between subject and object by prioritizing the former over the latter. Whilst admitting of the existence of structures, they were thus relegated to the status of being admissible only in so far as they were apparent in consciousness (Stryker 1980). In so doing, he returned to the very dichotomy in social thought which Mead had sought to overcome. This is where Goffman stepped in.

When it came to Goffman's work, a line of continuity may be traced with Mead in terms of the development of the self in opposition to Cartesianism. The self is found in a relationship between subject and object which emerges in a community of others in which individuals are shaped and which they reshape, through their actions. In the steps of Hegel and the German idealists since Kant, it was then possible for the Meadian self to become an object of knowledge, experience and development (Joas 1985). This implies that subjects are objects to themselves. With Mead, this was apparent in relationship between the 'me' and the 'I'. For Goffman, it was more sociological in form in terms of his analyses of roles.

Although Goffman's methods were undoubtedly unorthodox, in reading his work one cannot help but gain a great deal of insight into the workings of everyday life in terms of meaning production. Goffman was to see rules of interaction not simply as produced from within social encounters, but also as producing them. He admitted of the presence of structures within social life through the manner in which encounters are 'framed' in order to interact in the first place. However, it was social interaction, not social structure, which absorbed his interests. Nevertheless, he did not presuppose a symmetry of power between co-participants in the interaction order. People possessed differential access to knowledge and information which, in the 'information society', can act as a resource in interaction (Lyon 1994). Further, formal and informal rules exist which can prevent 'outsiders' joining anything from golf clubs and occupational groups to street gangs. Similarly, people are invested with skills and characteristics which they can drawn upon in influencing the actions and definitions of others. This is a legacy that has much to offer the study of social life and there is clear potential in his work for the production of a more general social theory (Giddens 1987; Rogers 1977).

For reasons of exposition, space and general influence on the development of social theory, I chose to emphasize Goffman in this particular journey. Yet within the development of interactionism, the same points on the relationship between social structure and social interaction could have been made in, for example, a consideration of the bounded nature of negotiations in organizations (P. M. Hall 1987; Strauss 1978; 1982). Similarly, there is the work of Howard Becker (1963) on the relationship between societal forces of social exclusion, which result from the power of a social group to define certain behaviour as anti-social, and its effects on the actions and self-definitions of those so labelled. In addition, as noted at the beginning of the chapter, those from within this tradition are now considering its merits and weaknesses through an encounter with postmodernism and poststructuralism (Denzin 1992).

There existed another route for social theory to pursue in order to devote itself to a study of the interaction order. This was to share Blumer's critique of the idea that people are often viewed as cultural dopes who are simply manipulated by structures and systems beyond their comprehension. Our focus now shifts towards an even more detailed analysis of the everyday methods that people employ in interpreting their social universes. This is a route that Schutz's phenomenology was to start, but certainly not to finish.

4

Social life as accomplishment

If, as Blumer suggested, the actor's point of view is a prime focus for an action-oriented social theory, then language and cognition are of central importance to its development. Language, after all, is the means through which people construct their worlds, share their experiences of it, communicate with each other and reflect upon their own experiences. Indeed, Alfred Schutz argued that people experience their social worlds as intersubjective ones which are then accessible to all through the mediums of intercommunication and language.

When it comes to a study of language and social life, the work of Wittgenstein cannot be ignored. Wittgenstein began his writings under the influence of Bertrand Russell, which included a brief association with what was known as the Vienna Circle of logical positivism. In his earlier work, the correspondence theory of truth was exemplified through the argument that the purpose of language was to state facts by 'picturing' them. In his later philosophy, however, he became critical of this insight (Monk 1990). The consequence of this move being that meaning was divorced from its usual basis in signification and different uses of language were collected under the generic term 'language games'. The search for hidden meanings and depth explanations then became replaced by the study of the *use* of concepts in everyday language:

> consequent upon the abandonment of the picture theory, the distinction between sense and non-sense is made entirely internal to language. It no longer depends on any correspondence to external reality but has to do

with the failure of users of the language to accord with its patterns of use.

(Anderson, Hughes and Sharrock 1986: 191)

Wittgenstein's intellectual legacy has paved the way for inquiries into knowledge production and use (Bloor 1983), the use of rules in social life (Holtzman and Leich 1981), as well as developments in the methodology of the social sciences (Clammer 1976). In relation to methodology, the work of Peter Winch (1990) has come to represent yet another assault, along with those of hermeneutics and phenomenology, on the applicability of cause and effect to the study of social life. To this was added the 'Ordinary Language Philosophy' of Gilbert Ryle (1900–76) and John Austin (1911–60), both of whom devoted their energies to the study of language.

A combination of phenomenology and ordinary language philosophy informs the development of ethnomethodology. Therefore, the first section of this chapter contains a more in-depth examination of these influences. Following this, there is a consideration of the diversities which exist within this broad tradition of thought. This will not only enable an evaluation of its insights, but also provide a basis upon which to continue this journey through the terrain of contemporary social theory.

The making of ethnomethodology

The term 'ethnomethodology' originated from some studies undertaken by Harold Garfinkel during his time at the Chicago law school in the mid–1940s. A researcher had 'bugged' a jury room in order to listen to their deliberations. Garfinkel, in analysing the tapes, focused upon the question of 'how the jurors knew what they were doing in doing the work of jurors' (Garfinkel 1974: 15). A study of these conversations then allowed him to consider what 'made' people jurors.

From his analysis of the juror's deliberations, Garfinkel found that they exhibited a methodical basis exemplified by their allusions to the adequacy of the evidence as presented in the court-room. Consequently, he characterized the juror's activities as the doing of 'methodology'. Some years later, in examining some cross-cultural area files, he found a set of words prefixed by 'ethno' (ethnobotany, ethnology, etc.). Garfinkel took this to mean, in more general terms, 'the availability to a member of common-sense knowledge of his society as common-sense knowledge of the "whatever" ' (Garfinkel 1974: 16). So evolved the term 'ethnomethodology'. As a body of thought it represents

an organizational study of members' knowledge of his ordinary affairs, of his own organized enterprises, where that knowledge is treated by us as part of the same setting that also makes it orderable.

(Garfinkel 1974: 18)

A new action theory: beyond Parsons and Schutz

As noted, the intellectual influences for ethnomethodology came from phenomenology and linguistic philosophy. However, the original impetus came from Garfinkel's time as a graduate student with Parsons, whose neo-Kantian emphasis constructed an analytic agenda which was concerned to identify the 'real' workings of society. The questions asked of social relations were of the order of 'what' and 'why'? The former being what is said or done, which then receives an answer expressed in causal terms. However, what of the 'how'? The issue here is one of a disjuncture between the 'concreteness' of people's activities in everyday life and their analytic representation in Parsonian action theory. This result being that 'real society' becomes only 'specifiable as the achieved results of administering the policies and methods of formal, constructive analysis' (Garfinkel 1991: 13). Given this, Parsons's action theory does not render justice to the very phenomena which it sought to understand because it seeks to impose a rationality on human conduct which is separated from the practical concerns of situated everyday life.

In contrast to this sacrifice of 'concreteness' to 'generality', ethnomethodology seeks to describe an order in everyday life that does not resort to an *a priori* analytic framework. This approach is apparent in Garfinkel's analysis of three problems in Parsonian theory of action. First, what is the status of the actor's accounts of their own actions? Particularly when these conflict with the analytic, causal accounts offered by social scientists. Second, as interactionists noted, people share their knowledge. What is the status of this insight in a theory of action concerned to generalize beyond the particularity of a social setting? Third, people are not 'cultural dopes' manipulated as puppets on a string of normative consensus, for they make strategic choices which involve the manipulation of their environments. These three gaps in Parsonian theory are referred to as the problems of 'rationality', 'intersubjectivity' and 'reflexivity' (Heritage 1984: 23). To each of these, ethnomethodology offers a unique solution.

Given these analytic failings, Garfinkel had to take a very different theoretical direction from that of Parsons. This quote, taken from Garfinkel's dissertation, indicates the nature of this route:

> At least two important theoretical developments stem from the researches of Max Weber. One development, already well worked, seeks to arrive at a generalized social system by uniting a theory that treats the structuring of experience with another theory designed to answer the question, 'What is man?' Speaking loosely, a synthesis is attempted between the facts of social structure and the facts of personality. The other development, *not yet adequately exploited*, seeks a generalized social system built solely from the analysis of experience structures.
>
> (Garfinkel quoted in Heritage 1984: 9, emphasis added)

To aim to describe these 'experience structures' has two important consequences for social theory. First, given this direction, the termination point for ethnomethodological interests actually becomes the starting-point for most other social scientific practices, including theorizing about social life. Second, social action is analysed in terms of sense, with a focus on *common sense*, without any particular recourse for this purpose to the notions of intentionality or motives. Bearing these points in mind, I now wish to turn to the intellectual resources which are mobilized to produce these outcomes.

Schutz argued that the object of social scientific study should be the 'natural attitude' in everyday life. *Verstehen* was not a resource for doing social science, but was the very topic which social science should devote its energies to studying. In Schutz's phenomenology, this was the common stock of knowledge that people draw upon in interpreting and ordering their social worlds. In contrast to this route, social science practitioners, such as Parsons and Weber, had projected their theories into the very phenomena which they should, in fact, be faithfully describing: for example, meaningful acts, everyday experiences and mutual understandings (Schutz 1972).

It follows from the above that social phenomena are viewed as constituted as meaningful *before* an analyst appears on the social scene. However, whilst the social world is intelligible, the 'lifeworld', which people draw upon for this purpose, is taken-for-granted by them. These basic 'meaning structures' are then analytically rearranged by social science with the consequence that they are not accurately represented. For this reason, Schutz (1979) argued that social scientific constructs must satisfy the 'postulate of subjective interpretation'. In this way, they would then faithfully reflect these everyday meanings. In contrast to this, one strategy for the generation of interpretative social theories was to construct 'ideal types' of action which serve as bridging mechanisms between subjective meanings and relations of cause and effect.

According to Schutz, such solutions failed to address the nature of the relationship between social scientific analytic categories ('second order' constructs) and the lifeworld ('first order' constructs). A central question thus remains unanswered: that is, a determination of 'the precise nature of the *phenomenon of meaning*' through an analysis of how it constitutes social life (Schutz 1972: 13, original italics). To focus upon how meaning constitutes social life would enable social scientists 'to analyze step by step the meaning-structure of the social world' (Schutz 1972: 13). A 'phenomenological reduction' is then required which permits the researcher to see how objects are constituted out of their appearances as encountered in 'streams of consciousness'. As such, the proper subject matter of the social sciences is not only the stock of knowledge which people draw in their daily lives, but also the 'typifications' which permit them to order their experiences in the first place. Through these interpretative procedures, experiences are ordered into particular groups with certain features, so that they might be intersubjectively recognizable.

From the above, we can characterize Schutz's work as inheriting Husserl's philosophical problematic and then translating it into a phenomenology of the lifeworld. At one level, this provided inspiration for the development of phenomenological social theories (Berger and Luckmann 1967; Rogers 1983). For Garfinkel, however, Schutz was to provide a basis for a descriptive, not analytic, sociology of everyday life which was to find any reference to the 'transcendental conditions' of action to be an undermining of its aims. To complete this move required that ethnomethodology draw upon linguistic philosophy.

Linguistic philosophy and ethnomethodology

It has been suggested that Parsons examined the external moderation of moral rules, without recourse to a description of everyday knowledge. Schutz, on the other hand, was concerned to examine this knowledge, but without reference to the moral dimensions of social life. Given this, Garfinkel sought to integrate the moral and cognitive dimensions. In essence, his journey involved the abandonment of epistemology in favour of method-ology. Quite simply, people get on with their daily lives by drawing upon a stock of background knowledge which makes sense of their social worlds. To 'know' what people are doing does not require any recourse to hidden motives or models of rationality, but the accurate description of everyday phenomena:

> 'know' consists really in a structure of activity. This is what the 'know' consists of. It is not that the member has it somewhere in the nervous traces or that he has it according to a theory of personal action, and that this will not permit someone to elicit what he has available to tell you ... The 'know' resides in the ability to generate ... recognizable sentences.
>
> (Garfinkel in Hill and Crittenden 1968: 47)

This idea of 'knowing' as available in the situated utterances of actors is found in the work of Wittgenstein, whose later studies can be read as the examination of philosopher's talk as *indexical* (Garfinkel and Sacks 1986). Wittgenstein suggested that philosophers cease asking questions which they cannot answer and turn instead to a study of meaning in terms of use *in situ*. In ethnomethodological parlance, this becomes translated as the abandon-ment of a need to use intentionality or motive to explain an action or utterance. The whole concept of an 'I', from Descartes and Kant, through to Freud, Mead and Husserl, becomes but a 'phenomenological residua' in social thought (Coulter 1979). It is a history based upon an ontological assumption which is then, illegitimately, used to explain human actions. In contrast to this, ethnomethodology seeks meanings in situated and practical usages in everyday life without reference to an ego. As a result, it represents a critique of aspects of the Enlightenment project. The correspondence theory of truth, according to which there is a difference between the perceiving of an object and what it 'really is', seeks to explain reality separate from the act of perception. According to the congruence theory of reality, on the other hand, there is no difference between these two parts. They are: 'synonymous and interchangeable' (J. M. Atkinson 1978: 176).

The intellectual armoury for this move is found in the 'later' Wittgenstein. He argues that there is no private or 'inner', or transcendental referent to which the analyst might allude in determining the meaning of an expression or action. 'Nothing', Wittgenstein asserts, 'is more wrong-headed than calling meaning a mental activity' (quoted in Thompson 1981: 29). Meaning is therefore to be determined via a study of use in context where there exists 'publicly available' linguistic forms. It is these 'forms of life' which serve as backgrounds to social activity (there are parallels here between Heidegger and Wittgenstein). In this way, ethnomethodology could develop without reference to an '"I" which, if it were only public, could explain us all' (Coulter 1979: 124). Ontological, as well as epistemological assumptions, are believed to be abandoned in the process.

We may translate this as the argument that words do not stand for ideas or objects as such, but are the tools acquired within a form of life which people then draw upon as the basis for achieving intersubjective understanding. Language and social relations, in other words, become inextricably linked:

> To give an account of the meaning of a word is to describe how it is used; and to describe how it is used is to describe the social intercourse into which it enters.
>
> (Winch 1990: 123)

As noted, this is accomplished without recourse to explanation in terms of the motive of individual egos or external relations of cause and effect. With this comes an alteration in the criteria through which social phenomena are understood:

> if the sociological investigator wants to regard them *as* social events . . . he has to take seriously the criteria which are applied for distinguishing between 'different' kinds of actions and identifying the 'same' kinds of actions within the way of life he is studying. It is not open to him arbitrarily to impose his own standards from without. In so far as he does so, the events he is studying lose altogether their character as *social* events.
>
> (Winch 1990: 108, original italics)

We can now return to the theme of rationality which Garfinkel exposed in Parsons's work. If it is to be understood, then it must be situated within a form of life. The task is then to describe its form from within, not to impose an explanation from without.

Winch argues that forms of life must be rule-governed and rule-following in order that intersubjective agreement can exist in the first instance. Rules thus occupy a central place in this analysis: 'all behaviour which is meaningful (therefore all specifically human behaviour) is *ipso facto* rule-governed' (Winch 1990: 52, original italics). Following Wittgenstein, rules are viewed as publicly available and intelligible within their social context. This does not necessarily mean that agents will know the rules upon which their actions are based, nor that they will always follow particular rules, merely that all social behaviour involves the acceptance or rejection of rules.

Important possibilities in ethnomethodological analysis are now opened up through such arguments: in particular, the study of naturally occurring conversations in everyday life. Conversation analysis (or 'CA' as it is abbreviated) has grown considerably since the 1960s. Under the pioneering work of Harvey Sacks (1963; 1972), this has led to a growing body of work (J. M. Atkinson and Heritage 1984; Boden and Zimmerman 1993). The themes of the correspondence and congruence theories of reality become apparent in these studies, for the ethnomethodologist can

> divorce the theory of action from its traditional preoccupation with motivational issues and recentre it on the knowledgeable ways in which, whether consciously or not, social actors recognise, produce and reproduce social actions and social structures.
>
> (Heritage 1990: 225–226)

Armed with these intellectual antecedents, ethnomethodology focuses upon a central problematic: 'how do social actors come to know, and know in common, what they are doing and the circumstances in which they are doing it' (Heritage 1984: 76). In order to see how these dimensions work, Garfinkel exposed the interpretative procedures of interaction which people routinely draw upon by devising a series of 'breaching' experiments. In one case, students returned to their homes, for fifteen minutes to one hour, and observed the scene as if they were lodgers:

> Many students became uncomfortably aware of how habitual move-ments were being made; of *how* one was handling the silverware, or *how* one opened a door or greeted another member . . . Many accounts reported a variation on the theme: 'I was glad when the hour was up and I could return home to the real me'.
>
> (Garfinkel 1967: 46, original italics)

For ethnomethodology, social order does not reside in the dictates of external rules as applied to situated activities. Instead, it emerges from within the practical circumstances of social life. To return to one of the problems in the theory of action – the actor's rationality – the illumination of social life through models of formal rationality in social science may be required for scientific theorizing, but it is not required, as Schutz had argued: '*in theorizing activities employed in coming to terms with the affairs of everyday life*' (Garfinkel 1967: 280, original italics). Everyday rationalities are data to ethnomethodologists, not impediments to their inquiries:

> the activities whereby members produce and manage settings of everyday life are identical with members' procedures for making those settings 'account-able' . . . When I speak of accountable . . . I mean observable-and-reportable, i.e. available to members as situated activities of looking and telling. I mean, too, that such practices consist of an endless, ongoing, contingent, accomplishment; that they are carried on under the auspices of, and are made to happen as events in, the same ordinary affairs that in organizing they describe.
>
> (Garfinkel 1967: 1)

In this sense, Weber's distinction between formal and substantive rationality is seen as a neglected one in social science (Garfinkel 1967: 281 fn). The former is employed as a model against which to judge the adequacy of routine actions. When translated, for example, into the study of formal organizations, rules are then seen as either placing limits upon actions, or something against which those actions may be judged, as opposed to being resources upon which actors routinely draw in the situated nature of their activities (Bittner 1974; Wieder 1974).

Summary

To remain faithful to the goal of understanding, ethnomethodological writings refer to indexicality, reflexivity, indifference and the documentary method of interpretation. Indexicality allows the theory of action to be tackled in a very different fashion to any we have come across before: for example, the link between particularity and generality in terms of objective mind (Dilthey). Normally, indexical expressions are regarded as impediments to constructive analysis because they are seen as in need of 'remedy' in order that they make sense. However, ordinary language will make sense only by examining use in context.

As Garfinkel's experiments demonstrated, each person will assume that the other will know a setting if their situated practices 'are to serve as measures to bring particular, located features of these settings to recognizable account' (Garfinkel 1967: 8). Thus, reflexivity is a routine feature of interactions that

> Members know, require, count on, and make use of . . . to produce, accomplish, recognize, or demonstrate rational-adequacy-for-all-practical purposes of their procedures and findings.
>
> (Garfinkel 1967: 8)

Actions, therefore, are not simply habitual, but subjected to 'routines' which are fragile. Because of this the actor has to be reflexive in order to continually monitor their own and others' actions and utterances to make sense of social action(s).

To study social phenomena in the above manner requires that the researcher exercises 'indifference'. The aims here is to faithfully describe the organized and routine features of natural language, whose indexical expressions are ordered and whose ordering is the direct result of the ongoing practical accomplishment of agents:

> Ethnomethodological studies of formal structures are directed to the study of such phenomena, seeking to describe members' accounts of formal structures wherever and by whomever they are done, while abstaining from all judgements of their adequacy, value, importance, necessity, practicality, success, or consequentiality. We refer to this procedural policy as 'ethnomethodological indifference'.
>
> (Garfinkel and Sacks 1986: 166)

Finally, the documentary method of interpretation, which Garfinkel gleaned from Mannheim (1952), refers to a form of reasoning, rather than a particular method of social inquiry. This allows a focus upon the way in which lay and professional accounts of social reality rest upon procedures of interpretation. Take, for example, the structuralist contention that a surface appearance stands for, and is indicative of, a deeper underlying pattern that is determining of human behaviour. This method of reasoning makes sense of the social world. These same methods are used in everyday life whereby understandings are the product of a circular process between an event and the background against which it takes place. This process embodies both indexicality and reflexivity because changes in social reality will only make sense against the context in which they appear. The consequences being that individual(s) are required to change their understandings and evaluations. These new meanings structures become, once again, the topics of ethno-methodological inquiry. We are now firmly on the original route that Garfinkel was to take ethnomethodology down:

> I have been concerned with the question of how, over the temporal course of their actual engagements, and 'knowing' the society only from within, members produce stable, accountable practical activities, i.e. social structures of everyday activities'.
>
> (Garfinkel 1967: 185)

The diversity of ethnomethodology

Looking back over its history, the reaction to ethnomethodology amongst the social scientific community has usually been one of refutation and con-demnation to varying degrees (Gellner 1968; 1974; Goldthorpe 1973; Hollis and Lukes 1982; MacIntyre 1973; Mennell 1975; B. Wilson 1970). These critiques have tended to focus upon its refusal to consider history, power and social structure, as well as the relativism engendered by its presuppositions. The result is said to be an idealist and empiricist social theory, which is inevitably conservative in orientation and has achieved little in the way of advancing an understanding and explanation of the dynamics of social relations.

At another level, ethnomethodology has been translated as an offshoot of symbolic interactionism (Meltzer, Petras and Reynolds 1975). Although some ethnomethodologists allude to the works of those such as Mead or Blumer to sustain their arguments, there are important differences in the basis of their understandings of social life (Denzin 1974; Zimmerman and Wieder 1974). However, there are those who self-define as ethnomethodologists and who are closer to interactionism than others. Goffman is sometimes mentioned in these terms, but as the discussion in chapter 3 and his own writings make clear, he is hardly a convinced ally of this school of thought. For instance, Goffman regarded social reality as more multi-layered than these one-dimensional views of social life seem to assume. Yet he was to provide inspiration for the writings of Harvey Sacks.

This state of affairs leaves many a social scientist somewhat bewildered in their attempts to situate ethnomethodology. For some, the very choice to have a chapter on this subject will lend credence to a discredited perspective. This view is mistaken because it fails to take account of the history, aims and achievements of ethnomethodological studies of social life.

Given this mixture of misunderstanding and critique, this section will concentrate upon the diversities which exist within this broad tradition of thought. For the sake of brevity, these may be considered as endogenous issues which are raised by those who are more sympathetic to its history and aims than those exogenous critiques noted above. This, I hope, will enable a measured evaluation of its basis and achievements, as well as its shortcomings.

The seeds of diversity

In its genesis, ethnomethodology contained the seeds of diversity and difference. The phenomenological input, for example, always possessed the potential for re-activation in the face of the assault by ordinary language philosophy. This is particularly manifested in its translation into conversation analysis. The critique of the mind–body duality which ordinary language philosophy brought with it was no friend of phenomenology with its emphasis on consciousness and intentionality. As Jeff Coulter puts it:

> A major corrective . . . to the Schutzian programme is to insist upon the relevance of what Wittgenstein termed 'criteria' for practical conceptualisation in everyday life. Criteria are defeasible, conventional evidences for the constitution of phenomena, and they are inextricably

linked to the differential distribution of practical interests in social existence.

(Coulter 1983: 123)

This tension between language as a medium for the expression of intentions, motives or interests and language as a topic for uncovering the methods through which ordered activity is generated, is an important one. Whilst there are overlaps between these approaches, those of the latter persuasion are concerned with the external observation of 'naturally occurring' statements made by individuals. The result is to downplay the phenomenological input of meaning in interaction. Whilst meaning clearly relates to linguistic categories, it is clear that the translation of Wittgenstein into ethnomethodology, in terms of meaning as use and the notion of publicly available linguistic forms, has lent itself to a desire to achieve a presuppositionless form of social inquiry that translates into a descriptive endeavour without a social subject.

Ironically, this lack of reference to a motivated subject who engages in conversation with some purpose or strategy in mind, has led to variants of ethnomethodology sharing its critique of phenomenology with structuralism (Lemert 1979; Rogers 1984). Conceptually, there exists a general agreement that the basis for understanding social action is environmental in nature, without reference to the mental states of individuals. Empirically, this is manifested in a concern with the sequencing of conversations, as opposed to considerations for their content. The result is that agents appear as decentred mechanics who, in drawing upon the natural attitude, take turns in conversations. The radical reflexivity which was once stressed is then: 'all but expunged from the ethnomethodological sensibility' (Pollner 1991: 373).

This abandonment of praxis, despite the parallels between Marx and Wittgenstein (Rubinstein 1981), leads to a displacement of the social 'self' with de-contextualized conversations becoming of prime focus in the study of social relations. Further, the analysis of conversations, without any reference to interest or motive, leads to functionalism. Take, for instance, the following quote from a leading ethnomethodologist:

> we will briefly illustrate a variety of ways in which the design of actions can contribute to the maintenance of social solidarity . . . it will be suggested that there is a 'bias' intrinsic to many aspects of the organization of talk *which is generally favourable to the maintenance of bonds of solidarity between actors* which promotes the avoidance of conflict.

(Heritage 1984: 265, emphasis added)

As suggested, this tension within ethnomethodology is exemplified by conversational analysis. This route here is an empiricist, rather than a hermeneutic one. CA seems to have travelled in two directions. First, through attention to the detail of 'descriptive accounts' in everyday life (Garfinkel and

Sacks 1986; Sacks 1972). Here, the idea of 'categorization devices' which people employ in order to make sense of their environments is found. Thus, Roy Turner (1974a) documents how people explain and predict the behaviour of formal mental patients in accordance with particular categories generated within interaction.

Second, CA has moved ethnomethodology even further away from its phenomenological input. This route entails a description of the sequential organization of interactions. Of course, it may be argued that such indexical expressions are windows through which the analyst can 'gaze upon the bedrock of social order' (Maynard and Clayman 1991: 399). Within this genre, there are studies on turn-taking in conversations, initiating topics and the starting and finishing of phone calls (Button and Casey 1984; Houtkoop-Steenstra 1993). Taped, naturally occurring conversations exhibit sequences which lend themselves to a processual mode of social inquiry.

At this point an argument may be employed whereby social settings are not of interest because people use conversational devices to account for what they do, regardless of the situation in which it takes place. The talk itself will then reflect methods of accounting which may even transcend, it is sometimes contended, cultural context. Therefore, these works may omit reference to not only the purposes of conversations, but also the settings in which they take place. What is or is not empirically admissible is then set according to such precepts. This allows the contention that political and economic resources are seen by 'other' social scientists to zoom down on everyday life as if from some 'conceptual ionosphere' (Benson 1974). Conversations are seen to exhibit symmetrical power relations. However, this is highly contentious, particularly with reference to the question of gender and conversational interaction (Tannen 1993); although there exist exceptions to such an approach (West and Zimmerman 1983).

If understanding of the interaction order is said to be more complete by using these methods, two further questions remain. The first has been considered: what happens to the practical creativity, as well as the constraints, in the interaction? This decentring of the strategic subject is manifest in CA reports which refer to 'members'. Members, presumably, who routinely and procedurally draw upon some impersonal interaction order. This desire to see social life from the 'inside' apparently free from presupposition is achieved at a very high cost:

> The radical stress on observable details risks becoming an unprincipled, descriptive recapitulation devoid of significance . . . minute descriptive detail is assembled in a hyper-realist profusion, until the reader loses any sense of meaning.
>
> (P. Atkinson 1988: 446)

Second, there is a methodological problem. This concerns the status of investigators who, in ignoring social context, appear to believe themselves capable of floating freely across language games without being fettered by the constraints of their own. This we can characterize as the hermeneutic absence in ethnomethodology. In this way, the analyst ignores the central question of translation between language games.

These problematics have been raised because, in various ways, they are addressed by those who once appeared in ethnomethodological anthologies. Amongst these we find a concern not only with language, but also with the meanings of interactions for the parties concerned. In addition, we find an attention to the social contexts in which such interactions take place in order that the connections between speech-acts and the forms of life of which they are a part are understood. For this reason we find a reluctance to submit to disembodied and de-contextualized studies of the sequencing of conversations.

This 'out-group' of the ethnomethodologically inspired includes Dorothy Smith, Aron Cicourel, Jack Douglas, Mary Rogers, Alan Blum and Peter McHugh. Their collective works provide for yet more differences within the ethnomethodological perspective which address some of those issues raised above. For instance, a recovery of the phenomenological notions of 'intentionality' and 'inner-time consciousness' and 'horizon' in order to address the limitations of a naturalistic ethnomethodological study of social action (Rogers 1983).

Aron Cicourel has been largely responsible for bringing ethnomethodological insights to a wider audience. Despite this, his attempts to avoid objectivism in interview and survey methods (Cicourel 1964) have, according to some, abandoned ethnomethodology as an alternative paradigm to conventional action theories (Sharrock and Anderson 1986). Yet Cicourel does seek to develop a theory of meaning which is sensitive to social context and is concerned with reflexivity:

> If we hope to construct a theory of meaning that enables us to understand how we assign sense to our everyday worlds and establish reference, then we cannot assume that oral language syntax is the basic ingredient of a theory of meaning. The interactional context, as reflexively experienced over an exchange, or as imagined or invented when the scene is displaced or is known through a text, remains the heart of a general theory of meaning.
>
> (Cicourel 1973: 140)

This search involves an empirical consideration of the sign language of the deaf with conceptual armoury provided for by Schutz and the linguist, Noam Chomsky. Chomsky's emphasis on competence by the users of language separates him from the structuralist tradition, but is taken as indicative of a deeper structure of rules which the surface utterances express (Chomsky 1980). In using these insights, Cicourel argues that it is necessary to understand what he calls 'interpretative procedures' which are 'socially relevant cognitive properties' (Cicourel 1973:168). It is these properties which provide for the competencies which enable people to produce everyday social structures and a sense of social order. These 'typifications' have then been analysed in relation to the processing of juvenile delinquents (Cicourel 1976) and provide the means through which micro events may be linked to macro considerations (Cicourel 1981) through, for example, the interplay between language, socialization and power (Cicourel 1993).

Dorothy Smith's (1987; 1993) work, which is further considered in Chapter 8, is unusual amongst the ethnomethodologically inspired. Although once thought of as worthy of inclusion in ethnomethodological anthologies (D. E. Smith 1974), an examination of such contemporary representations would seem to rule her out (see Coulter 1990). Broadly speaking, Smith sees in ethnomethodology the potential for examining the nature of the ideology which infuses women's everyday lives. At the same time, she is critical of conventional empirical and theoretical routes for getting at social 'reality' which end up sequestrating women's experiences. A more critical theory, aware of the 'relations of ruling' is required to understand this process which a descriptive sociology only serves to reproduce:

> Though women are indeed the expert practitioners of their everyday worlds, the notion of the everyday world as problematic assumes that disclosure of the extralocal determinations of our experience does not lie within the scope of everyday practices. We can see only so much without specialized investigation, and the latter should be the sociologist's special business.
>
> (D. E. Smith 1987:161)

Clearly, she is not in the business of describing the sequencing of alleged symmetrical verbal interactions. Her starting-point is a power imbalance in social relations and this steers her towards the field of critical linguistics (see Fairclough 1989). As John Thompson puts it, the domain of ideology, which is Smith's topic, is the place 'where the construction of meaning intersects with asymmetrical relations of power' (Thompson 1984:118). What we might refer to as 'mainstream' contemporary ethnomethodological writings seem to view these formulations as a distraction from the goal of accurate descriptions of the orderliness of social reality (Button 1991a).

It is this goal of description and its tenuous connection to the anti-positivist strand within the original development of ethnomethodology which concerns McHugh, Blum and their colleagues (McHugh *et al.* 1974). To find context free rules of interaction, as variants of CA seem to suggest, is to reproduce the very generalizing tendencies of positivism which do not exhibit a concern for situated meanings. In Pollner's (1991) characterization, this form of ethno-methodology has become more concerned with 'endogenous' rather than 'referential' reflexivity. The former refers to that which 'members' possess in a social setting, whilst the latter considers the process of constructing the object or field of analysis.

Here we find a tendency for ethnomethodology to gloss over referential reflexivity in the search for naturally occurring descriptions of social interaction. According to Blum and McHugh, this should be replaced by a relativism which sees truth in terms of time and convention. As McHugh puts it: 'the truth of a statement is not independent of the conditions of its utterance' (McHugh 1974: 329). Yet this is the theme which variants of CA appear to overcome by generalizing about conventions of language free of social context as if reasons *for* actions were causes *of* actions. If such practices are submitted to the original canons of referential reflexivity which ethnomethodology had called for, it would clearly fall short of meeting these standards. Instead, what is now produced is a supposed authoritative inquiry which fails to see how its own grounds of thinking are themselves constituted as a product of social relations (McHugh *et al.* 1974).

In the above manner, the world appears as a fixed entity, rather than a collaborative one involving people working together in an imaginative manner over problems which concern them. This Heideggerian inspired critique expresses the limitations of a form of ethnomethodological analysis which is pessimistic because it fails to see the possibilities which exists for different courses of social action. The result being a social universe which appears as a static, not dynamic phenomena:

> We . . . are not interested in terminating our analysis with descriptions of things, or in using our ability to speak about things in an orderly way as criteria of successful analysis . . . Our concern with such productions is reflected in our seeing them as occasions for renewing our own collaboration called analysis, because it is on such occasions that we become engaged with the question of possibility itself.
>
> (McHugh *et al.* 1974: 17)

In all of these modifications to the ethnomethodological school of thought, it is clear that it is a very broad tradition. Paradoxically, contemporary forms of its practice seem to repeat the very mistakes which were the inspiration for its beginnings: for example, the parallels with structuralism via a critique of the subject and with positivism through an abandonment of referential reflexivity in favour of a narrow form of scientism as apparent in the practice of forms of conversation analysis.

Summary

Ethnomethodology found its inspiration in Heidegger's idea that understanding is the business of life and Wittgenstein's ideas on language. It refuses to be shackled by theory, epistemology and philosophical speculation, in favour of being an empirical, some would say empiricist, programme of investigation. Here, therefore, lies an important change in social thought which many commentators have overlooked in their desire to trivialize and dismiss its implications for social scientific practices.

In general, ethnomethodology requires nothing less than a radical shift in the focus of social scientific inquiries. Sociologists, for example, should no longer assume Durkheim's notion of social reality as *sui generis*, or view human behaviour as following the impersonal and general rules of a role, or the covering laws of cause and effect. Instead, social order is a direct result of people's 'accomplishments' in their everyday lives. Psychologists should cease experiments which are of no relevance to the practical activities of people as they go about their daily lives and anthropologists should stop 'glossing over' the details of people's situated activities (Button 1991a).

Ethnomethodology is thus concerned with common-sense understandings in everyday life which are publicly available. These render intelligible the environments which people encounter in their situated activities. These cognitive methods are not derivable in some *a priori* sense through, for example, a general theory of the dynamics of society, formal rules or the universal properties of the human mind. Instead, in fusing the moral and cognitive aspects of interpretation, Garfinkel and his followers examine the practical and situated ways in which people make sense of their environment and of each other.

Ethnomethodology is believed to be a descriptive, not normative endeavour. There is a continual stress upon indexicality, reflexivity, accomplishment, intelligibility and knowledgeability in everyday life. The result being that the Parsonian problematic of social order is approached from the micro, not macro end of the theoretical spectrum. Conventional questions, such as 'Where does the natural attitude come from in the first place?', are either reframed or abandoned. The question of rationality, for example, becomes that which is situationally accountable. Questions of epistemology and ontology are transformed. The theory of knowledge becomes a description of the properties of social organization (Sharrock and Anderson 1991). Quite simply, questions of 'What?' and 'Why?' are reframed as those of 'How?' Even when it comes to the relationship between the individual and society or macro versus micro theory, these are 'resolvable in the work of sociological description, which is remorselessly reliant upon the documentary method of reasoning' (Sharrock and Anderson 1986: 54).

In these ways ethnomethodology is enabled to side-step conventional questions of truth. However, this has a cost in terms of an increased abstraction from the concerns which preoccupy not only social scientists, but also people in their daily lives. Ethnomethodology will remain unattractive to those who still wish to pursue something called 'the truth', or illuminate meaning, or relations of power and modes of oppression which exist within societies and even produce studies in the service of policy-makers. The unfortunate consequence being that an ethnomethodological 'in-group' seem to increasingly refer only to the works of each other and is itself a topic for textual analysis (Rogers 1984).

Despite these differences within ethnomethodology and the critiques that have emerged from other social scientists, there is a social theorist who has incorporated the insights of ethnomethodology, but who is not content to permit it the last word on society and social relations. The result is an attempt to fuse the macro and micro by examining the reproduction of society in social relations. It is to the work of Anthony Giddens that I now turn.

Section 2

Reproducing society within social relations

5

Society as enabling and constraining

Let me start by returning to our discussion of Goffman. According to Peter Manning (1992) Goffman makes three important advances in linking the macro and micro aspects of social life. First, the interaction order is connected to the production and reproduction of social structures. Second, via this link, it is possible to see how relations of power are implicated in social life and third, the identities of role incumbents are open to general analysis: for example, along race, class and gender dimensions.

Manning's inspiration for his observations does not come from Randall Collins (1981) or Aron Cicourel's (1981) 'aggregation hypothesis' which suggests that: 'macro-phenomena are made up of *aggregations* and *repetitions* of many similar micro-episodes' (Knorr-Cetina 1981: 25–26, original italics). Instead, the theoretical route that he takes is one of the 'hypothesis of unintended consequences' (Knorr-Cetina 1981) as derived from the work of Anthony Giddens. In this case, micro-events are seen to both produce and reproduce social systems by virtue of the intended and *unintended* consequences of human actions. The choice is now no longer between the micro or the macro in analysing society and social relations, for the overall intention is to transcend the agency–structure dualism in social thought. The task of the social analyst becomes, for example, one of charting the connections between social and system integration (Lockwood 1976). Therefore, for Giddens:

> unintended consequences *condition* social reproduction . . . Social systems appear to exist and to be structured only 'in and through' their reproduction in micro-social situations which are in turn limited and

modalized through the unintended consequences of previous and parallel social action.

(Knorr-Cetina 1981: 27, original italics)

To arrive at this position Giddens draws upon an extensive range of ideas, including classical social theory, which is then used to develop a 'hermeneutically informed social theory' (Giddens 1982: vii). He seeks to avoid the problems of the philosophy of consciousness and those of action theories in general, whilst acknowledging that society is not the creation of individuals, but without resort to structuralist explanations (Giddens 1984: xxi). In order to examine how he arrives at these positions in more depth, this chapter is divided into two sections. First, an overview of the development of his ideas via an encounter with other schools of thought and his resultant theoretical synthesis. All references to works in this section are by Giddens, unless otherwise stated. Second, an examination of the issues which it then raises in social analysis.

The intellectual development of structuration theory

The theory of structuration develops from encounter and synthesis. The former stems from a reaction to an 'orthodox consensus' in social science. This is taken as a combination of naturalism and functionalism (Giddens 1987: 24) which renders social science impervious to the insights of phenomenology, ordinary language philosophy and hermeneutics. The consequence being that the social sciences have remained in the shadow of the natural sciences long after they should have freed themselves from its shackles. Indeed, those who await a Newton of the social sciences: 'are not only waiting for a train that won't arrive, they're in the wrong station altogether' (1976: 13).

Structuration theory shares with micro-theoretical approaches the view that society is 'the outcome of the consciously applied skills of human subjects' (1976: 15). To sustain this view, without resorting to the limitations of action theories, various theoretical insights are mobilized. For instance, a scientific Marxism is abandoned as symptomatic of a natural science model, as are evolutionary theories of social change. On the other hand, a modified humanist-Marxism, concerned to historically analyse the connections between the objective and subjective features of social life becomes, from an ontological point of view, reconcilable with the aims of structuration theory (1976: 12).

A twist now enters structuration theory. Although Giddens retains a respect for the skilled accomplishments of actors in everyday life, he is also concerned not to abandon the idea of structure as a necessary part of socio-theoretical development (1976: 22). However, how is this achieved without resort to structuralism or structural-functionalism? Both of which downplay agency in everyday life. Or, without resorting to micro-theoretical approaches which downplay the role of structure in everyday life? To focus upon these questions, an examination of his encounters with these traditions of thought is required. This will then permit us to consider the synthesis of structure and action within structuration theory.

Encounters: taking aim at dualisms

Action theories are considered by Giddens as 'Strong on actions, weak on institutions' (1982: 29). For instance, in Schutzian-inspired social theory, the question remains as to how, given the reduction of consciousness to an individual ego, an outer reality may be constituted or reproduced. The Husserlian attempt to overcome the subject–object dualism, which Schutz inherited, simply ends up prioritizing the former over the latter. As one extensive study of his work puts it, Giddens's concern in this respect is to examine the reproduction of social practices whilst also insisting upon the opportunities which exists for innovation in social conduct (I. Cohen 1989).

As noted, ethnomethodology originally substituted the cultural dope approach to social analysis in favour of the skilled and accomplished actor in everyday life. To meet the postulate of subjective adequacy, Garfinkel placed situated rationalities over that of scientific rationality. However, whilst scientific rationalities should be connected to lay accounts, as Schutz (1972) argued, they are not simply illegitimate reifications, for there is still a need to make 'intelligibility intelligible' (Giddens 1976: 40). Mainstream ethnomethodologists, in their mobilization of ordinary language philosophy, do not escape from this requirement. For this reason, Giddens addresses the very issue that was raised in Chapter 4: that is, with an apparent air of indifference, how are ethnomethodological analysts able to both translate between and transcend language games?

To consider this question, Giddens employs hermeneutics. This allows him to tackle the question of the mediation between different frames of meaning in social analysis, as well as the empiricism, indicative of the orthodox consensus, which arises from ethnomethodological attempts to provide presuppositionless descriptions. Quite simply, one cannot make statements which refer to 'sensory observations' in a theoretically neutral way (1976: 135). The referential reflexivity which mainstream ethnomethodology abandoned, is now opened up to hermeneutic scrutiny:

> The process of learning a paradigm or language-game as the expression of a form of life is also a process of learning what a paradigm is not: that is to say, learning to mediate it with other, rejected,

alternatives, by contrast to which the claims of the paradigm in question are clarified.

(Giddens 1976: 144)

This scrutiny occurs at two levels. First, both the social and natural sciences are 'forms of life' which have to be learnt by their practitioners. Second, the relationship between lay and technical languages is not, as Schutz (1979) argued, one way. There is what Giddens calls a constant 'slippage' between the two. As such 'It would not be at all unusual to find a coroner who had read Durkheim' (1990: 42). This is an insight which he seeks to encapsulate in the notion of the 'double hermeneutic'.

In addition to the above, through its reading of ordinary language philosophy, ethnomethodology identifies rationality with accountability. However, the consequences of this is to strip social relations of an analysis of the purposes, motives or interests which routinely inform social conduct. 'Doing' should be viewed as more than making something accountable, it is also a practice and it is this which makes it an accomplishment on the part of actors in everyday life (1976: 44).

For Giddens, macro-theoretical approaches to social life are also deficient: for example, normative functionalism (Parsons), conflict functionalism (Merton) and historical materialism (1977; 1981a; 1985). As we saw in Chapter 2, this approach suggests that societies have 'needs' and the manner in which such needs are met is seen as an explanation of the social processes themselves. A number of criticisms of this approach can be made. First, human agency is subsumed under the internalization of societal values, whether for the purposes of social order in Parsonian theory or ideological control in Althusser's Marxism. This is manifest in the attribution of rationality to social systems rather than individuals.

Second, in the case of normative functionalism, explanations of power, which is an 'elemental concept' in the social sciences (1984: 283), is subsumed under consensually produced norms and values. The result is, as with interpretative social theories, problems in explaining asymmetries of power and the divisions of interest which exist within social relations and societies as a whole (1976: 157). In contrast to these views, structuration theory considers norms as the products of differing interpretations based on competing interests. As such, they are not simply enabling (Winch, Schutz) nor constraining (Durkheim, Parsons), but both enabling and constraining.

Third, in the dichotomy between synchronic and diachronic explanation, there is a neglect of history. This is manifested, for instance, in the separation of function (the relations between 'parts' and the 'whole') from 'happenings in time' (1976: 120). What results is a homeostasis, where concern is directed towards the maintenance and equilibrium of social systems which, in turn, structure social relations. Given Giddens's Heideggerian emphasis on an ontology of potentials, both the static and dynamics elements in society require an equal consideration. This results in a contrast between structuration theory and the conservative elements in both structural-functionalism and ethnomethodology which is apparent in their preoccupations with social order.

For Giddens, the only legitimate space for teleological explanation in social science is that which can be situated within the bounded conditions of action. Agency is ascribed to agents and is not a property of social systems as exemplified in the form of the explanation: 'the reason that people do X is to furnish the needs of the system Y'. As will be noted, in order to account for continuity in social institutions and relations across time, structuration theory does not resort to functionalist explanation. Similarly, whilst denying that systems have reasons or needs of their own, Giddens does not deny that systems possess properties which both enable and constrain practices (1979: 113). In sum, therefore, functionalism and structuralism fail to see society and social life as the product of active subjects, whilst action theories consider only the production, but not reproduction, of social systems in social relations. Now to an examination of the synthesis of these positions in structuration theory.

Synthesis: action and structure in structuration theory

In opposition to the dualisms of action and structure, Giddens directs attention towards the reproduction of structures within social relations. In their place we find the *duality of structure* and the process of *structuration*. Structure is seen to enter into 'the constitution of the agent and social practices and "exists" in the generating moments of this constitution' (1979: 5). This reproduction is a concrete, not philosophical question, manifested in 'the situatedness of interaction in time and space' (1984: 110). As he puts it:

> According to the notion of the duality of structure, the structural properties of social systems are both medium and outcome of the practices they recursively organize. Structure is not 'external' to individuals: as memory traces, and as instantiated in social practices, it is in a certain sense more 'internal' than exterior to their activities in a Durkheimian sense. Structure is not to be equated with constraint but is always both enabling and constraining. This, of course, does not prevent the structured properties of social systems from stretching away, in time and space, beyond the control of individual actors.
>
> (Giddens 1984: 25)

Structure thus becomes conceptualized as both the medium and outcome of the production and reproduction of social practices. To focus upon the structuration of social practices is to find an explanation for 'how it comes about that structures are constituted through action, and reciprocally how action is constituted structurally' (1976: 11). It follows from this, contrary to the propositions of structural-functionalism and structuralism, that structure is a dynamic, not static, phenomenon. How it is actually manifest, as either constraint or enablement or a combination of these, is held deliberately open and to be decided by empirical investigation. Given this, the duality of structure obtains its explanatory value only when considered against 'real historical situations' (1993: 6).

Giddens's writings exhibit an adherence to an ontology of potentials whereby the opportunities for innovative social conduct are deliberately held open in opposition to the idea of the constraining regularities of systemic forces. This provides for his primary concern to investigate 'the nature of human action, social institutions and the interrelations between action and institutions' (1991a: 201). Quite simply, if the possibility of always being able to 'act otherwise' were not the case, then Giddens would succumb to a structural form of explanation which he sees as a 'futile' and even 'harmful' search in the social sciences (1984: 214). These points noted, a further specification of the details of social reproduction is now required.

To return to an earlier discussion. The post-Wittgensteinian view is that society can be studied as a 'language'. In its ethnomethodological variant, this ended up having parallels with structuralism, whilst the idea of linking social context and account actually led to a severing of practical consciousness from social practice. In opposition to this, Giddens seeks to fuse these as 'crucial mediating moments between two traditionally-established dualisms in social theory' (1979: 4). The concept of *praxis* thus becomes mobilized as the connection between language and social practice. *Praxis* represents neither freedom nor determinism. It is

> an ontological term, expressing a fundamental trait of human social existence. To speak of human social activity as *Praxis* is to reject every conception of human being as 'determined objects' or as unambiguously 'free subjects'. All human action is carried on by knowledgeable agents who both construct the social world through their action, but whose action is also conditioned or constrained by the very world of their creation.
>
> (Giddens 1981a: 53–54, original italics)

The echoes of the 'humanist' Marx are clear. *The Constitution of Society*, the most systematic exposition of structuration theory to date, is actually described as a reflection upon Marx's famous phrase: 'Men (let us immediately say human beings) make history, but not in circumstances of their own choosing' (1984: xxi). At this point, a particular idea of agency becomes directly linked into the process of structuration.

We may identify two aspects of human conduct: capability and knowledgeability. Capability is taken to mean that someone 'could have acted otherwise'. Unlike the utilitarian influences on social theory, as manifest in rational-choice theories, this is not identified with the 'decisions' or 'choices' which people consciously make between various courses of action open to them, for most of social life is actually routinized. Yet according to the precepts of *praxis*, agency is identified with the ability to ' "make a difference" to a pre-existing state of affairs or course of events' (1984: 14). Given this, Giddens sees power as prior to both subjectivity and the agent's reflexive monitoring of their conduct (1984: 15). According to this view, which shares affinities with both Parsons and Foucault, power is not simply a repressive, but also an enabling force in social relations. It is the very means through which agency, defined as 'transformative capacity', is achieved.

Knowledgeability, on the other hand, refers to

> the fact that the members of a society know a great deal about the working of that society, and must do so if that society is recognizably a 'human society'.
>
> (Giddens 1981b: 163)

However, this is not to be equated with what is known 'consciously'. Why? Because it is bounded by two aspects: first, the unacknowledged conditions of action and second, the unintended consequences of action (Giddens 1981a: 19). This is where Giddens's theory of the make-up of individuals enters his formulations. In place of Freud's three-fold psychic organization of the individual, Giddens substitutes a basic security system, with its emphasis on ontological security and practical and discursive consciousness.

Practical consciousness is regarded as displaying an 'extraordinary complexity' (1984: 281). It is concerned with the routine monitoring of day-to-day conduct which, at the level of knowledgeability, is bounded by the above two conditions. At the level of capability, it represents what people know in order to get on with their daily lives, but through which the structural properties of social systems are also reproduced. Discursive consciousness, on the other hand, is revealed during times of departure from routine modes of action. It may arise when asking people the reasons for their actions or activities, or from an abrupt change in a person's circumstances. People then reflect upon the reasons and intentions which inform their actions, but not necessarily the motives for their actions. It is in the distinction between practical and discursive consciousness that one derives such insights on everyday life from reading Goffman.

Importantly for our purposes, what Giddens is doing here is making a distinction between the rationalization *of* action and the motivation *for* action. Motives play a part in social life only in 'unusual circumstances': for example, they inform what he refers to as 'overall plans or programmes' (1984: 6). These may be considered as a person's 'wants' which underlie the potential for action, but not necessarily the action itself. This distinction permits him to bring into his theoretical frame of reference, with its clear respect for the actions of people in their everyday lives, unconscious elements of motivation:

> Motivational components of action, which I take to refer to the organisation of an actor's wants, straddle conscious and unconscious aspects of cognition and emotion.
>
> (Giddens 1979: 58)

Lest this be misinterpreted, it is important to note that although a conception of the unconscious is thought essential to the development of social theory (1979: 58), Giddens is not suggesting conscious manifestations of action can simply be 'read off' against unconscious motivations; a point he makes in an interesting comparison between Goffman and Freud on 'everyday slips' (1984: 98–104). The problem with such psychoanalytic approaches to social life centres upon their downplaying of the influence of social forces on everyday actions (unintended consequences), in favour of viewing conduct as symptomatic of the psychological make-up of individuals (unconscious motivations). At the same time, action theories influenced by Anglo-American philosophies of action, have equated 'reasons' with 'motives' and thereby failed to examine the potential for unconscious motivations for actions. Similarly, they do not consider the very *social* conditions which work to structure activity, but which remain outside of the self-understandings of people in everyday life due to the bounded nature of their knowledgeability. These social conditions are referred to as '*the unintended consequences of intentional conduct*' (1979: 59, original italics).

The above represent the beginnings of a link between situated practices and the reproduction of social institutions through the unintended consequences of social action and hence, a synthesis between action and structure. To render this understanding more complete, a consideration of the ideas of rules and resources, which make up social structure, is required.

Giddens finds structuralist insights useful in the development of structuration theory, but they are deficient in some important respects (1977: 45–48). Indeed, he starts an essay on structuralist and poststructuralist thought by pronouncing that they are 'dead traditions of thought' (1987: 73). In placing his focus upon *praxis*, he may have accepted the decentring of the subject, but not its death. Structure, as external to human agency, is rejected because '*there is no such thing as a distinctive category of "structural explanation"*' (1984: 213, original italics). However, there does exist a second sense of 'structure' reflected in the intersection of presence and absence. In this sense, the underlying properties of social systems may be inferred from the surface manifestations of action (1984: 16). This ontological realism has conceptual mileage for structuration theory in terms of understanding and explaining the intentional reproduction of unintended consequences.

To consider this second sense of structure, Lévi-Strauss's work is found to be useful (Giddens 1979: 63–64). The problem being that Strauss omits time from his considerations with the result that social structure becomes manifested only in the first sense: that is, as a static 'thing', separate from its reproduction in the situated practices of everyday life. To overcome this, Giddens employs the insights of time-geography (1984: 110–119). The idea of social systems as having structuring properties which 'bind' time and space is thereby introduced (1979: 64). History is returned to social theory in a way which makes it possible for social systems to exist across time and space. Continuity, in terms of society displaying a 'systemic form', may then be admitted. This overcomes the limitations of action theories, but without succumbing to structure as separate from the actions of agents in social life.

Despite the existence of systemic forms, the basic ontology of human 'action' and 'doing' must leave open the possibility for innovation in social conduct. Therefore, systems are seen to be reproduced in social relations. The result is that structure is permitted a 'virtual order' because, from a logical point of view, it is not a property of social systems or collectivities:

> To say that structure is a 'virtual order' of transformative relations means that social systems, as reproduced social practices, do not have 'structures' but rather exhibit 'structural properties' and that structure exists, as time-space presence, only in its instantiations in such practices and as memory traces orientating the conduct of knowledgeable human agents.
>
> (Giddens 1984: 17)

Social systems exist only through the process of structuration. This allows for a definition of 'social institutions' as those social totalities which exhibit the greatest 'time-space extension' in social relations (1984: 17). Social systems and the situated activities of human beings are thus connected through structuration: that is, the reproduction of social systems in social practices. Therefore, in the course of their conduct, people draw upon structures, which exists out of time and space, which themselves comprise rules and resources:

> One of the main propositions of structuration theory is that the rules and resources drawn upon in the production and reproduction of social action are at the same time the means of system reproduction (the duality of structure).
>
> (Giddens 1984: 19)

So, action and structure are implicated, but what are the concepts of 'rules' and 'resources' being employed here? Rules exhibit two properties. These may be conceptually distinct, but in actual social practices cannot be separated. First, rules are drawn upon by people in everyday life in skilled and knowledgeable ways. The result is those regularities in language production and exchange that are so carefully described by ethnomethodologists. These rules 'are only tacitly grasped by actors' (1984: 22). As such, although skilfully drawn upon and applied, these rules cannot necessarily be formulated. Despite this, actors are dependent upon their 'structuring properties' for making sense of the social world. For this reason, social practices are both enabled and constrained by these rules of signification.

This leaves some problems. If such rules are implicated in social reproduction they could be linked, for example, to the maintenance of social order (ethnomethodology), or be interpreted as causal mechanisms which operate independently of human agency (structuralism). Giddens would then be open to the charge of systemic teleology, structural determination or the conflation of reasons with motives. Given the centrality of power in structuration theory and the capacity of the agent to 'make a difference' in their interventions, structural constraints cannot 'operate independently of the motives and reasons that agents have for what they do' (1984: 181). As such, there must be more to structure than these rules of signification. This is where the idea of rules as 'regulative' enters his formulations.

In the process of 'strategic conduct', actors 'draw upon modes of domination structured into social systems' (1982: 83). Here, the term 'domination' does not carry its usual negative connotations but power is, as noted, also related to the possibility of producing productive outcomes. These modes of domination are divided into 'allocative' and 'authoritative' resources (1984: 259). Whilst these vary with different types of social systems, allocative resources refer, in general, to the domination of nature by human beings. These include, for example, raw materials and technology and those goods which may be produced as a result of an interaction between the two. Authoritative resources, on the other hand, refer to the control of the social world and comprise the organization, in terms of time and space, social relations, plus the production and reproduction of the human body, as well as life chances as they affect the possibilities for self-development and self-expression (1981a: 51–52).

Both allocative and authoritative resources represent forms of asymmetrical power. These are manifest in agency which is defined, as noted, in terms of the capability of 'making things happen' or of 'bringing about particular states of affairs' (1981b: 170). These resources may be mobilized for the purposes of sanctioning the conduct of individuals in relation to the application of rules. Meaning production, power and normative sanctions are thus implicated in social practices; the result being the reproduction of social systems and structures. This is the 'regulative' sense of rule. It follows that, in terms of *praxis*, the 'correct' use of language (constitutive rules) cannot be separated from the environment in which they take place (regulative rules). To return to the opening paragraph of this chapter, Goffman's interaction order may now be linked to social structure as comprising rules and resources which are routinely drawn upon in social interaction.

In intentionally drawing upon resources, the unintended consequence is to reproduce social systems. However, if this power is a 'built-in' feature of domination within social systems, does this not constrain the actor in a Marxist sense? In considering this question, Giddens shares Weber's refusal to reduce the operation of power to the forces and relations of production. This places him at odds not only with historical materialism (1981a; 1985), but also with a Nietzschean conception of the 'will to power' as indicative of the continual desire for domination in social relations (1982; 1984). Although constraints may work, for example, at the level of a person's life chances (authoritative resource) structure is, to repeat, both enabling and constraining. Quite simply, people possess the capability to recognize objective social conditions which are then incorporated into their social conduct:

> No matter how complete the power of one individual or group might be over others, resources are always available whereby subordinates can reciprocally influence power holders.
>
> (Giddens 1987: 162)

This process expresses a transformative capacity which is equated with the exercise of agency. There is always a *dialectic of control* tempering domination within social relations. As such, no single person can completely influence the actions of others. Their very freedom of action is dependent upon their ability to perform a range of practices with a high degree of competence. Given that no one person is able to perform every practice as skilfully as their co-actors this, in turn, represents a constraint upon their actions (I. Cohen 1989).

Summary

In sum, action theories have a limited concept of action due to their inability to conceive of social institutions and the role of power in social life. In contrast, structuralist theories are said to submit agency to system determination which gives society a life of its own, separate from the actions of individuals. In its ontological emphasis, structuration theory replaces this dualism by the duality of structure and the process of structuration. Agency is then defined as a 'transformative capacity' which focuses attention upon strategic conduct in everyday life. Power is thereby central to this process.

Praxis is the link between practical consciousness which informs actions and the social conditions in which action takes place. In the course of social action, rules and resources, as part of social structure, are drawn upon with the effect of reproducing social systems (the unintended consequences of intentional conduct). Structure is both the medium and outcome of interaction because 'practices are situated within intersecting sets of rules and resources that ultimately express features of the totality' (1982: 82). Further, in order to explain continuity in social relations and overcome the limitations of action theories, the systemic aspect of societies are allowed for in the 'stretching' away of social systems in the dimensions of both time and space. Any systemic determination on localized conduct, however, is tempered by the necessity of systems and structures being reproduced in the situated activities of agents. Therefore, agency implies structure and structure implies agency.

Issues in structuration theory

Anthony Giddens's project is highly ambitious. In the attempt to synthesize the dualisms of action and structure, which is at the heart of social theory, it should come as no surprise that this has resulted in a number of works which criticize, elaborate upon and generally interrogate structuration theory. In this section, attention will first be devoted to matters of interpretation and applicability. I then wish to move on to examine whether action and structure is usefully thought of as a duality or a dualism.

First, there is a question over the accuracy and selection of Giddens's readings of the theoretical traditions which he mobilizes for the development of structuration theory. We can, for example, find authors who question his readings of Marxism (Wright 1989), poststructuralism (Boyne 1991) and postmodernism (Hekman 1990a). In this sense, structuration theory has been viewed as a kind of conceptual raiding party which, in its single-mindedness, often results in the loss of original insights from other theoretical traditions.

Readings of this type are symptomatic of the sheer breadth and depth of Giddens's work. For instance, he draws upon the traditions of Continental thought, via hermeneutics, whilst also wishing to appeal to the empirical (and empiricist) tendencies in Anglo-American thought. This is exemplified in his preference for an ontologically based social theory, where understanding is seen as part of human existence itself, rather than a method of social investigation *per se*. This is a difficult juggling act. There are those with an eye for the empirical utility of social theory who have described his work more as 'philosophization' (Rex in Mullan 1987: 19) and of lacking empirical applicability (Gregson 1989; Mouzelis 1991; Stinchcombe 1990).

Giddens (1984; 1991a) is clearly concerned to render structuration theory useful for social researchers and there are those who have sought to explicitly utilize his ideas for this purpose (C. W. Smith 1983). Yet he also argues that it represents a body of thought which acts as a corrective to empirical research through its illumination of key areas of social life which are frequently overlooked: for example, the relationship between human knowledgeability and the unintended consequences of social action. In addition, empirical implications should not be the only criterion upon which social theory is judged. The coherency of its formulations, the problems that it generates and the insights it offers, are also of importance (Giddens in Mullan 1987: 102).

In these terms, let us consider one of the problems that it generates and whether it is successful in its insights.

Consider the role of gender and agency in structuration theory. Although the women's movement has clearly identified weaknesses in sociological reasoning (Giddens 1987: 24), is gender domination not structured into social systems? If it is, the possibility of an engendered social structure is not considered by Giddens (Wolffensperger 1991). That said, he is admirably frank in reply to questions of this type raised by Linda Murgatroyd (1989): 'I have simply not accorded questions of gender the attention that they undeniably deserve' (1989: 282). This has begun to change in his works on the self and social and political relations (Giddens 1991b; 1992; 1994). However, does this example reveal a more general weakness?

If one thinks of time as a resource which has the power to organize social life, rather than chronologically (Adam 1995), then it has the potential to be mobilized for the purposes of excluding particular groups whose lives are structured according to dominant interpretations of time. If this is considered in terms of the burden of the division of labour between home and work, for example, the very timing of a union meeting or work meeting can act as an impediment to participation, the effect of which would be to force women back into the domestic sphere (Walby 1986).

The proliferation in part-time work in the 1980s could, of course, be seen as enabling. However, what happens to the insight when seen against the relationship between low pay and part-time work? It may then only be enabling in terms of the prior constraints of a gendered division of labour within a patriarchal-capitalist society. As people are always able to 'make a difference' in their actions, it is difficult to see how the persistence of such structured inequalities may be explained in the face of attempts, by women's movements, to change these practices. After all, both social systems and social structure are permissible in structuration theory only to the extent that they are instantiated in situated activities. This suggests that there are constraining influences on action, but only in so far as these are invoked in the course of human action. This does not appear to overcome a voluntarist–determinist dualism, because the latter is seen to exist only in the exercise of the former!

The point of this discussion is that structure and action may not be a duality, but a dualism. In the remaining part of this section, I would just like to highlight some of the issues around this question which authors have raised in respect to Giddens's work. Underlying these observations is what Roy Bhaskar (1993: 154) has termed Giddens's 'tendential voluntarism'. It is held that there is an underlying subjectivism in his work which prevents him dislocating structure from agency, as if such a move would automatically imply a surrender of social actions to deterministic social forces.

Giddens's overall attempt to collapse the action–structure dualism in social thought is mediated through particular lenses. These are ontological and provide a focus upon human 'doing' and 'being', which, in turn, gives structuration theory a particular conception of social reality. This is a reality where active subjects and social reality itself are taken as being one and the same. As such, whilst wishing to avoid the pitfalls of a philosophy of consciousness, any form of structuralist explanation which views social reality as external to social relations is also rejected. However, due to the nature of this separation, structuration theory cannot help but resort to subjectivism:

> It is only Giddens' insistence that a synthetic duality is the only alternative to a false dualism that prevents a realization that a dualism of action and (objective) structure is, in fact, the only way to understand structure and action as implicated in each other in a way that avoids subverting the integrity and influence of either.
>
> (Layder 1987: 31–32)

The duality of social structure views social change as dependent upon instantiated conduct. However, what of the durability of social systems, as in the case of the patriarchy and work example above? Quite simply, different amounts of time and effort may be required to effect change in social conditions. In such instances people might deliberately distance themselves from the very rules which they view as oppressive. The result being that the rules of language, upon which Giddens places so much stress, actually become topics for conflict rather than resources for actions. Subjects and objects are therefore deliberately distanced from each other and so become dualisms, not a duality (Mouzelis 1995). Further, during these times of struggles constraints may continue to operate independently of agency:

> Nations can fall, polities be deposed and economies bankrupted, *while* efforts are being made to change the factors responsible (for example, birth rates, despotism, illiteracy, ethno-centrism). As a general theoretical proposition this holds good however short the time interval involved. Yet this is what Giddens spirits away by making all cultural properties atemporal and according them only a pale 'virtual existence'.
>
> (Archer 1989: 89, original italics)

Another way of considering this issue is to examine the relationship between power and transformative capacity. Giddens does not see power as a property of social structures. Therefore, systemic constraint can never be complete as represented by the concept of the dialectic of control: 'the weak ... always have some capabilities of turning resources back against the strong' (Giddens 1981a: 63). Even in the case of solitary confinement, a 'hunger strike' or 'suicide', as the ultimate refusal of control, is seen as an option. Although this is a limited case and action is taken to be more fluid in social systems, is this link between power and transformative capacity adequate for the purposes of explaining social relations?

Power structures, once products of human actions, can become sedimented in social systems thereby effecting the *degree* to which agency can mobilize power in subsequent actions – as in the case of the relationship between women and paid-work. Therefore, it is this interplay between the dualisms of agency and structure which needs to be analytically and empirically considered, not the duality of structure. However, by theoretical fiat, structuration theory precludes this possibility: that is, structure is taken to be that which is reproduced in situated conduct, not something which may confront individuals as a durable constraint. Take, for example, the issue of contraception. In some instances, the church and the state become powerful contestants. The result can be a stalemate which actually blocks any transformation in contraceptive practices to the detriment of those who are subject to such relations of ruling (Archer 1990). Power cannot be simply considered in terms of agency, but is also the property of social systems which constrain group and individual actions:

> Do I have an opportunity to vote for my government? Do I have a
> wide or narrow range of jobs from which to choose? If I want to work,
> do I have to work in a job where wages keep me on or below the
> poverty line? These choices are not always my responsibility. They
> result from something that we can call 'social structure', and the ex-
> perience we have of these structures is often similar to that we have of
> the physical world, the constraints of which Giddens *can* recognise.
> (Craib 1992: 154, original italics)

Many of these issues stem from conceptualizing structure in terms of rules and resources. To consider constraint in terms of constitutive or regulative rules is highly problematic. When individuals who have not had a job for six months are faced with a reduction in their state benefits because it is said to reflect their personal inability to make themselves 'marketable', are we to consider these constraints as something reducible to the level of their comprehensibility of such sanctions? On the contrary:

> it is the *range of alternatives* which is restricted, and these restrictions
> do not stem from semantic and moral rules, but from the structural
> conditions for the persistence (and decline) of productive institutions.
> (Thompson 1984: 168, original italics)

Because of the link between agency and 'options' in terms of strategic conduct, Giddens seems to leave us with the idea that where there is no choice in terms of realizing our wants and desires, we can no longer be conceived of as an agent. As in the case of 'suicide' and imprisonment noted above, options of one are not options! The point being that wants and desires vary. It is the relationship of this variability to the social positions in which people find themselves which is largely unexplicated in structuration theory:

> One of the key tasks of social analysis is to explore this space of possibilities, both in terms of the differential distribution of options according to class, age, sex and so on, but also in terms of the kinds of wants and desires, the interests and needs, which are themselves differentially possessed . . . certain individuals or groups of individuals have greater scope for action and choice than other individuals or groups of individuals: freedom, one could say, is enjoyed by different people in varying degrees.
>
> (Thompson 1984: 170)

An analysis of this type would show that structure and agency are not antinomies. It would demonstrate that they are not implicated in the way that structuration theory argues due to a prioritization of the open-ended nature of *praxis* and its 'over-assertion' of human freedom (Craib 1992).

Summary

Despite the above issues, there is no doubt that structuration theory is an innovative approach to tackling the dualisms within social theory. At the level of the subject, structuralist lessons on its 'death' are criticized, yet without recourse to a Cartesian ego given the centrality of *praxis* and power in social life. Knowledge is not open-ended, but bounded, whilst capability is circumscribed by unacknowledged conditions and unintended consequences. Although most of the time people just 'get on' with their daily lives, an emphasis on practical consciousness means that individuals are knowledgeable about what they do. In addition, their conduct manifests strategic intentions, but their unintended consequences reproduce social systems.

In these formulations, structuration theory has taken on an enormous intellectual task. The myriad of influences which Anthony Giddens brings to his work provides it with the source of both its strength and weakness. On the one hand, there is no doubt that he has captured the imagination of the social scientific community. On the other hand, his synthesis of intellectual traditions leaves some at a loss and others challenging the resultant interpretations and conceptualizations. Despite these reactions, this is a theoretical enterprise which is still unfolding. At it stands, it is fruitful to use this work as an inspiration for matters which require further empirical investigation and conceptual specification. Overall, therefore, it stands as a corrective to the grander claims of both action and systems' theories.

In this enterprise, Giddens is not alone. There is a French social scientist who has emerged from within the tradition of structuralism to become a critic of objectivism. Practice, once again, becomes of central focus. However, the intellectual influences and experiences which inform the development of his ideas are different. The result is also a novel and often misunderstood project. It is also one that illuminates a gap in structuration theory: that is, an understanding of the relationship between social positions, aspirations and actions.

6

Habitus, capital and field: society in social relations

Since the 1950s, Pierre Bourdieu has published works covering the areas of social research, social theory, pedagogy, kinship, cultural studies, linguistics, economic change, religion, art, museums, literature, photography and philosophy. The resultant and continually emerging ideas have been framed by empirical investigations carried out under the auspices of a reflexive social science.

Bourdieu opposes the dichotomy between objectivism and subjectivism as represented by structuralism and phenomenology. Like Giddens, he has added his own interpretation to the agency–structure dualism in social thought. This relationship is conceptualized via a 'genetic linking' which is manifested in the relations between social divisions and mental schemata. However, as mental states are the embodiments of social divisions, the social sciences need to exercise a continual 'epistemological vigilance' over the blurring of the boundaries between everyday opinions and social scientific discourse (Bourdieu, Chamboredon and Passeron 1991). At the same time, it follows that: 'An adequate science of society must encompass both objective regularities and the process of internalization of objectivity' (Wacquant 1992: 13).

With this emphasis on social divisions, Bourdieu's work can be characterized as 'critical' in three ways. First, although according validity to people's everyday interpretations, they are not taken at face value for this would represent 'the illusion of immediate knowledge' (Bourdieu 1991a: 250). Received social categories are thus subjected to scrutiny in order that the social conditions which structure life chances and reproduce class distinctions may be analysed. Second, a reflexive social science is employed in order to examine the institutional conditions of knowledge production. Bourdieu is concerned to supplant not only the first illusion, but also a second: 'the illusion of absolute knowledge' (1991a: 250). This would suggest that agents are 'in error' and the scientist may place themselves in the position of 'all knowing'. Finally, these elements combine in his thought, in Heideggerian fashion, to open up the realms of the 'possible' by his exposing the basis of the 'actual', for 'Every established order tends to produce . . . the naturalization of its own arbitrariness' (Bourdieu 1977: 164). As such, Bourdieu is not content with either Lazarsfeld's positivism, or Adorno's speculations (Bourdieu 1984: Appendix 1).

In the process of his studies, Bourdieu brings a myriad of influences to his work. These include Weber, Marx, Durkheim, Mauss, Lévi-Strauss, Saussure, Heidegger, Wittgenstein and Austin. As with Giddens, this has led to different interpretations of his ideas, frequently stemming from a misunderstanding of the intellectual and cultural traditions in which he works (Bourdieu 1993a; Wacquant 1993). In addition, there is a tendency in Anglo-American circles to overlook Bourdieu's primary concern with empirical studies and focus upon it as another aspect of 'grand theory'.

These points noted, I cannot pretend to be able to satisfactorily counteract these interpretations within this chapter. However, instead of employing pejorative labels of convenience which only serve to alleviate the reader or speaker of the need for constructive encounter, consideration and dialogue, a more positive approach, I hope, will be available through the following format. First, a brief exposition of Bourdieu's ideas via an examination of his engagement with other traditions of thought and the subsequent development of his own ideas. In this section all unattributed references will be to Bourdieu's work. Second, by considering some of the unresolved issues in his work, a more general appreciation might be gained of its strengths and limitations.

Intellectual development

Encounters and utilizations

In Part I, post–1945 French social thought was characterized as being centred around differences between Sartre's existentialism and Lévi-Strauss's structuralism. Bourdieu's notion of a 'sociology of social experience' allows his intellectual formation during this period to be turned into an object of investigation. Indeed, this technique forms part of his work, together with colleagues at the Centre for European Sociology, on French intellectual life and the education system (Bourdieu 1988; Bourdieu and Passeron 1990; Bourdieu et al. 1994).

Following his graduation as an *agrégé de philosophie* Bourdieu taught in a provincial school. He was then conscripted to the army in 1956 to serve in Algeria. There he became more aware of the gap in understanding between French intellectuals, his own experiences and the plight of the Algerian people and French settlers. His subsequent research, mostly secondary analysis, was then supplemented by further fieldwork (Bourdieu 1962). One of the overall aims of these studies were

> to understand, through my analyses of temporal consciousness, the conditions of the acquisition of the 'capitalist' economic habitus among people brought up in a pre-capitalist world.
>
> (Bourdieu 1990: 8)

This fieldwork was to represent a basis for Bourdieu's intellectual development. It formed the beginnings of the methodological considerations which are now a central part of his work, whilst also providing the empirical bases upon which he was to subject the dominant intellectual trends of his time to critical scrutiny. In this sense, whilst reading Schutz and Husserl, he found that Merleau-Ponty's concerns with the human sciences and the 'everyday', or what he describes above as 'temporal consciousness', was 'one potential way out of the philosophical babble found in academic institutions' (1990: 5).

This period in Bourdieu's career marked his transition from philosophy to sociology culminating, more recently, in a sociological study of Heidegger (Bourdieu 1991b). An impetus for this transition came from the structuralist revolution in social thought. Led by those such as Lévi-Strauss and interpretations of the work of Saussure, structuralism was to enable the social sciences to become more 'respectable' in French academic circles. Nevertheless, the result was an unquestioning incorporation of ideas which were not concerned with establishing the limits of 'pure theory'. For this reason, Bourdieu sought to 'objectify objectivity', with Saussure's prioritization of *langue* over *parole* being one of the main targets of this strategy.

For Saussure, it will be recalled, speech is not seen as the medium of communication in human affairs, but an underlying system of objective relations which becomes devoid of reference to sense-experience. The analyst may then lay claim to being some kind of 'stage manager' who can play at will with their objectifying instruments. The result being that they become caught 'in a dream of power' (1992a: 31). The dream is one of congruence between the underlying rules or structures of concrete actions and the rational patterns of analysis used by the social scientist towards their goal of explanation. It is Lévi-Strauss's dream, for instance, of moving from social context to the establishment of some kind of universal human nature. Yet the consequence of this allusion to universal rules is to undermine the freedom of agents:

> To make transcendent entities, which are to practices as essence to existence, out of the constructions that science resorts to in order to give

an account of the structure and meaningful products of the accumulation of innumerable historical actions, is to reduce history to a
'process without a subject', simply replacing the 'creative subject' of
subjectivism with an automaton driven by the dead laws of a history of
nature. This emanatist vision . . . reduces historical agents to the role of
'supports' (*Träger*) of the structure and reduces their actions to mere
epiphenomenal manifestations of the structure's own power to develop
itself and to determine and overdetermine other structures.

(Bourdieu 1992a: 41, original italics)

In the processes of inquiries of this type hermeneutics is seen as a matter for
the subjects *of* research, not for the process of how they or their activities are
created as objects *for* research. Speech-act theorists, such as Austin, on the
other hand, counter this structuralist method via an 'internalist' approach
which links 'connotations' to social context. The result being, as in
mainstream contemporary ethnomethodology, language is viewed as an end
point of social analysis. For Bourdieu, however, there is another way to
approach the relationship between language and social life: that is, by linking
social conditions to language use.

   In contrast to the above approaches to the study of language, Bourdieu
considers the power of linguistic utterances to reside in the institutional
conditions for their production. The analyst may then ask with what power
or authority utterances are invested by examining the access that the speaker
has 'to the official, orthodox and legitimate speech' (1992b: 109). Institutions are not simply schools, prisons and factories, etc., but relatively stable
sets of social relations which provide their members with certain resources.
History becomes returned to the point where it is abandoned by both
ethnomethodology and structuralism, for it is under such conditions that
utterances are both produced and heard:

> efforts to find, in the specifically linguistic logic of different forms of
> argumentation, rhetoric and style, the source of their symbolic efficacy
> are destined to fail as long as they do not establish the relationship
> between the properties of discourses, the properties of the person who
> pronounces them and the properties of the institution which authorizes
> him to pronounce them.

(Bourdieu 1992b: 111)

This concern with 'properties' takes Bourdieu into other intellectual terrains
in the quest to illuminate his empirical findings. This requires an encounter
with the insights of classical social theory. In Part I, in an attempt to gain a
more productive reading than is usually the case, it was suggested that there
were some underlying problematics shared by various theorists from within
different traditions. Bourdieu puts this in a somewhat different way. To
paraphrase him, the ideas of classical theory are seen as a 'space of possible
positions', in whose antagonisms the chance of transcendence may be found

(1990: 35). With this in mind and to simplify the resulting synthesis, the following is an overview of Bourdieu's utilization of these insights.

Bourdieu employs Marx's concern with the reproduction of social relations, but tempers his economism by employing Durkheim's sociology of symbolism. In turn, Durkheim's ideas on morals and values are tempered by the manner in which symbolic systems are viewed as ideologically structured. Therefore, they are not seen to represent some consensually agreed upon state of affairs, but systems of domination, the form of which change in the transition from traditional to modern societies. In general, this may be expressed in terms of the move from the interpersonal to the institutional as seen in Bourdieu's work in Algeria (1962), right through to his extensive ethnographical and statistical analyses of French taste, where

> the conservation of the social order is decisively reinforced by what Durkheim called 'logical conformity', i.e., the orchestration of cat-egories of perception of the social world, which, being adjusted to the divisions of the established order (and thereby to the interests of those who dominate it) and common to all minds structured in accordance with those structures, present every appearance of objective necessity.
>
> (Bourdieu 1984: 471)

It is Marx and Durkheim who represent the objectivist position within the theoretical spectrum, albeit from materialist and idealist vantage points respectively. Bourdieu seeks to avoid such dichotomies. This is where Weber steps in. Using Weber's work, he seeks to analyse the relations that exist between lifestyles, life chances and the material resources which are at the disposal of particular groups. To return to the opening quote of this chapter, subjective views and social positions become related in what are referred to as the 'prereflexive assumptions that social agents engage by the mere fact of taking the world for granted' (Bourdieu in Bourdieu and Wacquant 1992: 168). What is called this 'doxic acceptance' forms the link between cognitive and objective structures. However, the problem with the objectivist position is that it fails to see the importance of practices and strategies; in other words, the role of agency in everyday life.

Bourdieu's stratification analysis holds that agents engage in forms of identification which permit them to distinguish themselves from other groups. Thus, the struggle for recognition is a central part of social life. The relationship between these strategies and social position, where the accumu-lations of forms of 'capital' are at stake, is understood dialectically:

> on the one hand, the objective structures that the sociologist constructs, in the objectivist moment, by setting aside the subjective represen-tations of the agents, form the basis for these representations and constitute the structural constraints that bear upon interactions; but, on the other hand, these representations must also be taken into consider-ation particularly if one wants to account for the daily struggles,

individual and collective, which purport to transform or preserve these structures.

(Bourdieu 1989: 15)

The resultant 'constructivist structuralism' provides for an empirical examination of the interplay between the subjective and objective features of social life, without abandoning the major contribution of the structuralist legacy to social science: that is, 'the *relational* mode of thinking . . . which identifies the real not with substances but with relations' (1989: 15–16, original italics).

Tools of analysis: capital, habitus, field and strategy

In examining the relationship between agency and social position, there are four tools of analysis which Bourdieu employs which require our consideration. They are capital, habitus, field and strategy. His novel approach to the questions of action and structure will become apparent in this discussion, whilst his interest in the multi-dimensional relations between phenomena, as opposed to their reduction to one dimension of social life, should be borne in mind when reading the following account.

Bourdieu speaks of the social world as a 'space' which is constructed out of a set of properties that are active at any one time. Social relations within this space exhibit the deployment of various forms of power or capital which may act singularly, or in accord with each other. The main types of capital in his work, each of which have their own subtypes, are cultural, social, symbolic and economic capital. These objective forms of power are held to be neither reducible to the intentions of agents as such, nor simply directive of their interactions. Agents are thus defined by their *relative position* to one another. The distribution of people within social relations, therefore, does not vary according to properties, or chains of properties in terms of their relation to the means of production. Instead, they are distributed according to the overall volume of capital in their possession, as well as its composition (1992b: 231).

Given this latter point, Bourdieu opposes *substantialism* which holds that no form of reality exists other than material conditions. This means that he modifies a Marxist economism that is seen to 'annihilate specificity' because of its inability to see the 'socially maintained discrepancy between the "objective" reality and the social representation of production and exchange' (1992a: 113). Again, Bourdieu is examining the dialectical relations between the subjective and objective features of social life. This also enables him to analyse non-material forms of capital in pre-capitalist and capitalist societies; an analysis which takes place without recourse to an economistic bias which imposes universal analytic categories upon disparate forms of social relations.

Non-material forms of capital include symbolic capital. This represents the power to confer meanings upon social reality whilst also providing for a social recognition of one's place within social relations. People in possession of such capital in a non-capitalist society may then go to a market, without any money, because the value placed upon them in terms of trust is as great as their wealth itself (1992a: 119–120). Within a capitalist society, the very accumulation of symbolic capital may actually depend upon its 'distance' from economic necessity. We can thus say that a set of macro conditions provides for the existence of non-material forms of capital which relate to micro lifestyles:

> As the objective distance from necessity grows, life style increasingly becomes the product of what Weber calls a 'stylization of life', a systematic commitment which orients and organizes the most diverse practices – the choice of a vintage or a cheese or the decoration of a holiday home in the country.
>
> (Bourdieu 1984: 56)

An aesthetic disposition then involves a set of experiences which are 'freed from urgency' and 'are an end in themselves' (1984: 54). In this sense, one is reminded of Goffman's notion of 'role distance' – a process enabled by the mobilization of resources.

To this conceptualization of social relations, the dimension of time needs to be added. This allows for the incorporation of the dynamic aspects of social life, in which the status ascribed to forms of capital changes over time. Here, Bourdieu is seeking to overcome the weaknesses of a synchronic view of social relations. This is where the *habitus* enters into his work as the key element in overcoming the 'sterile opposition' (1981: 305) which exists between history and sociology. To this extent, there are parallels between the habitus and Giddens's idea of structure. As Bourdieu writes:

> It is necessary to write a structural history which finds in each state of the structure both the product of previous struggles to transform or conserve the structure, and, through the contradictions, tensions and power relations that constitute that structure, the source of its subsequent transformation.
>
> (Bourdieu 1990: 42)

However, as will be noted, the idea of rules, found in Giddens's idea of structure, is replaced in Bourdieu's work by the notion of strategy.

Bourdieu (1981) divides history into that which is 'embodied' and 'objectified'. The latter, for example, is found in books, machines, buildings, monuments and laws. The word 'habitus' means something similar to the Greek word *hexis* which relates to deportment, manner and style, etc. The habitus itself is viewed as history embodied in human beings. Its existence is apparent in and through social practices as manifested in ways of talking, moving, getting on with people and of making sense of the environment.

Bodies may then be analysed from the interactions that take place between taste, social location and the formation of habitus (Shilling 1993).

The habitus is inculcated as much by experience as by teaching, whilst its power is seen to derive from the lack of thought which informs its manifestations. Quite simply, competent performances are produced on a routine basis, in the process of which objective meaning is reproduced. The habitus can thus be considered as a form of 'socialized subjectivity' (Bourdieu in Bourdieu and Wacquant 1992: 126) where the re-enactment of history takes place in the dispositions which people acquire over time and bring with them into social situations. It is a way of producing social practices and a way of perceiving and appreciating practices: 'the habitus implies a "sense of one's place" but also a "sense of the other's place" ' (1990: 131).

In this linking between the objective and subjective aspects of social life in the attempt to overcome the individual–society dualism, the former appears to be prioritized over the latter. The result is that the habitus may be read as a gun out of which the individual is shot, thereby determining their social trajectory. This, however, would clearly undermine Bourdieu's wish to examine the social conditions which underlie the flux of social life through downplaying the role of agency. As such:

> Habitus is not the fate that some people read into it. Being the product of history, it is an *open system of dispositions* that is constantly subjected to experiences, and therefore constantly affected by them in a way that either reinforces or modifies its structures. It is durable but not eternal! Having said this . . . most people are statistically bound to encounter circumstances that tend to agree with those that originally fashioned their habitus.
>
> (Bourdieu in Bourdieu and Wacquant 1992: 133, original italics)

From this, we may draw out three aspects to the habitus and its relation to practice. First, Bourdieu's concept of action stands close to Dewey's idea, as he acknowledges (in Bourdieu and Wacquant 1992: 122). This shares, along with Heidegger, Merleau-Ponty and Wittgenstein, a critique of the mind–body and subject–object duality which has so preoccupied philosophy and social theory. To be fully understood, therefore, it must be situated within this tradition of thought if its implications are to be adequately grasped.

Second, the habitus is not only a set of dispositions which an agent possesses when faced with the social world, for it also implies a 'transformative capacity'. This capacity will depend upon the social situations in which agents find themselves as the condition for its 'fulfilment'. In the absence of these, the habitus may become a 'site of explosive forces (resentment) which may await (and even look for) the opportunity to break out' (1993b: 87). Therefore, a disjuncture may occur between the practices generated by the habitus and the objective conditions required for their outlet. What Bourdieu calls the 'Don Quixote effect' can then arise where practices appear:

'ill-adapted because they are attuned to an earlier state of the objective conditions' (1984: 109).

This idea of a 'pre-objective' fit between disposition and position does not rule out the strategic choices which an actor makes in the course of their conduct. That said, Bourdieu is no ally of rational-action theory. As with the ideas of Park, Mead and Thomas, times of crisis will call for an adjustment between objective and subjective structures and at these points, a degree of rational choice may take over. However, this does not imply a methodological individualism which would simply reintroduce the very dichotomy he seeks to overcome. Instead, the individual must always be viewed as socially positioned 'within the limits of the system of categories he owes to his upbringing and training' (Bourdieu in Bourdieu and Wacquant 1992: 126). If the mind is the site of rationality, it is socially bounded, not asocial. Given this, we might characterize Bourdieu as being more interested with what it is to act *reasonably* rather than rationally.

The third and final point is that the habitus must, as the quote above suggested, be seen in relation to a *field*. Without this it would, once again, prioritize subject over object and lose the centrality of Bourdieu's dialectical method:

> The habitus . . . enables an intelligible and necessary relation to be established between practices and a situation, the meanings of which is produced by the habitus through categories of perception and appreciation that are themselves produced by an observable social condition.
>
> (Bourdieu 1984: 101)

Now the habitus represents a 'feel for a game' which is acquired during practical experience. It is the acquisition of technique with the result that practical sense has a 'fuzzy logic' to it (Wacquant 1992). Science seeks to totalize this aspect of social life, with the result that it does not capture its sense. For instance, to ask a person 'what they are doing' is to ask them a question for which they have no need, since the essence of practice is the very suspension of such questioning:

> Practice has a logic which is not that of the logician. This has to be acknowledged in order to avoid asking of it more logic that it can give, thereby condemning oneself either to wring incoherences out of it or to thrust a forced coherence upon it.
>
> (Bourdieu 1992a: 86)

As noted, this 'feel for the game' requires a social situation for its enactment. There are two ways in which the relation between habitus and field may be considered. First, the field structures or conditions the habitus to the extent that it provides for its realization. As such, the roots of a divided habitus may lie in a discrepancy between fields. Second, there is the part that the habitus plays in constituting the field as a place where the agent decides that it is worth investing their energy. It follows that there is a two-way relation between the habitus and field: 'Social reality exists, so to speak, twice, in things and in minds, in fields and in habitus, outside and inside of agents' (Bourdieu in Bourdieu and Wacquant 1992: 127).

Fields vary and are viewed as relatively autonomous from one another: for example, the artistic (1995) and scientific fields (1988). In general, the field of power informs all other fields and thus constitutes a 'meta-field'. There are also 'game fields'. These are seen by their participants as arbitrary constructs of which they are more or less aware and which contain specific rules where conditions of entry entail a kind of 'quasi-contract' between agents. In locations such as these one will find comments being made like: 'it's only a game'. Social fields, on the other hand, result from long and slow processes of 'autonomization'. These are games 'in themselves' rather than 'for themselves' (1992a: 67). The agent who enters these is equipped with the sets of beliefs which makes them work in the first instance. The earlier a person enters a game and the less aware they are of its learning, the greater is their ignorance of what the field grants them through such investment (1992a: 67).

In the two-way relationship between habitus and field, a congruence is established whereby the social world is understood because it comprises the person and so appears as self-evident. The result is an 'ontological complicity' (Bourdieu in Bourdieu and Wacquant 1992: 128) between a person and the social world of which they are a part. This is where the idea of social reality 'existing twice' provides for the possibility of analysing the field separate from those who comprise it:

> Fields present themselves synchronically as structured spaces of positions (or posts) whose properties depend on their position within these spaces and which can be analysed independently of the characteristics of their occupants (which are partly determined by them).
>
> (Bourdieu 1993b: 72)

A field is thus constituted by the power relations, or distribution of types of capital, which are mobilized in the struggles taking place within them. However, whilst fields are structured by these relations, the *form* of the struggles which take place within them will vary. It follows that the dynamics of one field may not be transposed into another, for the habitus within a field implies a knowledge of its laws, stakes and interests. The resultant struggles centre around what Bourdieu calls the 'monopoly of legitimate violence (specific authority) which is characteristic of the field in question' (1993b: 73). What is at stake is the conservation or subversion of the structure of the capital within the field. Those who are inclined towards conserving its power relations are defined as being engaged in *orthodoxy*, whilst newcomers to the field are likely to be subversive and engage in strategies of *heresy*.

The existence of heresy or heterodoxy in a field forces the doxa, or set of prereflexive assumptions, to awake from its slumbers. The dominant agents within the field will then seek to defend orthodoxy, with the overall aim being the restoration of common assent to doxic appearance. Once this is in place, the forms of domination within the field will operate through 'hidden persuasion' in what is taken to be 'the order of things' (Bourdieu in Bourdieu and Wacquant 1992: 168). This is ably assisted by the fact that even where the field exhibits overt antagonisms, there is still an agreement over what it is worth fighting for. 'Partial revolutions' may take place, but the players cannot question the basis of the game itself, otherwise they will be excluded (1993: 74).

From the above discussion we can say that the following elements appear to be the most significant in considering the constitution of fields. These are the 'interests' of agents in the field; what particular forms of capital are being deployed; the agents 'feel' for what is happening; the strategies adopted and their commitment to the fields' presuppositions, or doxa. Further, there is no mechanical set of laws which govern fields because agents adopt strategies leading to degrees of indeterminacy. To put it in economic terminology, this does not imply a conscious desire on the part of agents to maximize their own utility. In this sense, Bourdieu's use of 'strategy' and 'game' has unfortunate connotations which are rooted in a subjectivist tradition that finds its contemporary representation in rational-action theory (Bourdieu in Bourdieu and Wacquant 1992: 129).

To make this latter point as clear as possible let me recap on an earlier discussion. First, the habitus, as a set of acquired dispositions over time, acts as a generative mechanism, between structure and practice, which constitutes the field as meaningful. Second, the field conditions the habitus through being the place of its embodiment. A less-than-conscious ontological complicity therefore exists between the agent's habitus and the field. This is not indicative of a conscious rationality concerned to maximize self-interest. At the same time, actors are not the mere bearers of structures. The employment of strategies within a field provides for the generation of practices which are not simply reducible to any underlying rules of the field. An argument of this type would prioritize the construction of a macro-theoretical model against which the agent's practices are to be explained, thus countering Bourdieu's reflexive approach to the practice of social science.

Second and relatedly, there is an ambiguity surrounding the word 'rule' and hence its applicability to the study of social life. As found in previous chapters, it is often employed in a 'quasi-juridical' way to mean its employment in some conscious way by agents. Alternatively, in the structuralist sense, it is held to impose objective regularities on a game (1990: 60). Whilst Bourdieu is not suggesting that rules do not exist within fields, his reservations on this matter are summed up by his paraphrasing of Weber: 'Social agents obey the rule when it is more in their interest to obey it than to disobey it' (1990: 76). From this point of view, rules cannot be automatically invoked to explain social relations and it obliges the analyst to examine the conditions under which a rule operates. A practical mastery of a game is found; one acquired through experience, but which often works outside of the conscious control of agents.

We now return to the relationships between habitus, strategy and practical sense which Bourdieu employs in overcoming objectivism and subjectivism. The unconscious is not said to replace the conscious. Strategy is the means by which he seeks to avoid the structuralist notion of action without an agent, whilst struggles are those which take place between collectivities. As a result, he seeks to transcend two long-established and entrenched positions in the history of social thought:

> The good player, who is so to speak the game incarnate, does at every moment what the game requires. That presupposes a permanent capacity for invention, indispensable if one is to be able to adapt to indefinitely varied and never completely identical situations. This is not ensured by mechanical obedience to the explicit, codified rule (when it exists) . . . *Nothing is simultaneously freer and more constrained than the action of the good player.*
>
> (Bourdieu 1990: 63, emphasis added)

Summary

In the intersection between field, habitus and capital lies the dynamics of social relations which, at the same time, allows for the reproduction of society and the production of practices. The notion of *habitus*, for example, is used: 'as a way of escaping from the choice between structuralism without subject and the philosophy of the subject' (Bourdieu 1990: 10). The interplay of each of these is open to empirical examination. This provides for a multiplicity of practices via the formula: {[habitus] [capital]} + field = practice (1984: 101). Capital therefore functions only in relation to a field and there is a two-way relationship between the field and habitus. Nevertheless, an apparent diversity often conceals a unity which is the basis for such action: that is, class habitus as a generating and unifying principle (1984: 101). It is these common properties amongst people of particular classes which produce probable, but not determined, life chances.

Within the relationship between field and habitus lies the potentiality for a 'doxic appearance' enabled by the absence of overt struggles informed by particular interests. Given this: 'the misrecognition of the reality of class relations is an integral part of those relations' (1992a: 136). This is not to suggest the type of ideological determinations associated with Althusser's brand of structuralism. Instead, practices, aimed at transformation, are central to Bourdieu's work. As he puts it:

> The different classes and class factions are engaged in a symbolic struggle properly speaking, one aimed at imposing the definition of the social world that is best suited to their interests.
>
> (Bourdieu 1992b: 167)

Issues in the work of Pierre Bourdieu

Pierre Bourdieu's work has been subjected to a number of interpretations. In this section, I wish to draw attention to some of these which critically examine his preoccupation with power and strategy and his desire to generalize across particular social contexts. In the process, attention will be drawn towards possible inconsistencies in his methodological injunctions, as well as raising issues regarding his substantive findings on the dynamics of social relations.

Sitting within the tradition of French structuralism and seeking to overcome its limitations, inevitably leads to comparisons between Bourdieu and the tradition of poststructuralism, as represented, for example, by the writings of Gilles Deleuze, Jacques Derrida, Michel Foucault and Julia Kristeva. This interpretation is lent some credence through the manner in which power saturates Bourdieu's work (the question of power and poststructuralism will be considered in Chapter 9). Scott Lash (1990; 1993) argues that the potential for human practices to gain an autonomy from the operation of power is conceived to be 'only minimal' in Bourdieu's formulations, leading commentators to focus upon his somewhat one-dimensional view of human action (Alexander 1995).

Scott Lash raises important issues in Bourdieu's work. From a methodo-logical vantage point, this revolves around the possibility for the scientific field to operate independently of 'interests'. This clearly depends at what point interests inform the production of scientific work. There is a Weberian edge to Bourdieu's ideas on this subject, which reveals an ambiguity in his formulations. Interests, as Weber argued, inform the direction of scientific work. Thus, Bourdieu can be found saying:

> This interest may consist, as it does everywhere else, in the desire to be the first to make a discovery and to appropriate all the associated rights, or in a moral indignation or revolt against certain forms of domination and against those who defend them within the scientific world. In short, there is no immaculate conception.
>
> (Bourdieu 1993b: 11)

However, if interests inform the whole direction and production of scientific work, this would exhibit a Nietzschean 'will to power' as evident in poststructuralism. Bourdieu (1988) thus argues that scientific fields represent struggles over the very capital that enables scientists to make their 'scientific' pronouncements.

At this point in Bourdieu's formulations, reason seems to depart in favour of underlying power relations. Questions are then left over his 'invitation to reflexivity' where social scientists

> are instructed to reflect, not on the validity of statements and propositions, but on the social and power position of the producers of

these statements. Attention is drawn thus not to the autonomous 'universe of discourse' and its logic of 'true versus false' but to the field of power and its logic of 'friend versus foe'.

(Lash 1990: 264)

Bourdieu thus hovers uneasily between power as the final arbitrator of scientific discourse on one side and the view of a detached and rational scientific observer on the other.

Bourdieu does recognize that for the social sciences to be 'scientific': 'there must be specific, falsifiable, universal claims' (Dreyfus and Rabinow 1993: 40). At the same time, Bourdieu argues that the 'misrecognition' of class relations is an essential part of their functioning. However, does this not privilege the insights of the social scientific observer over the meanings that the lay actor attributes to their social reality? It was in this sense that Marx referred to 'false consciousness', Freud spoke of the 'unconscious', Gramsci spoke of the effects of 'hegemony' and Bourdieu now speaks of 'doxic appearance'. From this point of view, he sits within a tradition of critical theory which extends from Marx to the Frankfurt School (Calhoun 1995). In general, what is postulated here is a 'repressed truth' which claims 'to be able to liberate humanity by revealing it' (Dreyfus and Rabinow 1993: 41).

The substantive 'truth claim' to which Bourdieu can allude in solving this issue of judging the adequacy of his social scientific insights is the ubiquity of class relations as manifested in a universal struggle for symbolic capital. However, concerns are then voiced in relation to the idea that class is used as a universal explanatory principle in Bourdieu's work. The problem being that because it is so all-encompassing, it ceases to designate a particular social group – as it did for Marx and Weber – and thereby loses its explanatory power. Class then becomes

a metaphor for the total set of social determinants. Class structure is synonymous with social structure; class struggles are assimilated to sexual, generation, regional, ethnic, and occupations struggles; and class theory merges with sociological theory in general.

(Brubaker 1985: 770)

Bourdieu's substantive work thus exhibits the same tensions that are found in his methodological writings. In this case, it is between the richness of his ethnographic descriptions of particular practices and his desire to generalize from these (Brubaker 1985). This leads to the tendency, despite his wish to avoid this very problem, for an ahistorical structuralism to reassert itself. As such, it has been argued that he fails to see how changes over time occur in relation to the ways in which capitalism affects culture (Gartman 1991); how historical changes in 'doxa' are important for an analysis of gender relations (Risseeuw 1991) and how the relations between men and women are more complex and contradictory than his more one-dimensional analysis permits (Moi 1991).

The issue concerning the ubiquity of his explanatory concepts may also be applied to the relationship between language and institutions. Whilst serving as a corrective to Austin's (1976) idealist concept of speech-acts due to a consideration of the extra-linguistic sources of their power, the theory becomes too general. Here, as noted, Bourdieu establishes a correspondence between utterances and social position such that the power of speech is one which is 'delegated' to the speakers. This observation itself need not be denied. However, Bourdieu then generalizes to the idea that all utterances are those which are 'authorized'. As John Thompson (1984) argues, from whose work these comments are derived, not all instances of everyday speech are authorized in the way that Bourdieu suggests:

> Consider the case of a person who, in the course of a conversation among friends, seeks to embarrass or humiliate another, to silence or subordinate him or her, by commenting on some aspect of that person's appearance or past . . . or consider the case of a person who, when faced with the prospect of being left by a lover, threatens to commit suicide or to carry out some other act of self-mutilation. So many cases, it seems to me, in which to speak is to perform an act of power, but which it could hardly be said that the latter was the delegated power of a *porte-parole*.
>
> (Thompson 1984: 68, original italics)

To return to the connection with poststructuralism, Bourdieu tends to sever language from reason. The rational force of speech itself, or the conviction with which something is said, becomes explicable only in terms of reference to an outside institution. In other words, an utterance has no 'rational force' of its own (Thompson 1984: 69), leaving understanding reduced to the operation of power. There is no standard to which one can then allude for the purposes of reaching consensual agreement separate from the institutional authority which is bestowed upon the utterance of the speaker. The possibility that language involves communication which is 'supported by reasons' is absent and this also exposes an ambivalence in his methodological edicts:

> The justification of a claim to truth presupposes, not the suspension of power as such, but rather the suspension of systematically asymmetrical relations of power, that is, relations of *domination*. For it is the power to dominate others and to impose one's will on them that stands opposed to the demands for justification.
>
> (Thompson 1984: 71, original italics)

The link that Bourdieu makes between language, power and rationality could become one between rationality, reason and communication in the absence or suspension of power relations. Language could then exhibit a claim to validity and the desire to communicate in order to reach understanding. This argument will be raised in Chapter 7, but it is an issue which remains problematic in both Bourdieu's methodological injunctions and substantive writings.

Summary

The formation of Bourdieu's ideas takes place within the generation of a considerable body of empirical work. The result is a set of 'tools for thinking' to be used by social researchers. This encompasses the invitation to think with, beyond and even against Bourdieu (Wacquant in Bourdieu and Wacquant 1992: xiv) within an overall programme of a reflexive social science. This is not simply an existential call, but one aimed at the institutional conditions of knowledge production itself. The tools of the social sciences are turned back upon themselves, whilst also being used to illuminate the social conditions of action in society. This both recognizes and defends the possibilities that are afforded by rational, scientific dialogue without an allusion to some transcendental standard against which its observations might be measured (Wacquant 1992). This exhibits Bourdieu's tendency to turn philosophical problems, such as those concerned with 'truth': 'into practical problems of scientific politics' (Bourdieu 1990: 33).

Whatever else may be observed, the result of Bourdieu's social scientific practices create possibilities by uncovering the forms of domination that saturate social life. Reflexive analysis has the potential, therefore, to introduce us 'to the unthought categories of thought which limit the thinkable and predetermine what is actually thought' (Bourdieu 1990: 178). As one study of his work concludes, he wishes to 'lay bare' the pretensions of institutions to reflect some fixed reality (Robbins 1991: 176):

> It is through the illusion of freedom from social determinants (an illusion which I have said a hundred times is the specific determination of intellectuals) that social determinations win the freedom to exercise their full power . . . And so, paradoxically, sociology frees us by freeing us from the illusion of freedom, or, more exactly, from the misplaced belief in illusory freedoms. Freedom is not something given: it is something you conquer – collectively.
>
> (Bourdieu 1990: 15)

The tensions inherent in this project have been discussed. In particular, the nature of the relationship between universality and particularity and the connections between language, reason and power. It is at this point that a central thinker on the terrain of contemporary social thought is found who adheres to an uncompleted project of modernity, via his conception of language, communicative reason and their emancipatory potential.

Section 3

Unmasking society and social relations

7

The linguistic turn in critical theory

Jürgen Habermas sits within the tradition of critical theory. Some of the ideas that he has taken-on-board and utilized include those of Weber, Freud, Mead, Durkheim, Parsons, Piaget, Chomsky, Luhmann and the moral-developmental theory of Kohlberg, as well as the traditions of hermeneutics, pragmatism and ordinary language philosophy! He is a defender of an incomplete and modified Enlightenment project who has also inherited Marx's critique of capitalism.

As noted in Part I, the Marx-Hegel connection is important for understanding certain aspects of twentieth-century social theory. There was also the creative tension between Hegel and Kant. For one member of the critical theory tradition this is 'one of the most productive elements' (Honneth 1993: 37). It is not surprising, therefore, that Habermas has utilized their works in order to understand the relationship between knowledge and human interests (Habermas 1989a) and develop his ideas on 'discourse ethics' (Habermas 1993). Yet this philosophical tradition has provided for misunderstanding when it comes to interpreting the works of Habermas. As Taylor and Montefiore put it:

> Notoriously . . . this enterprise has been little appreciated or under-
> stood in Anglo-Saxon philosophy of the last half-century or so . . . This
> inevitably makes it difficult for someone from within this culture to gain
> a familiar sense of the ground plan of the house of critical theory.
> (Taylor and Montefiore 1980: 1)

Take this, together with the myriad of ideas which are evident in his work and the fact that he has subjected them all to critique and we gain an insight into why his ideas are so complicated, wide-ranging and often misunderstood. Despite this, the exercise of perseverance is more than compensated for by the considerable insights that Habermas offers into the operation of societies and the dynamics of social life.

I cannot pretend to be able to redress any imbalance in interpretation within a single chapter and there are those who have performed an excellent service in this regard in book-length studies of his work (McCarthy 1984; Outhwaite 1994; White 1990). Here I simply wish to provide some foundations upon which a further exploration of his work might proceed. First, there is a consideration of the intellectual antecedents and development of his ideas, paying particular attention to the role of rationality, language and the relationship between the system and lifeworld. In the second part of the chapter, some issues which his work raises will then be outlined in order to assess some of its strengths and weaknesses.

The domain of communicative reason

There is a core theme that informs much of Habermas's thought. This is exhibited, to one degree or another, in his earlier work on structural changes in the public sphere, written in 1962 but only recently available in English (Habermas 1989b), his use and criticism of Freudian psychoanalysis (1989a), his linguistic turn (Habermas 1984; 1987) and more recently, his writings on law and democracy (Habermas 1996): that is, the pathologies which arise in the lifeworld which result from systemic imbalances. These imbalances serve to impede the production of meaningful communication which is aimed at the formation of understanding and a 'democratic will' amongst peoples. They interfere with the symbolic reproduction of the lifeworld and are exemplified at a macro level via economic crises and questions over the legitimacy of the state apparatus (Habermas 1993: 148).

In Marx's work, pathologies in the lifeworld were caused by the capitalist system and represented in the state of alienation. In the case of Weber, the triumph of formal rationality over substantive rationality was to form an 'iron cage' of modernity. For Habermas, both of these analyses are limited. Whilst Marx had sought to transcend Hegel's idealism, so Habermas seeks to transcend the limitations of Marx's materialism whilst not abandoning it to idealism. Similarly, he seeks to generate a theory of rationalization using Weber's work but, in so doing, also overcome the pessimism of Nietzschean inspired social theory where reason becomes viewed as the 'will to power'. Therefore, in order to situate Habermas's work, we must consider the nature of these critiques. We shall then be in a position to examine the main elements of the theory of communicative action.

Thinking with and beyond Marx, Weber and the Frankfurt School

Labour was of primary significance for Marx. Alienation was not derived from Hegel's 'mentalist' conception, but from the actual material conditions of capitalist production. However, in his later work or 'mature' work, as encapsulated by Althusser's (1969) notion of an 'epistemological break', Marx appears to reduce ideas to material interests, instead of viewing them in a dialectical fashion. The result is a paradox in *praxis* philosophy:

> Marx reduces the process of reflection to the level of instrumental action. By reducing the self-positing of the absolute ego to the more tangible productive activity of the species, he eliminates reflection as such as a motive force of history, even though he retains the framework of the philosophy of reflection.
>
> (Habermas 1989a: 44)

Marx thus reduces the potential for reflection to the mode of production and that, in turn, to labour. The social self is then linked to the environment in such a manner that there is no social sphere in which people might reflect upon their situation. Therefore, although Marx acknowledges not only the relationship between production and nature, but also the transformation of societies via class struggle, a mechanical view of history remains apparent. A desire for recognition and the pursuit of understanding in human relations is reduced to instrumental action as represented by labour. Marx ends up giving primacy to the application of knowledge towards particular goals over the achievement of understanding within human relations. The consequences of this dilemma was expressed in a different form in Chapter 1 where the question was posed: where are the resources for spontaneous radical change, within an all-encompassing system such as capitalism, actually derived?

Relatedly, Habermas argues that Marx did not adequately differentiate between natural-scientific knowledge, with its implications for control as manifested through technical knowledge harnessed in the process of production, with that of 'critique'. Instead, in positivistic fashion, Marx argued that the 'objective' conditions of capitalism would, as it evolved over time, create the necessary conditions for 'subjective' proletarian emancipation: 'Marx regarded the productive forces unleashed by capitalism as an objective presupposition for overcoming it' (Habermas 1984: 367). Once again, this is a mechanical view which repeats the subject–object dualism in social thought. It does not allow for human interpretation, reflection and understanding which are, to a degree, independent of the labour process:

> In his empirical analyses Marx comprehends the history of the species under categories of material activity *and* the critical abolition of ideologies, of instrumental action *and* revolutionary practice, of labour

and reflection at once. But Marx interprets what he does in the more restricted conception of the species' self-reflection through work alone.
(Habermas 1989a: 42, original italics)

An analysis of the evolution of human learning and understanding, which is not simply reducible to labour, is absent from Marx's work. Of course, a similar problematic preoccupied the Frankfurt theorists for whom Habermas worked in the early stages of his career. Habermas thus identifies a need to incorporate the dimensions of labour *and* interaction in order to develop a more adequate critical theory. Without this, interaction collapses into labour and is open to manipulation by the sort of 'technical' or instrumental knowledge that is constitutive of a positivistic social science with its consequences for control, not emancipation.

Here we can detect the influence of Adorno and Horkheimer's (1979) critique of instrumental reason. Within capitalist societies increasing areas of social life are informed by the logic of a system governed by instrumental action. What Habermas (1989a) refers to as the 'empirical-analytic' sciences, simply add to a purposive-rationality oriented towards the achievement of particular ends. This stands in contrast to those areas of social life which are normatively informed: for example, familial relations. Habermas must now retain the critical edge of Marx within a reconstructed historical materialism that refuses to surrender to instrumentality as the principal mode of characterizing modern societies. A realm of interaction that aims at the achievement of understanding must then be delineated; a realm which contains an evolutionary human-learning process that

cannot be ascribed exclusively either to society or individuals. Certainly the personality system bears the learning process of ontogenesis and, to a certain extent, only individuals are capable of learning. However, social systems can form new structures by utilizing the learning capacities of their members in order to cope with problems that threaten system maintenance. In this respect the evolutionary learning process of societies is dependent on the competence of their individual members. These in turn acquire their competence, not as isolated monads, but by growing into the symbolic structure of their social world.
(Habermas 1981: 269)

Society is dependent upon this realm for its reproduction. This allows for a theory of culture that is not simply reducible to labour. Similarly, it permits a reconstruction of historical materialism which recognizes that the wage–labour relationship produces distorting effects within the lifeworld. In the process, the base-superstructure model, with its economistic approach to social and political relations, is abandoned, together with a mono-causal analysis of power relations as reducible to wage labour; to say nothing of any direct faith in the proletariat as *the* instrument of socialist revolution. With these grounds in mind, we can now make more precise links with our previous discussions on reason and rationality.

Adorno, Horkheimer, Marcuse and Lukács were all, to one degree or another, influenced by Weber's theory of rationalization. As we saw in Part I, instrumental rationality is seen to penetrate the lifeworld to such an extent that modernity represents 'disenchantment'. For Adorno and Horkheimer, in their initial attempts to explain the ideological incorporation of the working classes within capitalism, rationalization and the Enlightenment end up as the prime suspects. Once again, in a similar twist, only from a different starting-point, the idea of progress in the unfolding of human history was destroyed. The result being that they 'surrendered themselves to an uninhibited scepticism regarding reason' (Habermas 1992a: 129).

In charting the development of social theory, history, once again, is seen to offer little hope. Yet each of these theorists is taken to task by Habermas for their failure to diagnose modernity in order to recognize the existence and potential of what he calls 'communicative reason'. A brief examination of his critique of Weber, Adorno and Horkheimer will assist in understanding how he forges this realm in order to argue that a modified Enlightenment project is yet to be completed.

Weber's theory of rationalization views the economy and the state as subsystems of purposive-rationality; the prime cause of capitalism then being the process of rationalization. At the same time, Weber was to abandon any idea of laws in history. Dilthey's historicism urged connections to be made with the meaning-constituting activities of human subjects in order to abandon dialectical and evolutionary theories of history which were viewed as deterministic (Habermas 1984: 153). Yet whilst Weber urged social scientists to start with the meanings that people attach to their social environments, at another level we find him espousing determinism as exemplified in the idea of the 'iron cage'. This gap in Weber's analysis is filled by a Nietzschean-style pessimism, accompanied by the call for an ethic of personal responsibility in the face of historical uncertainty and the continual and never ending struggle for power.

This gap in Weber's reasoning may be summed up as follows:

> Weber did not adequately distinguish between the particular value *contents* of cultural traditions and those universal *standards* of value under which the cognitive, normative, and expressive components of culture become autonomous value spheres and developed complexes of rationality with their own logics.
>
> (Habermas 1984: 249, original italics)

This is symptomatic of the more general problem of viewing society and social relations in terms of a subject–object dualism. The end result being a series of critiques, epitomized by Adorno and Horkheimer, of the contemporary forms of 'subjective' reason from the vantage point of an 'objective' reason which itself has fallen into disrepute (Habermas 1984: 377). From this point of view, it was inevitable that the end result was pessimism, commonly manifested in the idea of a 'reification of consciousness'.

Habermas seeks to avoid such conclusions. Take, for example, Weber's conflation of a particular form of societal rationalization with the entire notion of rationality. For Weber, it was the institutionalization of purposive rationality, beginning with Protestantism and culminating in legal systems, that explains the rise of capitalism. This form of rationality, as noted earlier, involves the selection of means for the attainment of particular ends based upon an interpretation of the intentions of other actors who are, or might be, party to the interaction. However, this does not allow for the possibility that other forms of rationalization exist within modernity. An analysis of these would open up theoretical avenues and lead Habermas to the realm of communicative reason.

To develop an adequate critical theory, the need exists to reconsider the possibilities that modernity offers, without succumbing to the same errors that beset previous theorists. This requires that Habermas avoid the pitfalls of instrumental rationality via a critique of the underlying philosophy of consciousness upon which these theorists relied. In particular, this is manifest in the inadequacy of their theories of action and systems (Habermas 1984: 145). Expressed in this way, we can return to the conceptualization of the relationship between agency and structure in terms of the forging of the domain of communicative reason which

> refers neither to a subject that preserves itself in relating to objects via representation and action, nor to a self-maintaining system that demarcates itself from an environment, but to a symbolically structured lifeworld that is constituted in the interpretive accomplishments of its members and only reproduced through communication.
>
> (Habermas 1984: 398)

To achieve this requires not only extensive historical excavations over the terrain of social theory and philosophy, but also the development of an entirely new basis for critical theory which does not get trapped in the philosophy of the subject. For this purpose, Habermas turned his attention towards the development of the theory of communicative action (TCA) that is informed by four main themes. First, the construction of a theory of rationality which seeks to overcome the above problems, which is not content to let relativism as exemplified, for example, by Winch's (1990) work, to have the last word on the subject. Second, the development of the theory of communicative action itself. Third, an examination of the 'dialectic of rationalization' for the purposes of constructing a theory of modernity which is then able to analyse socio-pathological states in contemporary society. Finally, the bringing together of action and systems theory within a new conceptual framework (Habermas in Dews 1992: 104–105). The result is a highly complicated set of intriguing and challenging ideas. In the next section attention is turned to the development of the TCA where all references are to works by Habermas, unless otherwise stated.

The theory of communicative action

Consider the following proposition. The maintenance of societies results from the co-ordinated activities of its members. This whole process takes place through communication which, at particular times and places, must be oriented towards agreement and understanding in order that such co-ordination occurs in the first instance. Thus far, we might hold that these propositions are unproblematic. However, consider another component: 'the reproduction of the species *also* requires satisfying the condition of rationality that is inherent in communicative action' (Habermas 1984: 397, original italics). There is now a fundamental aspect to the lifeworld which rests upon a form of rationality that encompasses understanding, via language, based upon normative consensus.

From an evolutionary perspective, Habermas will move on in the two volumes of the TCA to argue that although society is dependent upon this realm for its very reproduction, over the course of time there is an increasing 'uncoupling' of the lifeworld from the system. First, however, he turns his attention to an account of the origins and constitution of the lifeworld and from there, to an examination of the relationship between the lifeworld and the system over the course of history.

The origins and constitution of the lifeworld

To consider the constitution of the lifeworld, Habermas develops his ideas on intersubjective communication. Following our earlier discussion on Mead, it should be clear that this mode of communication does not denote the coming together of autonomous subjects, but how it is that people are formed in and through their interactions with others. Nevertheless, whilst Habermas refers to his general attempts at a reconstructive science as 'universal pragmatics', Mead's work is found to be limited in terms of his accounts of the development of the self and the lifeworld. It is at this point that Durkheim, read from the point of view of his theory of evolution, enters Habermas's formulations.

Durkheim's lifelong concern was 'to explain the normative validity of institutions and values' (Habermas 1987: 47). Durkheim's principal legacy regarding society as an active moralizing force enables Habermas to discuss the concept of rationality without succumbing to the trap of instrumentality. As Durkheim argued, norms are held to be valid due to the moral authority which they contain, not simply because their infringement is attached to particular sanctions (Habermas 1992c: 73). From this point of view, Habermas now considers the origins of the lifeworld within a normative framework. Furthermore, Durkheim's focus upon the *conscience collective* permits him to correct the ontogenetic emphasis of Mead's ideas and recover them at a phylogenetic level (Habermas 1987: 46). Briefly, how does this take place?

For Mead the moral authority of the group rested upon the internalization of the 'generalized other' within the individual. In turn, this is based upon an initial set of group sanctions for the purposes of maintaining social control. However, there remains an issue: 'groups must have first been constituted as units capable of acting before the sanctions could be imposed in their name' (Habermas 1987: 45). According to Mead's formulations it appears that individuals can become members of a group only once a collective consciousness has formed! With this paradox in mind, Mead resorted to ideas on the personality for his explanatory resource, with the result that he failed to provide an account of the origins of the collective lifeworld itself.

In contrast to Mead, Durkheim rooted his analysis in terms of beliefs which were 'the expression of a collective consciousness rooted deep in tribal history and constitutive of the identity of groups' (Habermas 1987: 46). However, there are gaps in Durkheim's ideas through an absence of the linguistic component of the lifeworld. After all, the everyday world of the profane is channelled through linguistic communication which aims at intersubjective understanding. Instead of seeing the sacred and profane in this way, Durkheim collapsed both normative consensus and the process of reaching understanding through speech acts under the umbrella of the collective consciousness (Habermas 1987: 57). What we are witnessing here is yet another repetition of the subject–object dualism in social thought. In Durkheim's work this is manifest through his duality of human nature in terms of self-interested activity and morality. The result being, in evolutionary terms, he failed to answer the question 'How do institutions draw upon social solidarity in order to maintain their validity?' (Habermas 1987: 57). This may be resolved only

> if we bear in mind that profane everyday practice proceeds by way of linguistically differentiated processes of reaching understanding and forces us to specify validity claims for actions appropriate to situations in the normative context of roles and institutions.
>
> (Habermas 1987: 57)

Linguistic communication fills the analytic gap between institutional reproduction and normative consensus. It may be characterized as having a 'mediating function' that links individuals to the collective consciousness. Therefore, both normatively grounded symbolism and linguistic communication are fundamental constituents of the lifeworld which, together, account for the origins of the lifeworld. Durkheim's focus upon norms, the sacred and the moral, thus end up as supplements to Mead's theory of intersubjective communication. With a normative background in place, our everyday speech can then be argued to presuppose its basis in consensual validity. Overall, this fusion yields 'the structure of linguistically mediated, normatively guided interaction, which is the starting point for sociocultural development' (Habermas 1987: 46).

To complete this connection Habermas must draw upon one more analytic resource: ordinary language philosophy. As we have noted before, this 'has taken the place of the traditional problem of consciousness' (Habermas 1990: 117). In furtherance of the concept of intersubjective communication, language becomes the medium for reaching understanding, learning and achieving co-operation. As Habermas puts it so eloquently:

> From the structure of language comes the explanation of why the human spirit is condemned to an odyssey . . . Only at the greatest distance from itself does it become conscious of itself in its irreplaceable singularity as an individuated being (*Wesen*).
>   (Habermas 1992b: 153, original italics)

At this stage in the development of Habermas's thought the discussion becomes highly technical. For our purposes we can consider this in the following manner. To complete the forging of the potential of communicative reason, Habermas employs Austin's speech-act theory (Austin 1976). If the potential for communicative reason exists in language itself then there exists a scientific, as opposed to a normative basis, for critical theory. He then ends up employing the analytic tradition of philosophy for the purposes of working on a continental problematic which, as noted at the beginning of the chapter, can lead to interpretative misunderstanding. Briefly, how is this achieved?

Austin divides performatory utterances – speech-acts which are also performances of an action – into locutionary, illocutionary and perlocutionary statements (1976). Simply put, the first involves the act of actually saying something; the second refers to what is done in the act of an utterance – for example, a promise – and the third produces particular effect in others. From this Habermas seeks to make a distinction between illocutionary and perlocutionary statements by arguing that the former are oriented towards understanding and the latter employed in strategic action. In other words, once again, albeit at a different level, instrumental action in terms of being oriented towards success is perlocutionary, but this is parasitic upon communicative action as oriented towards reaching understanding as exemplified by illocutionary speech acts. The latter are therefore primary and speech acts take place against the background of normative consensus in the life world:

> The illocutionary components express the fact that the speaker is explicitly raising a claim to propositional truth, normative rightness, or

subjective truthfulness, as well as the particular aspects under which he is doing so.

(Habermas 1987: 72)

As Habermas recognizes (1984: 328), one might then ask how we can link this into everyday usages of language? He seeks to use these ideas to arrive at a general classification of 'linguistically mediated interaction' (1984: 329). The issue here being, if he is not to repeat the mistakes that Weber and others have made in relation to the general problem of rationality, that what should be examined is not the motivations for actions, but the relationship of these to the structures of the lifeworld itself for this is presupposed as the background to actions:

> Communicative action takes place within a lifeworld that remains at the backs of participants in communication. It is present to them only in the prereflexive form of taken-for-granted background assumptions and naively mastered skills.

(Habermas 1984: 335)

Whilst Habermas finds the insights of ordinary language philosophy important for the development of communication action, it is also limited for reasons which we have come across before. First, the absence of any hermeneutic input in terms of the translation between language games. Second, it shares an idealism along with hermeneutics. Therefore, although Gadamer (1975) was correct in overcoming Wittgenstein's limitations by connecting language use with the history through which we inherit our language, he shares a failure to see the ways in which language 'serves to legitimate relationships of organized force' (Habermas 1990: 172. Also see Holub 1991: ch. 3). Third, the analyses of those such as Wittgenstein, Austin and Searle remain particularistic and hence they fail to develop a general theory of language games (Habermas 1989a: 354).

Recalling Habermas's critique of Durkheim, we can characterize communicative action as a 'switching station for the energies of social solidarity' (1987: 57). We are bound together by the rationally motivating force of communicative reason that is embedded in the background to our everyday utterances:

> The concept of communicative rationality does not just apply to the processes of intentional consensus formation, but also to the structures of a state of pre-understanding already reached within an intersubjectively shared lifeworld. The latter demarcates in the shape of a context-forming horizon the respective speech situation; at the same time, as an unproblematic and prereflexive background it plays a constitutive role in the achievement directed toward reaching

understanding. Lifeworld and communicative action thus relate to one another in a complementary fashion.

(Habermas 1991: 223)

In relation to a theory of rationalization, if communicative reason holds across societies, then it represents a form of rationality that cannot be viewed as a subsystem of purposive rationality (the Weberian problematic). Instead, the point of reference becomes 'the potential for rationality found in the validity basis of speech' (Habermas 1984: 339). Communicative action can also be examined in terms of how it 'mediates between the ritually preserved fund of social solidarity and existing norms and personal identities' (1987: 77). This is the very realm upon which the reproduction of society and social relations is dependent.

Despite these arguments we are still left with a fundamental question. If this is the basis for the lifeworld, how is it that its potential has not reached fruition? We witness conflict and misunderstanding as much, if not more, than we see consensus and understanding. Clearly, Habermas does not intend to furnish us with yet another idealist social theory and wishes to retain Marx's critical spirit, if not the substance of his work. This is where the relationship between the system and lifeworld enters his formulations.

The uncoupling of system from lifeworld

From an evolutionary perspective, to chart the space that is now occupied by communicative reason Habermas poses the following hypothesis: the socially expressive and integrative functions within society which were once part of ritual are now performed by communicative action. A 'linguistification of the sacred' has occurred over time which may be expressed in the following manner:

> the authority of the holy is gradually replaced by the authority of an achieved consensus. This means a freeing of communicative action from sacrally protected normative contexts. The disenchantment and disempowering of the domain of the sacred takes place by way of a linguistification of the ritually secured, normative agreement; going along with this is a release of the rationality potential in communicative action. The aura of rapture and terror than emanates from the sacred, the *spellbinding* power of the holy, is sublimated into the *binding/ bonding* force of criticizable validity claims and at the same time turned into an everyday occurrence.
>
> (Habermas 1987: 77, original italics)

Given this, Habermas can maintain that any analyses of modernity in terms of instrumental rationality is bound to be limited. Furthermore, if the use of language involves particular claims to validity which, under given social conditions, may be resolved by a consensus based upon such reason, then the potential exists to reach human understanding under the umbrella of an incomplete, but highly modified, Enlightenment project. At the same time, however, in terms of a theory of human action, we have seen that Habermas must distinguish between communicative and strategic action so that the potential of the former is realized and that he does not commit the error of reducing all human action to the latter.

At this point Habermas emphasizes that there is not, as Weber had maintained, a state of competition between two modes of action in the lifeworld – one being oriented to success and the other to understanding. Instead, the competition exists between

> *principles of societal integration* – between the mechanism of linguistic communication that is oriented to validity claims – a mechanism that emerges in increasing purity from the rationalization of the lifeworld – and those de-linguistified steering media through which systems of success-orientated action are differentiated out.
>
> (Habermas 1984: 342)

Two domains now appear. This is a dualism that views social integration as part of the lifeworld and system integration as part of the system. In order to consider this further, he turns to the ideas of Parsons and Luhmann; although not without criticism (see Habermas 1987; Holub 1991: ch. 5). In the process he furnishes us with a theory of social change that sees an increasing 'uncoupling' of the system from the lifeworld. System reproduction and the differentiation of more and more autonomous organizations increasingly rely not upon communicative action, but what Habermas terms the 'delinguistified media of communication' (1987: 154). Normative consensus is replaced by the non-normative regulation of individual decisions which extends beyond the consciousness of individual actors (1987: 117).

According to these formulations, society must comprise both system and lifeworld. If accepted, the question is how to connect the two? For Giddens it rests on duality, for Parsons on the system and for those such as Mead, Garfinkel and Schutz, on the lifeworld. For Habermas, we need both in order to explain the evolution of societies. Society becomes a system

> that has to fulfil conditions for the maintenance of sociocultural lifeworlds. The formula – societies are *systematically stabilized* complexes of action of *socially integrated* groups . . . may stand for the heuristic proposal that we view society as an entity that, in the course of social evolution, gets differentiated as a system and as a lifeworld.
>
> (Habermas 1987: 152, original italics)

The thesis being that as new systems emerge over time, they are increasingly separate from those structures which contribute to social integration. As social systems become more differentiated, they rely less on structures of social integration and more on systemic mechanisms that are not anchored in the lifeworld. The result is norm-free objectified structures. The consequences for the lifeworld and the individuals who comprise it are clear:

> in modern societies, economic and bureaucratic spheres emerge in which social relations are regulated only via money and power. Norm-conformative attitudes and identity-forming social memberships are neither necessary nor possible in these spheres; they are made peripheral instead.
>
> (Habermas 1987: 154)

Yet, as noted before, the transmission of culture and socialization relies upon the domain of communicative action. This cannot take place through the mediums of power and money. The result being that the processes of commercialization and bureaucratization generate 'disturbances, pathological side effects in these domains' (Habermas in Dews 1992: 172). Again, the consequences are apparent:

> The reproductive constraints that instrumentalize a lifeworld without weakening the illusion of its self-sufficiency have to hide, so to speak, in the pores of communicative action. This gives rise to a *structural violence* that, without becoming manifest as such, takes hold of the forms of intersubjectivity of possible understanding.
>
> (Habermas 1987: 187, original italics)

The reification of consciousness does not then arise, as it does for those trapped in the tradition of Cartesianism, from the forward march of instrumental rationality. Instead, it derives from the ways in which the norm-free and purposively rational co-ordinating mechanisms of system reproduction continually undermine the potential of communicative reason, aimed at social integration, within the lifeworld. The material conditions for undistorted communication therefore remain absent due to the distorting effects of money and power as exemplified by increased state intervention into the operation of capitalist societies – a phenomenon that orthodox Marxism is not able to satisfactorily analyse.

Summary

To return us to Weber's problematic with a Marxist edge, whilst rescuing the potential of critical theory from the clutches of the subject–object dualism in social thought via an analysis of language use, is a formidable task. Habermas stands as a defender of a foundationalist social theory, via a modified Enlightenment project, in a world which has allegedly become subject to the process of postmodernization.

Habermas reaches back in time to construct an evolutionary social theory which argues for a normative basis in the lifeworld. The result is that our everyday utterances, as a matter of course, raise claims which are open to consensual validation. Communicative reason is then seen to form the bedrock of social relations. As such, there is potential where Weber found only fatalism and the possibility of consensus where Marx found only instrumentality.

Habermas formulates a basis for critical theory in the very structures of language itself. This places him at odds with Adorno. For Adorno, under the influence of the literary theorist Walter Benjamin (see Benjamin 1991), high art, rather than empirical studies became 'the last refuge of critical practice in a world completely dominated by total administration' (Aronowitz 1992: 308). He became increasingly anti-scientific and rejected any attempt to grasp social totality in the name of reason. Habermas, through his extensive excavations accompanied by considerable theoretical power, may thus be characterized as having saved critical theory from its retreat into negativism.

Issues in the theory of communicative action

Habermas's work is so rich and wide-ranging that it should come as no surprise that there is a great deal to choose from in the way of critical commentary that stems from a variety of disciplines. In this section I wish to consider a core issue in his work which illuminates our central theme of the relationship between action and structure. More specifically, this concerns his utilization of systems theory.

For Zygmunt Bauman, Habermas provided a source of inspiration, until, that is, he turned to a 'positivistic re-hashing of Parsons' (Bauman 1992: 217). Further, in what is one of the most telling critiques of Habermas's use of systems theory by an otherwise sympathetic critic and translator, Thomas McCarthy concludes:

> Habermas once criticized Marx for succumbing to the illusion of rigorous science, and he traced a number of Marxism's historical problems with political analysis and political practice to this source. The question I have wanted to pose here is whether in flirting with systems theory he does not run the danger of being seduced by the same illusion in more modern dress.
>
> (McCarthy 1991: 139)

We have seen that Habermas uses the insights of systems theory to make a series of distinctions between communicative and purposive rationality or, expressed in another way, between communication and power. However, this begs questions. First, does the use of systems theory for this purpose actually undermine the aims of critical theory? Second and relatedly, does this distinction fail to see the ways in which the lifeworld itself is regulated by power as opposed to some normative consensus?

It has been argued that if we are to explain macrosocial phenomena, then simple recourse to actors' intentions for explanatory purposes is inadequate. However, as Giddens has argued in recognizing the importance of analysing the unintended consequences of social action, it does not follow that functionalism, in its attribution of teleology to social systems, has a monopoly over this analytic sphere. Nevertheless, in order to maintain his distinction between system and lifeworld, Habermas uses not only Parsonian functionalism, but also the works of Luhmann (1982) who argues that with the increasing complexity of society, it is the 'system' which possesses its own rationality and this is separate from the rationality of the interacting subjects who comprise it.

With the introduction of this distinction, the potentiality of communicative reason is assumed to be preserved against the encroachment of strategic action. However, is this satisfactory? Reason, rooted in the structures of language within the lifeworld, is viewed as a final arbitrator. What we then witness is the increasing encroachment of system rationality upon the lifeworld to such an extent that the societal sphere of the communicative lifeworld shrinks significantly. We are then left wondering how so much might be invested, for the purpose of generating a viable critical social theory, in something which has been so successfully reduced by the forces of systemic power?

For the purpose of analytic illumination, we can approach this issue in another way. The theoretical utilization of systems theory enables Habermas to create a duality between an independent lifeworld and the operation of power. However, for Axel Honneth, writing in the tradition of critical theory, this is a 'fiction' which

> results not only from Habermas's evolution-theoretic explanations of the emergence of modern societies in terms of the uncoupling of system and lifeworld but also from the terminological constraints into which he falls with his distinction between two forms of integration of social action.
>
> (Honneth 1991: 299)

This distinction between two forms of social action – action oriented to success and action oriented to understanding – is highly problematic. Paradoxically, it permits criticisms from two different angles. First, from neo-functionalist approaches to social relations which regard Habermas as still being trapped in Marxist notions of 'contradictions', only this time between the system and lifeworld, whilst remaining insensitive to cultural influences in the desire to locate a new basis for universal reason (Alexander 1991).

A second basis for critique comes from writers such as McCarthy (1991), Honneth (1991) and Joas (1993), where we find the argument that this dualism cannot be maintained through the utilization of systems theory. The result is that the concrete struggles of groups of people within their everyday lives, against the continuing encroachments of purposive rationality, become surrendered to a domain which is assumed to be separate from the exercise of power. To attribute a self-maintaining purposive-rationality to material reproduction, separate from the activities of those who comprise it, actually loses the very power of insight that Marx possessed: that is, to critique supposed natural systems as human constructions which are symptomatic of a particular mode of production within a given epoch. Habermas ends up surrendering materialism to idealistic formulations expressed in terms of the acts of some 'lifeworld contemplation' in the face of systemic encroachments:

> whereas Marx saw *stringent material conditions* as being necessary for the efficacy of counter-cultural ideas, Habermas attaches *speculative cultural conditions* to the emergence of effective critical thought.
> (Archer 1989: 69, original italics)

McCarthy puts this general argument in a slightly different form. Luhmann's separation between politics and administration permits a distinction to be made between procedural decision-making and the legitimacy which is required to ensure its mass support. One is viewed as goal motivated, the other providing the legitimacy for its effective functioning. In following Habermas's argument, the political system, as the producer of mass loyalty, takes precedence over the communicative process in which values and norms are formed (McCarthy 1991: 127). If we empirically examine the relationship between the informal and formal aspects of an administrative system, the interactions within it cannot be simply explained through reference to the functionally co-ordinated activities of its members which are seen as oriented towards collective goals. This is often found expressed in terms of what is deemed 'functional' for system maintenance.

A recognition of this tension is evident in Habermas's work. Despite this, he still maintains that 'action within organisations falls *under the premises* of formally regulated domains of action' (1987: 310, original italics). However, the achievement of social integration in organizations may equally be achieved through interactional threats or fear of sanctions and the giving and taking of orders (McCarthy 1991: 130). To attribute this role to system integration, by theoretical fiat, fails to see how organizations are co-ordinated in social, as well as system, terms:

> All of this is meant merely to say that system integration and social integration, as they are defined by Habermas, seem to be extremes rather than alternatives that exhaust the field of possibilities: the denial of one does not entail the other . . . Moreover, if softened to correspond to the inside/outside differences in methodological perspectives, it seems clear that most, if not all, domains of social action can be looked at in both ways.
> (McCarthy 1991: 130)

A similar critique of the system–lifeworld distinction is made by Nancy Fraser (1989). She argues that the idea of non-normative and non-consensual co-ordination of action through systems is not tenable. Indeed, however dubious the nature of consensus might be or the status of the norms invoked in the course of interaction, 'virtually every human action context involves some form of both of them' (Fraser 1989: 117). From this point of view, strategic action is neither analytically, nor practically, distinct from an horizon of shared meanings and norms. In the workplace, for example, the co-ordination of actions will take place against the presumption of normative consensus: 'Thus, the capitalist economic system has a moral-cultural dimension' (Fraser 1989: 118).

Fraser goes on to argue that we cannot hold human actions as being devoid of a strategic component. The dichotomies – between labour and interaction and the system and lifeworld – whilst apparently mirroring empirical reality in terms of the lifeworld of familial relations and the systemic domain of paid work are, in fact, highly problematic when it comes to gender relations:

> Feminists have shown through empirical analyses of contemporary familial decision-making, handling of finances, and wife battering that families are thoroughly permeated with, in Habermas's terms, the media of power and money. They are sites of egocentric, strategic, and instrumental calculation as well as sites of usually exploitative exchanges of services, labor, cash, and sex – and, frequently, sites of coercion and violence.

> (Fraser 1989: 119–120)

The restriction of power to systemic properties is thereby limited, for it does not capture the operation of power within the lifeworld itself. The distinction between the official economy (system) and family (lifeworld) is incapable of analysing the relationship between women's unpaid labour and the official economy. From this point of view, Habermas repeats the Marxist problematic of reducing *reproduction* to *production*.

Summary

Habermas's overall project is to escape from the philosophy of consciousness and ground critical theory in communicative action. In the process he seeks to avoid the idealism that is apparent in approaches to the study of language. Now, as we saw in relation to issues in Bourdieu's work, as soon as one admits of the role of power in language, any notion such as communicative reason departs in favour of viewing action in terms of the employment of the strategic resources at the disposal of actors oriented towards particular ends. Quite simply, it would not be the better argument that wins the day, but the deployment of power.

In view of the centrality of language in social life, we must question, given the above, the possibilities of ever reaching a position where discourse might be free from domination. However, this is not what Habermas actually says: 'People who impute this to me make it a bit too easy for themselves' (Dews 1992: 180). From an historical point of view, he argues that there are trends in world history that are witnessing the erosion of prejudices. That is certainly not to suggest that they do not exist, as a number of tragic events in recent times have made only too clear. What Habermas argues is that the very use of language presupposes an ideal-speech situation as a regulative principle. This is very different from saying that it has a factual existence.

From a socio-theoretical and philosophical point of view, with a political project in mind, Habermas reaches back into the history of social and philosophical thought in order to critique the philosophy of the subject so that he might develop his notion of communicative reason. This also requires that, from the point of view of a 'discourse ethics', he examines the procedures through which this might be achieved. He refers to this as 'practical discourse'. As he so eloquently expresses it in his summary of the works of Albrecht Wellmer on this question:

> Like all argumentation, practical discourses resemble islands threatened with inundation in a sea of practice where the pattern of consensual conflict resolution is by no means the dominant one. The means of reaching agreement are repeatedly thrust aside by the instruments of force. Hence, action that is oriented toward ethical principles has to accommodate itself to imperatives that flow not from principles but from strategies necessities.
>
> (Habermas 1992c: 106)

This is a tall order given the saturation of social life by power effects and strategies. However, it is the interpenetration of the distorting effects of the system on the lifeworld that prevents the possibility of reaching such agreement.

We are left with a powerful theory of contemporary social relations. A theory that is a 'reconstructive science' whose aim is to examine our 'pre-theoretical' knowledge by seeking to 'isolate, identify, and clarify the conditions required for human communication' (Bernstein 1985a: 16). We are also left with a thinker who argues that consensus might be achieved based on something called communicative reason, but only once the distorting effects of power are removed from everyday discourse; a thinker who argues that human emancipation is only attainable in a society which is rationally organized and that the conditions of such organization is the institutionalization of universally valid norms. As such, those social institutions which embody 'norms with a valid claim to universality are a necessary condition of human emancipation' (N. Smith 1993: 42).

The end result is a linguistically based critical social theory that is said to possess the potential to fuse indexicality with a pragmatic emphasis on practicality (McCarthy in Hoy and McCarthy 1994: 72). All of this takes place under the umbrella of a modified project of modernity that stresses the one-sided nature of social theories which concentrate on instrumental rationality to the exclusion of communicative reason. In sum, Habermas refuses to surrender the concept of transcendence, whilst remaining critical of such a conception, to the relativism of so much recent social and philosophical thought.

Despite the undoubted power of Habermas's ideas, issues remain. For Nancy Fraser (1989) these were revealed through the need to substantially modify his insights in order to be applicable to an analysis of gender relations. These general critiques, however, are not simply applicable to Habermas, whilst it should be noted that he has consistently demonstrated his willingness to enter into discussions concerning his ideas, thus translating his own theories into personal practice. These are critiques that have been applied to social theory in general. Therefore, it is now necessary to examine the arguments and insights of feminisms.

8

Where did all the women go?

An argument was noted in Part I whereby social practices and the production of social theory as part of those practices, exhibit a bias by reflecting interests and values associated with a masculine identity and perspective on social life. The result being that mainstream social theory, much of which we have covered so far, is said to represent a partial and incomplete view of society and social relations. Such is the power of this critique that any book which seeks to chart the contemporary terrain of social theory will itself be incomplete without due consideration being given to its main themes and ideas.

In chapter 2 it was suggested that feminist theories may be divided into three broad perspectives. First, there are the works of those such as Wollstonecraft, informed by liberalism and individualism, for whom women's nature was rational and gender-neutral. From this point of view, femininity can be viewed as an artificial condition which subordinates women within a patriarchal culture. The implication is that women should become integrated within dominant modes of thought. This may be characterized as the integrationist perspective.

Within the second perspective, feminist theorists examine the basis of society and its social practices. This necessitates subjecting the history of social theory to critical scrutiny in terms of its production being shaped by masculine perspectives and experiences. Shunning liberal individualism, it is the social process of gender construction that becomes the object of its study: that is, the manner in which social relations confer meanings upon sexual differences. Its basis therefore being the ways in which patriarchal practices are themselves the causes of exclusion. As such, they cannot form the basis of an integrative strategy. We may term this perspective one of critique whose aim is to expose gender bias. Quite simply, women cannot achieve equality on foundations set by men. Instead, what is required is a process of building a more adequate social theory through utilizing studies on women, by women, in order that their perspectives and experiences are recovered from the realms of marginality.

A third broad perspective now exists which aims at the heart of the Enlightenment project itself. This does not seek to replace a masculine truth with the equal 'bias' of a feminine truth. Instead, it is argued that differences and diversities amongst women mean that there cannot be one essential category of *woman*, but multiple experiences, identities and truths; in other words, there are *women*. This is the perspective of postmodern feminisms:

> A postmodern feminism would reject the masculinist bias of rational-ism but would not replace it with a feminist bias. Rather it would take the position that there is not one (masculine) truth but, rather, many truths, none of which is privileged along gender lines.
>
> (Hekman 1990b: 9)

The purpose of this chapter is to examine the second perspective and in the latter section it will introduce some of the ideas of the third, the basis of which will be clearer as we move on through Chapters 9 and 10. As will become evident, however, feminist theorists, as with social theory in general, do not automatically embrace postmodernism. On the contrary, many are highly critical of its arguments and presuppositions.

The development of feminist social theory

The second phase of feminist theorizing may be characterized in terms of deconstruction and reconstruction. Both of these strategies have profound implications for the ways in which we theorize about agency, structure, society and social relations. Deconstruction is understood to be an examin-ation of the ways in which masculine perspectives inform and produce 'the most fundamental and most formal aspects of systematic thought in philosophy and in the social and natural sciences' (Harding and Hintikka 1983a: x). The desired end being to expose the ways in which such biases shape dominant modes of thought. The reconstructive project, on the other hand, involves the identification of women's experiences which can then 'provide resources for the construction of a more representatively human understanding' (Harding and Hintikka 1983a: x).

With a combination of the deconstructive and reconstructive modes in mind, we can focus upon an examination of social theory in terms of its inbuilt biases and provide an account of the reconstruction of a more representative social theory. Therefore, I shall begin with an account of the issues associated with contemporary social theory and then move on to provide an overview of the development of modern feminist thought.

Where did all the women go?

Thus far, questions concerning the applicability of social theory for explaining and understanding the position of women in society have been raised without a detailed exposition of the arguments concerned. In this section, I explore these in more depth. As will become apparent, what we uncover is a systematic exclusion of women from the concerns of social theory due to an over-reliance upon partial modes of thought, that exist within society in general, that place men at the centre of its analytic foci.

The 'engendering of modernity' (Marshall 1994) is a project that captures the strategies of both deconstruction and reconstruction. At the level of deconstruction, the most influential social theories and theorists find themselves subjected to a number of criticisms; in particular, the manner in which the social world is divided into the realms of the public and the private. This is of significance if we trace it in the following manner.

With the growth of modernity, social theory has placed the socialized individual, as opposed to the pre-social autonomous ego, at the heart of its analysis. As we have seen throughout our journey, the idea of the social self and its relationship to society is central to this development. It is the very tensions between a socialized and pre-social individual and its ramifications for understanding and explanation that provides social theory with much of its dynamism. However, the social self is a gendered concept: that is, the very processes of socialization ascribe particular characteristics and modes of behaviour to individuals on the basis of their sex. This process, in turn, is based upon dominant normative standards. Differences in anatomy, for example, often assumed to be the most physical, as opposed to social aspects of the self, are constituted as meaningful in entirely different ways according to political relationships of male dominance (Millett 1992). The ramifications for gender relations as a whole, as well as the self-conception of women and men in particular, are clear. Yet the causes and effects of these insights are absent from much modern socio-theoretical discourse. Alternatively, when present, they are accounted for in a manner which owes more to dominant presuppositions than to analytic scrutiny.

The attribution of characteristics to social structure follows similar patterns. Take, for instance, an account of women's place in society according to traditional Marxist analysis. Here it is held that gender categories have arisen which may be explained through reference to class oppression. A one-way causal relationship between capitalism and the evolution of the family is thus posited such that the latter serves the needs of the former. However:

> The fact that the family continues to coexist with a capitalist economy does not prove it serves the latter, still less that it serves only the latter.

All their coexistence proves is that the prior institution, the family, and the wage labour system, etc., are compatible. What does need to be stressed, however, since it seems not to be evident to many authors, is that compatibility is necessarily mutual. Coexistence does not imply a hierarchical relationship, still less a one-way causality.

(Delphy and Leonard 1992: 33)

The manner in which the family affects capitalism, in terms of the constituent relations between men and women, is an equally important area of concern. Of course, this does not suggest that the subordination of women is without a material basis, simply that it is limited not to the means of production, but also to that of reproduction (Barrett 1988). Therefore, how social structure is theorized will inevitably affect the content of the theory itself. If social structure is conceived of in the absence of any gendered component then it will limit the analytic power of the theory. Given this, feminist theorists have preferred to conceive of social structure in terms of patriarchy, defined as the manner in which men as a social group exploit, dominate and oppress women as a social group (Walby 1990: 20).

This joint absence of considerations of gender relations – at the levels of the self and social structure and the relations between them – inevitably leads to gaps, or gaping chasms, in social theory. These points have been noted in relation to the works of Giddens, Bourdieu and Habermas, amongst others. What is argued to be reproduced in the texts of these and other authors are partial versions of society and social relations. To return to the public–private dichotomy, the very areas of social activity in which women participate appear to be absent on grounds which leave more to the realms of common sense than to the type of critical scrutiny that theorists reserve for other spheres of life.

This point may be illustrated in relation to the world of work:

We think of paid work as being work and exclude other kinds of work (e.g. housework, DIY and voluntary work) from our definition. We tend also to have a conception of paid work derived from an analysis of manual work in manufacturing industry, which was perhaps more appropriate to nineteenth century conditions than the present day. Workplaces are generally thought of as strictly demarcated from the home and family life. Similarly, we think of workers as people who leave home in the morning to travel to these workplaces and who work for a certain number of hours that has nothing to do with the home.

(Beechey 1986: 77)

The above might well be an accurate characterization of paid work undertaken by men, but it is not useful for the purposes of understanding women's paid work (Beechey 1986: 78). Domestic work is viewed as a peripheral activity which is not directly related to economic issues. Giddens, for example, is open to the criticism that far from being peripheral to economic activity, as he has suggested, women are part of the fundamental process of 'producing people' and 'things'. This constitutes

> an important focus for analysing patterns of interaction and structures of power outside of the domestic sphere, and helps fill a big lacuna still current in sociological theory.
>
> (Murgatroyd 1989: 156)

As noted in chapter 5, whilst being refreshingly honest in meeting such criticisms, Giddens's suggestion that psychoanalysis is a useful paradigm for understanding the differences between men and women (Giddens 1989: 284) sits somewhat uneasily with his reservations concerning its general explanatory power. Given the centrality of an analysis of gender relations and a recognition of the need to explain the position of women in society in relation to power inequalities through their confinement to domestic contexts (Giddens 1989: 286), why is there an absence of any discussion of the gendering properties of social structure from a general theoretical analysis which places power at its centre?

A similar point can be made in relation to the work of Habermas. His distinction between system and lifeworld fails to account for the patriarchal aspects of both economic and administrative systems and thus the content and effects of the systemic operations of money and power as they apply to women. His 'colonization thesis' thus

> tends to replicate, rather than to problematize, a major institutional support of women's subordination in late capitalism, namely, the gender-based separation of both the masculine public sphere and the state-regulated economy of sex-segmented paid work and social welfare from privatized female childrearing.
>
> (Fraser 1989: 137)

Conceptions of agency and structure within contemporary social theory are found wanting when applied to women. Clearly, the very idea concerning how society is divided into different realms and by what causes and with what consequences, is a central issue for social theory. It requires problematization, as opposed to being bracketed by definitional fiat or even ignored altogether. That noted, the question is now begged as to what an adequate feminist social theory might consist of? The next section is therefore devoted to an outline of the development of feminist ideas with the caveat that the reader should be aware that this is highly selective. In order to commence this thematic overview, I shall start with Shulamith Firestone's (1988) critique of Marx and Engels. This work represents a distinct and radical development in social theory.

Bringing women back in: forging feminist theory

Firestone begins her study by noting that class analysis, particularly in the work of Engels (1942), is a 'beautiful piece of work, but limited' (Firestone

1988: 14). Indeed, the original division of labour between men and women was observed by Engels as based upon child-rearing. As such his 'outstanding achievement' was to see 'women's oppression as a problem of history, not biology' (Delmar 1976: 287).

Despite the potential of Engels's work, Firestone finds it limited because it rests upon the reduction of sexual class to the economic sphere. On the other hand, to concentrate on the psychosexual realm of human behaviour which underlies the economic sphere is also inadequate because it is ahistorical. In this way Firestone rejects both Marxist and Freudian accounts. Yet she also retains an explicit preference for a materialist theory of history in order to account for women's subordination. How does she overcome these apparent limitations? Firestone argues that there is a third way: 'we can attempt to develop a materialist view of history based on sex itself' (Firestone 1988: 15). How is this accomplished? The following is an outline of her argument.

Simone de Beauvoir spoke of women as the 'other'. Femininity is then constructed in terms of being all that the masculine is not:

> One is not born, but rather becomes, a woman. No biological, psychological, or economic fate determines the figure that the human female presents in society; it is civilization as a whole that produces this creature, intermediate between male and eunuch, which is described as feminine.
>
> (de Beauvoir in Humm 1992: 48)

In true existentialist fashion, de Beauvoir argued for a greater role of rationality in the lives of women in order that they might transcend their position in society. *The Second Sex* (1972) may thus be characterized as having two targets: one is male-institutions and the other, as in Wollstonecraft's work, is women themselves (Crosland 1992).

Firestone's debt to de Beauvoir is apparent in her work. She writes of de Beauvoir's thoughts on representation whereby men describe the world: *'from their own point of view, which they confuse with absolute truth'* (de Beauvoir quoted in Firestone 1988: 148, original italics). However, as Marx and Engels had argued, Hegelian notions of 'transcendence' must be rooted in actual history. As one part of humanity (men) have transcended nature, for Firestone this cannot be the origin of women's oppression. Further, where de Beauvoir was clearly ambivalent concerning the potential of women's unification, Firestone displays fewer uncertainties. The reason is that she locates women's subordination in the power which men exercise over their reproductive potential:

> it was women's reproductive biology that accounted for her original and continued oppression, and not some sudden patriarchal revolution, the origins of which Freud himself was at a loss to explain . . . throughout history, in all stages and types of culture, women have been oppressed due to their biological functions.
>
> (Firestone 1988: 74–75)

Not only is the dominant culture sustained in this way, but women are alienated because of their reproductive capacity and the historical division of labour which surrounds child-rearing. It follows that women must recover the means over which their bodies are controlled in order to become liberated. New reproductive technologies provides the means as long as its power is utilized by women, for women. The works of Marx and Engels, for whom production, not reproduction, was paramount, is inadequate to this task. Male theories cannot contribute to this task because the basis of women's inequality lies in the control of their biology by men, not in economic relations. Where Marx and Engels spoke of proletarian revolt, Firestone now speaks of sexual revolution:

> not only the full restoration to women of ownership of their own bodies, but also their (temporary) seizure of control of human fertility ... just as the end of the socialist revolution was not only the elimination of the economic class *privilege* but of the economic class *distinction* itself, so the end of feminist revolution must be, unlike that of the first feminist movement, not just the elimination of male *privilege* but of the sex *distinction* itself.
>
> (Firestone 1988: 19, original italics)

Ideas of this type are part of a whole body of radical feminist scholarship. Adrienne Rich (1980), for example, has been a central contributor to the development of lesbian theories. She speaks of 'compulsory heterosexuality' in order to signify how women's history, culture and values are distinct from the dominant patriarchal culture. Her use of the terms 'lesbian existence' and 'lesbian continuum' are not intended to supplant one set of compulsions for another, but to indicate that women lack choices in their sexual predispositions and emotional attachments. Similarly, Andrea Dworkin focuses upon the exploitative nature of patriarchy where men not only exercise power over women, but also decide 'how women will suffer' (Dworkin 1987: 194). Along with Catharine MacKinnon (1988), she has been pivotal in the debate on pornography and the representation of women (see Tong 1989: 112–123).

In terms of Firestone's work, the question of whether an account of women's position within society might be adequately captured by an emphasis on biology has led feminist theorists to seek other explanations, but ones which might equally account for the pervasive nature of gender divisions within societies. Juliet Mitchell (1974), for instance, employs psychoanalysis for the purposes of developing her ideas within a Marxist historical framework. After Freud, Alfred Adler, Karen Horney and Clara Thompson had all emphasized an environmental component to the growth of personality. In utilizing these insights, together with those of Althusser, Marx, Lacan and Lévi-Strauss, Mitchell aimed to explain the causes of women's oppression. In the process, 'woman' is not seen as a static category, but one which is historically located.

We may recall Althusser's argument that ideology 'flows through' the individual creating social and self-images. In addition, social structures are viewed as both autonomous and contradictory with the economic sphere being 'ultimately determining'. In Mitchell's work, the key structures in society become production, reproduction, sexuality and the socialization of children. Each of these is argued to play an important role in the unfolding of history. The problems of prioritizing any one of these elements is evident from the following quote:

> A modification of any of them can be offset by a reinforcement of another (as increased socialization has made up for decreased repro-duction). This means that a mere permutation of the form of exploitation is achieved.
>
> (Mitchell 1971: 120)

Mitchell seeks to understand not only the social, political and economic forms of women's oppression, but also the realm of sexual ideology. Although men are exploited by the state and class society, women's oppression centres upon patriarchy and ideology. Freud's insights, reworked through Lacan, permit her to see how subjectivity is 'sexed', thereby linking power, identity and social practice within an overall explanation based on social structure. Social reforms, which seek equality of opportunity at a political level, are thus doomed to failure given that women's oppression is part of her collective psyche. The roots of women's inequality are thus seen as more complicated than Firestone's analysis would suggest.

Mitchell's utilization of Freud's work, involving as it does a focus upon the role of the unconscious, aims directly at Cartesian-based theories. Her concentration upon women's psyche is directly concerned with the nature of the mental representations that women carry with them. The emphasis is less upon biology, than the social construction of gender within a capitalist society. In this way, the family comes to occupy a central place on the analytic stage through forming part of the ideological superstructure.

Although the family found its economic function most aligned in peasant-based forms of production, over time a growing dislocation has occurred between the economic and ideological functions. The result is to place a particular burden upon women where the family becomes the centre of contradictions generated by a system that both promotes, yet destroys, individualism and private property: 'The housewife-mother is the guardian and representative of these' (Mitchell 1974: 161). The effects of this pressure upon women are clear and their causes apparent in a dual system of oppression:

> It produces a tendency to small-mindedness, petty jealously, irrational emotionality and random violence, dependency, competitive selfishness

and possessiveness, passivity, a lack of vision and conservatism. These qualities are *not* the simple produce of male chauvinism . . . *They are the result of the woman's objective conditions within the family* – itself embedded in a sexist society.

(Mitchell 1974: 162, original italics)

A psychoanalytic approach to gendering is also apparent in the works of Nancy Chodorow (1978). However, it is the specific relationship between the mother and the child, in the pre-Oedipal stage that becomes of central importance to identity formation and from there to cultural formation. 'Mothering' within the family-unit is of prime analytic concern and the root of gender oppression. To put a complex argument as simply as possible. Focusing upon the pre-Oedipal stage, Chodorow contrasts a mother's identification with her daughter with the separation that takes place between the mother and son, a process that is accompanied by the unconscious sexualization of this relationship by the mother. Despite a 'primary love' for the mother by the son, at the Oedipus stage, he represses this desire. The result is to be pushed out of the pre-Oedipal relationship into the realm where the tie with the mother is severed and his love for her curtailed through repression. This process is enabled by his being constituted as 'other'.

The overall result of this process for the male is one of individuation. He achieves a defensive autonomy via the repression of his desires. The female, on the other hand, continues with the pre-Oedipal phase for a longer period and the mother experiences her as aligned, rather than differentiated, from her own sense of self. The female child's experiences of merging and separation at this stage thereby form an entirely different basis of personality. Here we find an emphasis upon empathy and less of a differentiation of self from the object-world.

These gender differences, between what we might term a 'concrete' and 'generalized' 'other', appear in social thought. The latter refers to the means whereby 'we' consider what individuals have in common from a general set of normative principles. The former, on the other hand, refers to a reverse of the commonality-individuality process to 'view each and every rational being as an individual with a concrete history, identity and affective-emotive constitution' (Benhabib 1992: 159). With this in mind, alongside Chodorow's theories on personality formation, we have an explanatory resource with which to approach the differences in perspective which exist between men and women in relation to the social world. Here I am thinking, in particular, of gender differences in ethical deliberations and actions as encapsulated by the debate between Carol Gilligan and Lawrence Kohlberg whose work, as noted, is utilized by Habermas (see Larrabee 1993).

Given the above, in both her elaboration and critique of the Freudian account, Chodorow develops powerful ideas on gender identification and formation. Her account reveals a sociological component which is informed by 'objects' in the world, including the mother, as opposed to being motivated by the Freudian concept of 'drives' where the idea of 'object' becomes arbitrary. The Freudian ahistorical component of self-formation is thus grounded in a manner that takes account of cultural context:

> This self is intrinsically social, and, because it is constructed in a relational matrix and includes aspects of the other, it can better recognize the other as a self and, ultimately, attain the intersubjectivity that creates society. This self's full historical grounding contrasts with that of the drive-determined individual. The grounding of the object-relational self derives from an appropriation and interpretation of experienced relationships and accordingly varies by individual, culture, period, gender, and so forth.
>
> (Chodorow 1986: 204)

The appeal of Chodorow's work, which has been very influential on the development of psychoanalytic feminisms, appears three-fold. First, it offers an explanation of a woman's participation in her own repression without recourse to Freudian ideas on penis-envy, or via the invoking of a male norm. Second, it indicates that the participation of the father in child care may actually assist in the escape from gender-oppression and finally, there are her observations that women seem to gain little in the way of gratification from heterosexual relationships because men are not able to express intimacy due to their lacking the means for meaningful communication (adapted from Lawler 1995: 90–91).

The process of gender formation and its consequences for women does not necessitate a resort to psychoanalysis. Here one would turn the feminist gaze upon the process of knowledge production as being as important as that which is produced. If the process of knowledge production is itself exclusionary, so too will be its product or content with a corresponding effect on self-image. As Dorothy Smith puts it:

> The universe of ideas, images, themes – the symbolic modes that are the general currency of thought – have been either produced by men or controlled by them. In so far as women's work and experience have been entered into it, it has been on terms decided by men and because it has been approved by men.
>
> (D. E. Smith 1987: 19)

The exploration of these 'relations of ruling' occurs through a process of social construction (D. E. Smith 1993). The assumed universality of men's standpoint is consequential for the formation of culture, the result of which is the production of partial images, ideas and practices. In order to develop her notion of ruling interests, Smith utilizes Marx's ideas, in the process of which she posits a ruling class whose interests are served by this outcome. However, this does not take place on the lines suggested by Marx, for the resulting disjunctures between images, ideas and experiences have particular ramifications for women. These social forms of thought are then argued to be

> made for us by others, which come to us from outside, and which do not
> arise out of experience, spoken of and shared with others, or out of the
> need to communicate with others in working contexts.
>
> (D. E. Smith 1987: 55)

This, however, is not a model of hegemonic and intended manipulation by a ruling elite. Instead, it is 'a set of positions in the structures that "rule" (manage, administrate, organize, and otherwise control). These constitute the bases of common perspectives' (D. E. Smith 1987: 56). The public–private dichotomy is then viewed in terms of an increasing public sphere dominated by male interests and a diminishing private sphere occupied by women. The sphere in which women have the potential to draw links between their experiences and the images and ideas through which they can make sense of them, is thereby institutionally limited.

Drawing upon phenomenological, ethnomethodological, Marxist and symbolic interactionist insights, without being constrained by the limitations of each, Smith argues that this whole process creates a 'bifurcated consciousness'. On one side there is the male, rational and neutral world. On the other, the subjective and emotional world of the female. Yet this is a gendered process. Therefore, to accept a phenomenological focus would be to prioritize the subjective side, but this is not conducive to a feminist social theory because it ignores the material and social bases which give rise to this process. Similarly, whilst Marxist categories are invoked for explanatory purposes these only serve, as with dominant modes of thought in general, to 'subordinate the actualities of the world' (D. E. Smith 1987: 86). For these reasons, the starting-point for analysis must be a woman's standpoint. Her bifurcated consciousness provides the very resources upon which new modes of thought can be constructed. Ontological exclusion is now employed in the service of epistemological correction as a strategy that is central to standpoint feminisms in general (Hartsock 1983; Harding 1986; Jaggar 1983):

> The feminist standpoint theories focus on gender differences, on
> differences between women's and men's situations which give a
> scientific advantage to those who can make use of the differences.
>
> (Harding 1991: 120)

If an examination of patriarchal relations of ruling is required to account for women's location within society and her sense of self, this begs questions concerning the socio-structural composition of patriarchy itself. It is the means through which women are constituted not as subjects, but the 'other'; they are the objects, not the subjects, of discourse. They are not seen as having 'an autonomous source of knowledge, experience, relevance and imagination' (D. E. Smith 1987: 51). Yet if this is an important project for the development of feminist theory, mainstream concepts of structure are, once again, inadequate for this task.

The need to recast ideas on social structure has led those such as Walby (1986; 1990) and Delphy and Leonard (1992), to argue that class categories cannot be simply manipulated to incorporate women but must, instead, be subject to major critique and restructuring. Without such a project being undertaken, inequalities within the 'private' world of the family would be overlooked in the conceptual prioritization of the 'public' realm of work. Explanations for women's oppression would then be sought in the realms of sexuality and motherhood, rather than being seen as also rooted in the material advantages that men enjoy over women. Therefore, both the public and private dimensions need to be incorporated in a feminist account of social structure.

In these terms, the family should be seen as an economic system which itself generates inequalities: 'The family as a system in space and in time is a social institution which pre-exists them and sets parameters to their choices' (Delphy and Leonard 1992: 265–266). There exists what may be characterized as a dual system of production which involves both domestic and industrial components. Of central analytic interest is the position that women occupy in both spheres, without the prioritization of one over the other. For instance, one might emphasize the public sphere to the detriment of the private and thereby reduce gender to class relations.

With these arguments in mind, a distinction has to be made between degrees and forms of patriarchy. This dynamic form of analysis would allow for changes over time without committing oneself to the fallacy of uniform progress, the Marxist notions of regress and stasis, or the radical-feminist positions of 'no change':

> Degrees of patriarchy refers to the intensity of oppression on a specified dimension, for instance the size of the wages gap between men and women. Forms of patriarchy refers to the overall type of patriarchy, as defined by the specific relations between the different patriarchal structures.

(Walby 1990: 174)

Situating changing relationships in this way, between forms and degrees of patriarchy, allows for a diachronic approach that corrects for the synchronic tendencies of structuralism. The relationship between the public and private may then be analysed without resort to either sexuality or labour as determinant in the last instance. Instead, what we find is an examination of the relationship that occurs between six structures:

> the patriarchal mode of production; patriarchal relations in paid work; patriarchal relations in the state; male violence; patriarchal relations in sexuality; and patriarchal relations in cultural institutions including religions, media, education. In different times and places some of the

structures are more important than others. The elimination of any one does not lead to the demise of the system as a whole.

(Walby 1990: 177)

In this way, it is possible to conceive of forms of resistance to oppression, thereby avoiding the deterministic strands of structuralism. The production and reproduction of women's subordination is also historically understood and explained according to two main forms of patriarchy: the public and the private. The former viewing women's subordination as based upon structures which lie outside of the household unit and these take a collective form. Private patriarchy, on the other hand, has the analytic potential to view an individual man as the main beneficiary of the direct control of women within the household. At the same time, however, the maintenance of private patriarchy is enabled by the exclusion of women from the public arena:

> Patriarchal relations outside the household are crucial in shaping patriarchal relations within it. However, the effect is to make women's experience of patriarchy privatized, and the immediate beneficiaries are also located there.

(Walby 1990: 178)

Structures, rationales, strategies and outcomes of actions, are thus infused with male power. In addition, the means through which society and social relations, as well as science in general, conducts its studies and justifies its findings, are themselves part of the same process. Therefore, when it comes to the conduct and products of social theory, it requires nothing less than deconstruction, followed by reconstruction.

Summary

The practice of feminist theory may be characterized in the following manner. In the first place it necessitates an uncovering of the ways in which ideas contain, both overtly and covertly, misogynist perspectives. These may take subtle forms, but the strategy involves exposing how male values come to predominate and perpetuate particular views of the social and natural worlds. In the process it uncovers how silences and absences also structure ways of thinking about women.

From these deconstructive modes, we move on to its reconstructive elements. It is not sufficient to simply explain the relations of dominant modes of thought, but to then develop understandings of the ways in which partial representations of women suppress alternative identities that may be available to them. This strategy provides for women to be able to see themselves in a different way to the dominant conceptions that exist of their roles and places within social relations. Here, in particular, because feminist theory will not countenance a simple separation of the public from the private and questions the demarcation between nature and culture on a gendered basis, it possesses the power to threaten identities, as well as to create new ones.

From the above, feminist social theory develops the means to move beyond patriarchal thought. However, this requires the formation of alternative research programmes which recover women's perspectives in order to inform social, political and economic changes. In sum, as Elizabeth Gross (1992) puts it, from whose work these characteristics are derived, feminist theory involves both a refusal of the props upon which patriarchal theory and practices sustain themselves, as well as a positive affirmation of the alternatives that are made available through such critiques.

Issues in feminist theory

In this section I wish to outline some of the issues which have informed debates within feminist theory. My intention is to provide a further basis upon which to consider the insights of this very broad body of scholarship and to demonstrate that many of these not only mirror, but also add a new dimension to our ways of thinking about the social world. Here I shall focus upon two aspects to these debates which are not mutually exclusive topics. First, the concept of patriarchy and second, debates concerning essentialism in feminist theory.

Feminist theory is a project for positive change. If patriarchy is to be employed towards this end, it has to avoid the problems of structuralism where deterministic concepts have a tendency to rule the day. Within the development of feminist theory this concept has, as with structural ideas in social theory, been subjected to criticism for being ahistorical, deterministic and of little analytic utility by virtue of its abstraction (Barrett 1988). The result being that it is 'too specific an expression to describe very diffuse and changing forms of male domination' (Cockburn 1990: 98).

Patriarchy has the potential to be employed in feminist theory as a 'catch-all' to describe what is a diverse set of social relations. From its early use by Millett (1969), via the work of Spender (1980) through to Dworkin (1987), it may be read as an analytic monolith against which social 'reality' is not only to be explored, but then explained. For instance, take the work of Dale Spender. She holds that language creates reality and that language is produced by males, for males, as the dominant group within society. This is seen as an intentional process whereby the use of 'he' to refer to both sexes is regarded as a deliberate policy of exclusion and dominance. Clearly, language of this type can and does act in this way, but to consider this as intentional according to dominant and absolute criterion of patriarchy is highly problematic:

> Though the effect of the use of 'he/man' language may be to subjugate the female sex, it is ludicrous to suppose that every man who has ever

used such language intended to do that by his use of it. Many men may have had every intention of *not* doing women down, yet they may still have done so, precisely because their language has an effect that is not apparent to them.

(Assister 1983: 27, original italics)

This thesis does not adequately distinguish between the use of language and the utterance of particular words, whilst it is infused with idealism in the form: 'language makes reality'. The materialist version of this would be: 'reality makes language'. In this sense, patriarchal ideology would be held as either unconnected to economic conditions, or as directly reducible to them; the former taking no account of the material basis of women's oppression. The latter, on the other hand, opens up the issue of the 'unhappy' relationship between Marxism and feminism.

At this point Mitchell's work becomes of central importance in the development of feminist theory; in particular, her emphasis upon the psychic aspects of gender relations whilst, at the same time, exposing their historical and material constitution and potential for revision and change. This use of psychoanalysis and its relationship to women's self-image is of clear importance through allowing for the investigation of the representation of women in relation to the public organization of sexual structures (Coward 1982).

The fusion of Marxism and psychoanalysis to generate a theory of patriarchy is, however, problematic. Are its explanations context bound or universal? Quite simply, is psychoanalysis predicated on law-like generalizations, or is it sensitive to historical context? In contrast to Mitchell, if the former reading of Freud is taken, then it is incompatible with a theory that seeks to understand how particular historical structures limit women's potential. In this way, an unhappy relationship between psychoanalysis and feminism appears for two reasons. First, there is a tendency to repeat a determinism, only this time it takes a psychic form such that social relations are held to mirror their structure. Second, Mitchell's dual systems of ideology and capitalism views feminist struggles as taking place in the realm of ideology and a socialist struggle as taking place against capitalism.

The separation of these two spheres is highly problematic. Mitchell employs it in order to argue that the arrival of socialism will not end women's subordination and thus not to repeat the reductive trap of Marxism. However, to use Freud specifically, or in terms of a modified psychoanalysis in general, is still to risk 'psychic essentialism' (Segal 1987). What is then witnessed is a repeat of the structuralist tendencies of patriarchy, only this time in the unconscious, not the economy.

Issues such as these have opened up a debate in feminist theory over the utility of psychoanalysis (J. Rose 1990; E. Wilson 1990). As Elizabeth Wilson puts it:

The last thing feminists need is a theory that reaches them only to marvel anew at the constant recreation of the subjective reality of subordination . . . Psychoanalysis is of interest in its account of sexual identity and its construction – indeed, in many ways it is fascinating. More useful to contemporary feminists may be theories of social change that speak to aspects of the self not harnessed to the Phallic taskmaster. To change the conditions of work – in the world and in the home – might do more for our psyches as well as for our pockets than an endless contemplation of how we came to be chained.

(E. Wilson 1990: 224)

The debate over patriarchy has also taken another route with essentialist consequences. Take, for example, the work of Firestone (1988). She sought to replace the centrality of class as the motor of a materialist history. However, there are those who have taken this to the conclusion that 'sexuality is to feminism what work is to marxism' (MacKinnon 1988: 106). Accompanying radical feminist explanations of women's subordination, therefore, is a tendency towards biological determination such that the two sexes appear fundamentally incompatible. This can translate into the call for all women to become political lesbians (Leeds Revolutionary Feminist Group 1982).

Importantly, when it comes to political lesbianism as a variant of radical feminism, it should be noted that this does not necessarily mean alluding to biological essentialism to sustain its arguments. However, there is a clear tendency within aspects of feminist discourse to base arguments upon a particular view of the origins of women's oppression which is not only seen as universal, but determining. The problems of being ahistorical and taking no account of cultural differences within and between societies becomes, once again, apparent. The form of argument is reductionist whereby social and cultural factors are provided with biological causes (Grosz 1990). Quite simply, if biology is destiny, then perhaps we should abandon social explanations to physiology and anatomy?

Concerns of this type have led feminist theory to examine relations between men and women without recourse to the formulation of theoretical bases which have an absolute ontology, a series of indispensable attributes, or objective properties upon which all others depend (de Lauretis 1990). This is precisely the fault that has been found in mainstream theory; for it also resorts to so-called 'essences' in its working assumptions. We thus move from an 'old' essentialism whereby women were seen as inferior to men, to a 'new' essentialism that asserts the superiority of women (J. R. Martin 1994).

On these and other grounds radical feminism has been subjected to criticism. These critiques, however, also come from within this perspective. Audre Lorde, for example, criticized Mary Daly for her presentation of black women as victims, rather than seeing them as making a positive cultural contribution to their own history. Lorde's theoretical position is a fusion of

Enlightenment rationality with an understanding of emotion derived from the experiences of African women. As this quote illustrates, women may share particular experiences, but this should not be placed at the service of a 'white' lesbian theory encompassing *all* experiences:

> The oppression of women knows no ethnic nor racial boundaries, true, but that does not mean it is identical within those differences. Nor do the reservoirs of our ancient power know these boundaries. To deal with one without even alluding to the other is to distort our commonality as well as our difference.
>
> (Lorde in Humm 1992: 139)

If biological explanations suffer from essentialism, so social explanations might fail to account for the ways in which people remain so firmly attached to their gender-identities. For Brenner and Ramas (1990), the relationship between the social and the natural must be incorporated into feminist theory in order to account for this ubiquity. Nevertheless, questions are still begged as to the idea of 'woman'. It is here that one detects a clear movement in feminist theory towards rethinking ideas on the 'self'. This has consequences for the formulation of patriarchy as a useful explanatory device; to say nothing of the direction and nature of feminist politics.

The self in feminist theory has travelled through periods of autonomy, selfhood and determinism and provided a basis upon which to evaluate patriarchal practices according to women's latent potential. This has witnessed a movement through the agency–structure debate which, in the terms presented above, has travelled through patriarchal concepts based on sex, gender, psychoanalysis and the economy, in order to make sense of the public–private divide. New ideas then enter the terrain of feminism because analyses of this type are seen to take place against the backdrop of modernity with its fixed ideas of the self: for example, power belongs to a class (men) and is exercised by them over women as a class. However, if we see individuals as the vehicles of power and as constituted by its effects, this whole edifice begins to crumble:

> The individual is not to be conceived as a sort of elementary nucleus, a primitive atom, a multiple and inert material on which power comes to fasten or against which it happens to strike, and in so doing subdues or crushes individuals. In fact, it is already one of the prime effects of power that certain bodies, certain gestures, certain discourses, certain desires, come to be identified and constituted as individuals. The individual, that is, is not the *vis-à-vis* of power; it is, I believe, one of its prime effects.
>
> (Foucault 1980: 98)

As with some developments in social theory, there are feminisms which have moved into these realms in the pursuit of explanations. If the techniques of power are not attributable to a particular group and are transmitted and exercised throughout the social body, any idea of essential subjectivity is called into question. The projects of deconstruction and reconstruction, as part of Enlightenment thought itself, may then be jettisoned, leaving the critical gaze of a new feminism to be turned against what is seen as outmoded forms of thought. Nevertheless, this is not a linear progression; far from it. As a result, debates now exist within feminist thought between what I have characterized as the second perspective and postmodern feminisms, with contributions by those who seek to move beyond the political paralysis implied by the latter (Landry and MacLean 1993).

Summary

Ideas of the self, agency and social structure have been criticized and reconstructed in order to provide for an adequate explanation of the position of women in society. The result is an extraordinary growth in feminist scholarship since the mid 1960s. This journey has witnessed an array of ideas through its encounters with Marxism, psychoanalysis and phenomenology – to name but a few.

The response to this intellectual journey, by women and men, often takes a reactionary form; including from people who consider themselves broad-minded. This appears to be an inevitable feature of any body of ideas which questions the status quo. However, feminisms add an important dimension to this process: they also aim at intimacy and what are assumed to be the most 'personal' aspects of people's lives. This derives from their focus upon the public–private divide not as some commonsensical manifestation of a natural process, but a socially constructed topic to be investigated in terms of its ramifications for women's places and identities within society. Ideas on selfhood and identity, thereby fuse with power, social structure and sexuality.

At the same time this may be evaluated as a project within modernity. This, as noted before, is seen to possess the potential not simply to liberate, but also to stifle. First-wave feminism was to be informed by the liberal individualism of the Enlightenment and second-wave feminism was to turn its analytic tools into those which could be used by women, for women. However, a new perspective was to develop which found their underlying ideas on the self to be problematic.

These changes are mirrored within mainstream social theory with a turn towards new ideas. For many, these ideas represent a negation, not a celebration, of the aims of feminism. In light of these arguments and insights, therefore, Chapters 9 and 10 are devoted to an examination of poststructuralism, with reference to the work of Michel Foucault and postmodernism. In each of these, issues will be raised with regard to agency and structure and both will contain references to the ways in which these ideas have been utilized by feminist theorists.

Section **4**

Modernity under the microscope

9

The making of the modern subject

The thematic continuity for understanding contemporary social theory in this book has been the relationship between agency and structure in the unfolding of modernity. For some, modernity is an 'attitude' which orientates thinkers in particular ways. Yet in one way or another, all contemporary social theories have challenged aspects of these background assumptions; in particular, the concept of the autonomous ego who stands at the centre of the social universe. In the history of ideas presented here, this tendency has been traced back to Hume.

Despite modifications to the idea of the self, it is argued that from the Enlightenment onwards social thought has exhibited a movement away from an *analysis* of representations towards an *analytic*:

> From Kant on, an analytic is an attempt to show on what grounds representation and analysis of representations are possible and to what extent they are legitimate.
>
> (Dreyfus and Rabinow 1982: 28)

Michel Foucault (1992) characterizes this as the desire to achieve a correspondence between reality and the language which describes that reality, from whose propositions an ahistorical and normative basis for ways of life may be derived. In practice, differences between cultures can then be judged according to reason and the authenticity of any dialogue is based upon the participants abilities to reach a particular standard. However, as has been noted, the power of reason is double-edged: in its judgements it can also exclude on the basis, for example, of race and gender.

The end result of this desire is that we have become both the subjects and objects of knowledge. According to this view the beginnings of the human sciences are not seen to be the result of a need to address some 'scientific' problem which demanded analysis, or some 'pressing rationalism', but the decision to include people amongst the objects of science occurred 'when man constituted himself in Western culture as both that which must be conceived of and that which is to be known' (Foucault 1992: 345). We should look upon this as 'an event in the order of knowledge' (Foucault 1992: 345).

As abstract as this may at first appear, it is of central importance for understanding contemporary ideas and practices. Therefore, it is for good reason that Habermas (1986) entitles one essay on Foucault's thought 'Taking Aim at the Heart of the Present'. Suspending, for the moment, a discussion of the relative merits of these arguments, the point is that Foucault has offered us a new perspective on society and social relations. For this reason, his work is worthy of inclusion in this tour of modern social theory. Given this, I shall first consider the intellectual influences on his ideas and the development of his thought and then outline some of the issues which his work raises for understanding social life.

Michel Foucault: against (and in) modernity

From our discussions in Part I, we can take two broad positions in relation to 'truth'. First, truth is ahistorical and second, truth is constituted in history. If we take the second, however, we also often attribute the history of ideas, discoveries, inventions, etc., to individuals. The idea of the 'individual' is then 'fixed', whilst their actions are understood and explained within the flux of history. The result being that the individual appears to transgress historical context. In this way we can read Marx's work in terms of the 'true' subject in history eventually revealing itself in an historical ending: communism. In the meantime, the potential of the individual is stifled due to the exploitative effects of capitalism. The humanist and structuralist elements in Marx's work are thereby juxtaposed in an uneasy tension. For Weber, on the other hand, history had no laws and the subject was simply enjoined to act responsibly in the face of historical uncertainty.

With this theme in mind, we have another approach to the history of social theory through the conceptualization of the subject. On the one hand, there stands the isolated individual whose excavations over history will eventually reveal a truth lying within it. On the other hand, knowledge is regarded as historically located. Attempted resolutions to this paradox, aside from that of Marx, have also been considered in relation to Husserlian phenomenology and Saussure's structuralism. The latter 'dissolved' the subject as the rules of language gained analytic and ontological primacy over a phenomenological emphasis upon the attribution of meaning to social reality on the part of a transcendent individual.

In essence, it was within the analytic space of this problematic that Foucault worked: 'my problem has always been . . . the problem of the relationship between the subject and truth' (Foucault 1991b: 9). Nevertheless, we find a very different emphasis from previous perspectives and it is this that causes difficulty in situating Foucault. For instance, consider his approach to the work of Kant. Foucault historically situates Kant in terms of his ideas being a response to a particular problem at a point in time. Kant then derived an elaborate defence of the critical capacity of reason, as well as a formulation of its limits, in the face of uncertainty. Yet despite this, it results in a mode of thought which is assumed to be universally applicable.

With this historical legacy in place, what we should then examine is an

> analysis of ourselves as beings who are historically determined, to a certain extent, by the Enlightenment. Such an analysis implies a series of historical inquiries that are as precise as possible; and these inquiries will not be oriented retrospectively toward the 'essential kernel of rationality' that can be found in the Enlightenment in any event; they will be oriented toward the 'contemporary limits of the necessary,' that is, towards what is not or is no longer indispensable for the constitution of ourselves as autonomous subjects.
>
> (Foucault 1984: 43)

What analytic tools does Foucault use for this purpose? Once we have examined these, we can then consider his arguments on power and the subject. Unless otherwise stated, all references in the following two sections are to works by Foucault.

Beyond structuralism and hermeneutics

In order to situate Foucault's thinking, we need to understand the background against which he formulated his views. If we return to an earlier discussion on the intellectual climate in post–1945 France, two views emerge in relation to Husserlian phenomenology. First, structuralism, and second, a hermeneutics which did not resort to the transcendental subject, but argued that the source of meaning production should be sought in the social practices and texts which are fundamental to human activity. For the purposes of this section, we may trace this latter intellectual lineage from Heidegger. In the process, we shall be required to consider the generation of meaning without reference to an autonomous subject and to utilize the idea of discourses without allusion to underlying rules of structure. In other words, we have to move beyond the limitations of structuralism and hermeneutics in order to develop an 'interpretive analytics' (Dreyfus and Rabinow 1982).

The fusion of these different ideas in Foucault's work results in an approach to the history of thought that is freed: 'from its subjection to transcendence' (1989: 203). In this journey we are also required to take two further steps. First, the relationship between the subject and truth should be viewed as an effect of knowledge itself. As Foucault put it:

> what if understanding the relation of the subject to the truth, were just an effect of knowledge? What if understanding were a complex, multiple, non-individual formation, not 'subjected to the subject', which produced effects of truth?
>
> (Foucault in Elders 1974: 149)

Knowledge should not, therefore, be viewed as 'theoretical' separate from the realm of 'practice'. Instead, knowledge becomes a practice which has the effect of constituting particular objects – non-theoretical elements – which are part of practice itself. Relatedly, the theory of knowledge and the subject of knowledge become fused and the subject and truth are not related in the ways suggested earlier, but are seen as part of a relationship between knowledge and power that is socially constructed:

> The important thing here, I believe, is that truth isn't outside power, or lacking in power: contrary to a myth whose history and functions would repay further study, truth isn't the reward of free spirits, the child of protracted solitude, nor the privilege of those who have succeeded in liberating themselves. Truth is a thing of this world: it is produced only by virtue of multiple forms of constraint. And it induces regular effects of power. Each society has its régime of truth, its 'general politics' of truth.
>
> (Foucault 1980: 131)

What Foucault is doing here is rejecting certainty in social and political life and arguing that there is no universal understanding beyond history and society. In the process a 'history of the present' is written, according to which history is not excavated to reveal a deeper meaning but, instead, is viewed as a 'battleground' between relations of power. Now this begins, albeit in a different guise, to look like structuralism: that is, to view events as manifestations of a deeper, underlying reality. How is this issue tackled in his work?

In commentating on those who have labelled him a structuralist, Foucault writes: 'I have been unable to get it into their tiny minds that I have used none of the methods, concepts, or key terms that characterize structural analysis' (1989: xiv). Fine! Beyond assertion, however, what are his justifications for this position? After all, the opening for the type of analysis we have considered so far occurred in Althusserian structuralism. Ideologies are seen as ways of constructing subjects and their perspectives on the world, all of which takes place against the backdrop of a Marxist model of social reality.

The first point we might observe here is that Foucault eschews grand theoretical projects of the Althusserian type. Perhaps the most simple way to view his relationship with structuralism is by examining his analysis of historical 'events'. What we find here is a refusal to read historical 'events' as manifestations of deeper social structures, or as located on particular levels, accompanied by a focus upon the seemingly marginal as indicative of relations of power. Events are thereby seen to differ in their capacity to produce effects:

> The problem is at once to distinguish among events, to differentiate the networks and levels to which they belong, and to reconstitute the lines along which they are connected and engender one another. From this follows a refusal of analyses couched in terms of the symbolic field or the domain of signifying structures, and a recourse to analyses in terms of the genealogy of relations of force, strategic development, and tactics. Here I believe one's point of reference should not be to the great model of language (*langue*) and signs, but to that of war and battle.
>
> (Foucault 1980: 114, original italics)

If Foucault does not reach for structuralism, neither does he resort to grounds in the universal preconditions of human understanding (Heidegger). What he calls genealogy, following Nietzsche, is an analysis of cultural practices without a reference point outside of history itself. The motivating question underlying this approach is: 'What are we today?' (1988a: 145). For it is history which makes us what we are and what we think of ourselves as being. This is a very different starting-point from, say, an analysis of the limits which are continually placed upon what is seen as our 'hidden' creativity as found in a critical social theory based in philosophical anthropology (see Honneth and Joas 1988). The manifestations of such a project we have covered in relation to a 'dialectic of freedom' whose aim is to determine the good and bad elements in the Enlightenment. Genealogy, in contrast, does not involve a search for any 'origin':

> On the contrary, it will cultivate the details and accidents that accompany every beginning; it will be scrupulously attentive to their petty malice; it will await their emergence, once unmasked, as the face of the other. *The genealogist needs history to dispel the chimeras of the origin.*
>
> (Foucault 1984: 80, emphasis added)

We have come across other universal grounds for analysis through the employment of modified forms of reason; none more powerfully argued than by Jürgen Habermas. Yet the issues motivated by such an approach are still couched in terms of the ability to provide grounds for distinguishing between the true and the false, not in terms of the formation of truth itself. It is via this focus in Foucault's work that we uncover the legacy of Nietzsche.

Unlike Kant, Nietzsche did not ask what the grounds or basis for our knowledge was, but why knowledge was necessary in the first place. He argued that it was the belief we have in knowledge that is of importance, not whether it is true or false. This belief is seen to be indicative of a 'will to truth' which, as part of the 'will to power', involves the desire to affirm life as it appears to us. Truth now becomes inverted to be a fiction that is 'invented':

> What urges you on and arouses your ardour, you wisest of men, do you call it 'will to truth'? Will to the conceivability of all being: that is what *I* call your will! You first want to *make* all being conceivable: for, with a healthy mistrust, you doubt whether it is in fact conceivable. But it must bend and accommodate itself to you! Thus will your will have it. It must become smooth and subject to the mind as the mind's mirror and reflection. This is your entire will, you wisest men; it is a will to power; and that is so even when you talk of good and evil and of the assessment of values.
>
> (Nietzsche in Hollingdale 1977: 224, original italics)

With the Nietzschean turn in place, the object of Foucault's analyses became the production of discourses that provide justifications for actions: 'my problem is to see how men govern (themselves and others) by the production of truth' (1991c: 79). With a focus upon how the truth is constructed in a manner that permits, from the point of view of practice, a distinction to be made between the true and the false, Foucault's use of language as an analytic resource becomes distinct from any we have come across before.

Thus far we have considered the role of language in social life in a number of ways: Saussure's structuralism; as a 'form of life' (Wittgenstein) analysed in terms of speech-acts (Austin, Searle); a fusion of speech-act theory onto the problematic of rationalization (Habermas) and the relationship between utterance and institutional authority (Bourdieu). We could undertake genealogical analysis by, for example, examining the rules of language governing an utterance and then derive a set of rules which produced the utterance in the first place. Our results may then be transposed from context to context. Once again, however, Foucault throws a spanner into the works of these approaches.

Foucault's analysis of discourse does not contain the idea of knowledge production via a meaning-producing subject, or rules that govern speech-acts, nor an allusion to rationality that poses some absolute value in reason (1991c). Given this, his approach cannot be situated within any of the above positions. Nevertheless, he sees discourses as a unity of statements in what is termed a 'discursive formation'. The question is: what provides their unity? Foucault rejects four possible answers to this question. First, that there is a well-defined field of objects to which they refer; second, that they possess a clear normative basis; third, that they possess what he calls an 'alphabet of notions'; and finally, that they are characterized by 'the permanence of a thematic' (1989: 37).

With these possibilities rejected, what we uncover is the existence of possibilities and differences in structures and rules. Where it does become possible to describe these 'systems of dispersion' in terms of objects, statements, concepts or themes that make up a 'regularity' then we may say:

> for the sake of convenience, that we are dealing with a *discursive formation* . . . The conditions to which the elements of this division (objects, mode of statement, concepts, thematic choices) are subjected we shall call the *rules of formation*. The rules of formation are conditions of existence (but also of coexistence, maintenance, modification and disappearance) in a given discursive formation.
>
> (Foucault 1989: 38, original italics)

In a description of the events of discourse the question then becomes 'How is it that one particular statement appeared rather than another?' (1989: 27). However, there exists the potential for terminological confusion in Foucault's idea of 'statements'. Dreyfus and Rabinow thus propose the term 'serious speech acts' (1982: 48). This neatly encapsulates Foucault's adherence to the study of relations between speech acts and their continual formation and transformation where they are validated by particular procedures and the increasing army of 'experts' which characterize modern societies. It also takes account of Foucault's acceptance of the idea we have come across before to the effect that speech-acts are formulated against a background of everyday assumptions, whilst the idea of 'serious' retains his emphasis upon the generation of meaning within discourses.

With these themes and arguments in mind, we can now say that Foucault did not resort to a depth-hermeneutics whereby, via an excavation of the background assumptions which inform everyday interpretations, a 'truth' is revealed to exist. Further, that he was not content to view meaning as ultimately residing in a transcendental subject, nor to eliminate meaning through the employment of structuralist insights. His concerns were to empirically examine the effects of social practices without recourse to some idea of their intrinsic homogeneity. It is to an understanding of this project in relation to power and the subject that I now turn.

Power and the modern subject

The above situates Foucault's approach to analysing social phenomena in terms of the politics of truth, but it says little of the effects of these discursive regimes. For this purpose, Foucault turned towards analyses of the exercise of power in contrast to a consideration of the forms of knowledge which create a sense of social order. In more specific terms, his objective became 'to create a history of the different modes by which, in our culture, human beings are made subjects' (1982: 208).

To return to our earlier discussion. The position which the analyst occupies in this process of inquiry is still not that of the 'bearer of universal values' (1980: 132). It is, however, as someone who is situated within society and does not speak *for* the truth, but engages in a 'battle' regarding its status and the political and economic role that it plays in social relations (1980: 132). In other words, what is taken as being self-evident in the present, is viewed as part of an historical process. From this point of view Foucault's (1991d) study on imprisonment and punishment aimed

> to write a history not of the prison as an institution, but of the *practice of imprisonment*: to show its origin or, more exactly, to show how this way of doing things – ancient enough in itself – was capable of being accepted at a certain moment as a principal component of the penal system, thus coming to seem an altogether natural self-evident and indispensable part of it.
>
> (Foucault 1991c: 75, original italics)

Three lines of inquiry are required in order to understand how the subject is objectified. First, how particular sciences contribute to this process. Second, a study of the 'practices' that divide people from others, as well as within themselves: for example, the mad and sane, the sick and healthy and the criminal and non-criminal. Third, in what ways people then turn themselves into subjects (Foucault 1982: 208). Just to reiterate: the form of this analysis is opposed to the search for origins and ideal significations, as well as the notion that we possess an intrinsically rational and coherent sense of self.

At this point we find another central aspect to Foucault's work which causes interpretative confusion. Quite simply, it is the tension which exists between his approach to the study of social relations and a deep-seated idea within Western cultures: that is, the belief that the condition of freedom is the absence of power and thus power is always repressive. To commit oneself to this tradition would be to fall into the trap that Foucault's Nietzschean-inspired genealogies seek to avoid. For instance, when it comes to the individual in relation to the means of production, or as involved in relations of signification, we turn to economic history, linguistics and semiotics to shed light on these matters. When it comes to power all we ever ask is: 'What legitimates power?' (1982: 209). However, with the individual implicated in these relations, this approach cannot suffice. In order to understand how the subject is objectified, this idea of power needs total revision. This is where Foucault's 're-conceptualization' of power is of central importance and we need to understand what he means by this before I continue with our discussion.

Power is not inevitably vested in the state, nor localized in, say, relations between the citizen and state. Instead, the effects of the domination of power are attributable to various 'dispositions, manoeuvres, tactics, techniques, functionings' (1991d: 26). Its properties are invested in those over whom it is exercised, so it not only exerts pressures upon people, but is also transmitted by them: 'Power comes from below; that is, there is no binary and all-encompassing opposition between rulers and ruled' (1979: 94). Power is part of the social body as a whole – in the machinery of production, families, limited groups, and institutions (1979: 94). Thus, power is not a property – of capitalism, patriarchy, or the bourgeoisie – it is a strategy that has evolved as part of the characteristics of modern society. Nor should power be identified with an individual who possesses or exercises it by right of birth:

> Not the domination of the King in his central position, therefore, but that of his subjects in their mutual relations: not the uniform edifice of sovereignty, but the multiple forms of subjugation that have a place and function within the social organism.
>
> (Foucault in Kelly 1994: 34)

Given this, if we conceive of power as emanating from one source, we will not understand its effects. When it comes to politics and power, the sovereign's head must be cut off. Further, to think of power as repressive (the repressive hypothesis) is to neglect its positive aspects. In this sense, power becomes 'a machine in which everyone is caught' (Foucault 1980: 156).

Yet a question still remains: if power is transmitted in this way, where does it come from in the first place? This is one of the most difficult concepts to grasp. After all, if knowledge and power are linked, one thinks of Marx and the idea that those who are in charge of the means of production are, at the same time, in charge of the means of mental production. An illuminating discussion of this issue can be found in an interview with Foucault, conducted by Jean-Pierre Barou and Michelle Perrot (Foucault 1980: 146–165).

Let us take the example of a factory: here, relations of power may be seen in terms of how 'individuals try to conduct, to determine the behavior of others' (1991b: 18). The system of power is pyramidal and it occurs between the managers and the managed. However, the strategic apex (the managers) is not the source of power, nor is a principle or goal which organizational members are expected to invest with legitimacy in terms of their practices. Power and its techniques are used throughout the factory. Therefore, it cannot be simply identified with a particular group:

> These tactics were invented and organised from the starting points of local conditions and particular needs. They took shape in piecemeal fashion, prior to any class strategy designed to weld them into vast, coherent ensembles. It should also be noted that these ensembles don't consist in a homogenisation, but rather a complex play of supports in mutual engagement, different mechanisms of power which retain all their specific character.
>
> (Foucault 1980: 159)

We can draw three points from this quote. First, in his analysis of power Foucault is concentrating on the local and contingent. Therefore, as noted before, he is not prepared to 'read off' practices against some universal idea of rationality. Rather, he is concerned to examine the ways in which particular rationalities are deployed, leaving the connections to be established amongst them open to investigation (Dean 1994). Second, power should not be seen, from this point of view, as existing above, but alongside developments in the forces and relations of production. Power is transformed along with, but not by these changes and may be found in both socialist and capitalist societies (1980: 160). Third, the workings of this form of power can be traced far back into history.

In terms of tracing the history of this form of power, it was during the seventeenth, eighteenth and nineteenth centuries that a new form of political rationality found its target. When faced with the issue of population growth, political economists examined it in terms of wealth accumulation and the productive capabilities of labour, with the causes of poverty being conceived of in terms of disease, idleness, etc. The social reformer and philosopher Jeremy Bentham (1748–1832), on the other hand, 'poses the question in terms of power – population as object of relations of domination' (1980: 151). It was the economic changes occurring in the eighteenth century that

> made it necessary to ensure the circulation of effects of power through progressively finer channels, gaining access to individuals themselves, to their bodies, their gestures and all their daily actions. By such means power, even when faced with ruling a multiplicity of men, could be as efficacious as if it were being exercised over a single one.
>
> (Foucault 1980: 151–152)

The differentiation of the population thus required this new form of power. The simple domination of one group by another was no longer a feasible technique given the increasing complexity of society. Contrary to simple ideas of coercion, power has both a political and economic cost. If you are too violent in controlling a population, you risk revolt. If you intervene too frequently, then resistance and disobedience may result. Disciplinary technologies and regulatory procedures must inform and produce a normative basis which spreads throughout the social body, whilst masking the operation of power that underlies this process. In this way, the modern subject becomes inextricably linked to the society of which they are a part through turning themselves into an object:

> There is no need for arms, physical violence, material constraints. Just a gaze. An inspecting gaze, a gaze which each individual under its weight will end up interiorising to the point that he is his own overseer, each individual thus exercising this surveillance over, and against, himself. A superb formula: power exercised continuously and for what turns out to be a minimal cost.
>
> (Foucault 1980: 155)

The body, space and time are routinely controlled. What Foucault calls 'bio-power' relies upon the scientific categorization of the population, in terms of being an object of systematic and sustained political intervention, as well as encompassing a focus upon the human body as an object of control and manipulation. Collectively, these 'technologies' centre around the 'objectification' of the body. They form a 'disciplinary technology' whose aim is to forge the individual, with 'normalization' being one technique. This is best exemplified in enclosed situations, such as a prison, school, hospital or, as above, the factory, where the control of space and time is more readily apparent. It is here that we find

> a whole micro – penality of time (lateness, absences, interruptions of tasks), of activity (inattention, negligence, lack of zeal), of behaviour (impoliteness, disobedience), of speech (idle chatter, insolence), of the body ('incorrect' attitudes, irregular gestures, lack of cleanliness), of sexuality (impurity, indecency).
>
> (Foucault 1991d: 178)

This disciplinary technology permits supervision and control with interiorization being the most effective deployment of power. In this respect, Foucault suggests that there are three ways in which 'self-examination' has developed over time. First, the Cartesian form such that thoughts are considered in relation to their correspondence with reality. Second, the ways in which our thoughts correspond with, or relate to, rules. Third, the relationship between a thought which is 'hidden' and some inner impurity:

> At this moment begins the Christian hermeneutics of the self with its deciphering of inner thoughts. It implies that there is something hidden in ourselves and that we are always in a self-illusion which hides the secret.
>
> (Foucault 1988b: 46)

The discourse of constituting the subject as object thereby also requires the discourse of the subject and this too, has changed over the course of history. The means of exposing the truth of ourselves in Christianity involved being subjugated to a master. This model of obedience means that once the confession was verbalized, it was accompanied by a renunciation of the sense of self and 'will' as part of a continual process of self-renunciation: that is, disclosing oneself to an authority. This is a 'permanent verbalization'. However, what then occurs is that the interpretative sciences come to play this central role. After all, it is they who 'claim to be able to reveal the truth about our psyches, our culture, our society – truths that can only be understood by expert practitioners' (Dreyfus and Rabinow 1982: 180):

> From the eighteenth century to the present, the techniques of verbalization have been reinserted in a different context by the so-called human sciences in order to use them without renunciation of the self but

to constitute, positively, a new self. To use these techniques without renouncing oneself constitutes a decisive break.

(Foucault 1988b: 49)

This is accompanied by the state performing 'a modern matrix of individualization' (1982: 215). Together, these are the new forms of 'pastoral power'. Nevertheless, whilst claiming to speak the truth, these interpretative sciences are actually part of the rationalities which inform a political technology that saturates everyday life. Importantly, however, this should not be conceived of as being a deterministic relationship.

To illuminate the indeterminacy of these practices and hence the possibilities for their transformation, the focus of Foucault's investigations changes. He now considers not so much the ways in which we are constituted as both subjects and objects, but the effects of this on our relations with others and the implications for the relationship between power, truth and the self. Now these are not discrete topics, but ultimately complementary strategies of historical investigation (Foucault 1988c: 15). The body then becomes not only the object or target of power, but also the centre for resistance and opposition. After all, contemporary society is increasingly characterized by struggles against the exercise of power:

opposition to the power of men over women, of parents over children, of psychiatry over the mentally ill, of medicine over the population, of administration over the ways people live.

(Foucault 1982: 211)

Foucault asks the empirical question 'what happens' when power is exercised? As opposed to becoming involved in endless debates over what power 'is' and where it comes from (1982: 217)? Resistance to forms of power is the starting-point for this investigation. These are struggles for new subjectivities which encompass the right to be different and distinguish oneself from the ways in which the effects of particular 'technologies of the self' routinely constitute people: 'These struggles are not exactly for or against the "individual", but rather they are struggles against the "government of individualization"' (1982: 212). This makes sense if we remember that the individual is not constituted before the effects of power because

it is already one of the prime effects of power that certain bodies, certain gestures, certain discourses, certain desires, come to be identified and constituted as individuals.

(Foucault 1980: 98)

There is a clear tension between struggles for new identities and the totalizing forms of power characteristic of modern society. These forms are considered to be more rational and economic, but this does not imply that people are more obedient. Nor does the exercise of power imply that people are not capable of acting in the first place. Indeed, its very exercise presupposes the condition of freedom:

> It is a total structure of actions brought to bear upon possible actions; it incites, it induces, it seduces, it makes easier or more difficult; in the extreme it constrains or forbids absolutely; it is nevertheless always a way of acting upon an acting subject or acting subjects by virtue of their acting or being capable of action.
>
> (Foucault 1982: 220)

Summary

We are now in a position to summarize the ways in which Foucault gives us a new perspective on social relations. In particular, if we think of structure as determining and action as freedom, we simply replicate the voluntarist–determinist duality in social thought. This stems from seeing the individual as the centre of social relations through invoking the idea of a transcendent subject. In so doing, we will not understand the dynamics of modern society. In these terms, we should not view power and freedom as opposites. Instead, they exist in antagonism or, as Foucault characterizes it, an 'agonism' or 'permanent provocation' (1982: 222).

The connection between Foucault's writings and the Frankfurt School were noted in Part I. However, we should not over-extend such parallels. As Barry Hindness (1996: 149) notes, for this tradition of critical theory the autonomous agent provides the 'postulated ideal' against which a real state of affairs is then evaluated. For Foucault, there are no such utopias. Yet there are similarities between Foucault's characterizations of modernity and the writings of Weber. Although Foucault did not regard himself as a Weberian, if that is seen in terms of viewing rationality as an 'anthropological invariant' (Foucault 1991c: 79), interesting comparisons can still be made between these thinkers (Gordon 1987; Warren 1992). In both we can trace the influence of Nietzsche's idea of the 'will to truth' which is exercised in the name of reason so that order might be achieved out of what would otherwise be a chaotic and unstable world.

Despite these observations, given the particular influences and directions of his thought, Foucault's questions were of a different order to those we have come across before. As he puts it:

> What is this Reason that we use? What are its historical effects? What are its limits, and what are its dangers? How can we exist as rational beings, fortunately committed to practicing a rationality that is unfortunately crisscrossed by intrinsic dangers?
>
> (Foucault 1984: 249, original italics)

This does not suggest that he is in favour of irrationality, simply that his approach to understanding our contemporary practices has the effect of questioning the rationale upon which they are based.

Finally, we should note that Foucault's methods for these inquiries did not follow Schutz's postulate of subjective interpretation, nor a depth-hermeneutics such that an underlying truth may eventually be revealed to the actor. Both positions force one into a regime of truth which then stands as the final arbitrator, whereas it actually serves to hide yet another meaning and so forth. We can thus summarize Foucault's interpretation of current practices as 'interpretative analytics' which is

> a pragmatically guided reading of the coherence of the practices of the society. It does not claim to correspond either to the everyday meanings shared by the actors or, in any simple sense, to reveal the intrinsic meanings of the practices. This is the sense in which Foucault's method is interpretative but not hermeneutic.
>
> (Dreyfus and Rabinow 1982: 124)

Issues in the work of Michel Foucault

Foucault's studies have proved to be both highly influential and controversial. Much of his influence is explained by the failure of 'conventional' accounts to explain the ubiquity of power and the struggles in contemporary societies for new forms of identity. Power is frequently evaluated against and reduced to a series of conceptual monoliths: the state, class, race and gender relations. This is not to suggest that his work does not illuminate the dynamics of these relations. On the contrary, when it comes to understanding the dynamics of race and ethnicity (Rattansi 1994) and sex and gender (Diamond and Quinby 1988; Weedon 1987), it is clear that his works have been of considerable use. That noted, his studies are not without their conceptual flaws. In this section, I wish to bring your attention to some of these.

We have seen that Foucault offers a new approach to the relationship between agency and structure, as expressed in terms of an 'agonism' between power and freedom. However, he simply asserts that we should resist power, but does not provide the grounds upon which such a resistance can take place. As one theorist, who also employed a relational theory of power, put it:

> no kind of resistance is possible if we follow Foucault's analyses. For if power is always already there, if every power situation is immanent in itself, *why should there ever be resistance? From where* would resistance come, and *how would it even be possible?*
>
> (Poulantzas 1978: 149, original italics)

We end up with mixed messages. At one level, 'power is a machine that no-one owns'. At this point, Foucault reads as a structuralist bidding yet another farewell to the subject. At another level, he recognizes struggles for new subjectivities but in abandoning the idea of the subject to 'discursive formation', it is difficult to conceive of *any* basis upon which to build change. We can develop this point further in relation to the centrality of a normative basis upon which to conduct feminist-inspired critiques.

The attraction of Foucault's work for some feminist researchers is clear in terms, for example, of its avoidance of essentialism through supplanting naturalism in favour of cultural constructionism. He thus brings our attention to the ways in which we experience ourselves not in some state of nature, but in a symbolically mediated fashion, thereby shedding light on the gendered nature of the self and social relations. Nevertheless, whilst he is correct in questioning the idea of a 'natural' body, it is also argued that: 'the body exists as a physical entity prior to any cultural work' (Soper 1993: 32). Yet he refused such ideas on the basis of being epistemologically sceptic regarding the status of acultural explanations, whilst his studies analysed the effects of political rationalities as the routine denial of differences via tactics of incorporation and neutralization.

If feminism takes these kinds of insights too far, it risks losing its basis for critique; hence the clear 'tensions' between feminism and Foucault (Ramazanoglu 1993). If everything, including desire, is up for discursive grabs, then what may be viewed as 'authentic' in social life? A feminist social theory built on this basis risks nothing less than a negation of feminist politics which, necessarily, requires some common interest or cause as a unifying principle upon which to base change. The underlying reason for this is a central issue in the use of Foucault's work. It may be further illuminated through a consideration of his concept of power.

There are a variety of interpretations that may be applied to Foucault's work. His pluralist concept of power, for example, lends itself to an American liberal political science tradition, as well as having parallels with Weber and the Frankfurt School in terms of analysing the effects of instrumental rationality under conditions of modernity. The basis for these multiple interpretations may be understood if we take the requirements of genealogical critique to be politically engaged, in order to take power effects seriously and hence retain the domain of human meaning, whilst also remaining normatively neutral. However, the result is that Foucault

> adopts a concept of power that permits him no condemnation of any objectionable features of modern societies. But at the same time, and on the other hand, his rhetoric betrays the conviction that modern societies are utterly without redeeming features. Clearly, what Foucault needs, and needs desperately, are normative criteria for distinguishing acceptable from unacceptable forms of power.
>
> (Fraser 1989: 33)

Foucault's rejection of humanism, in order to avoid the problems of intellectual traditions built upon Cartesian philosophy, seems to imply that values do not require justification. How, therefore, can Foucault claim that 'discipline' is a bad thing as part of the routine political judgements which he makes in the course of his inquiries (Fraser 1989: 42)? His refusal to engage in these debates is perhaps a strategy of resistance to the premises of humanism which, of course, he sought to avoid. However, when we act, do we simply do so strategically in order to gain the upper hand in a never ending game of power relations? As we have seen, explanations of human agency as being motivated by the desire to gain some strategic advantage over one's 'adversaries' are limited.

Foucault's price for analysing the processes of objectification and subjectivism of the subject is therefore high. It is, without doubt, illuminating to question the belief that the production and operation of norms takes place in the absence of the exercise of power. However, does power saturate our lives to the extent that Foucault suggests? If it does, then we are caught in endless games of power with strategic action being the only dimension to *all* human actions. Whilst Foucault (1984: 351) spoke of 'creating oneself' in his discussion of a genealogy of ethics, this stands in clear tension with his idea of power which rules out, by fiat, the possibility of reaching consensual agreement. We should not be surprised to find Habermas levelling this critique at Foucault and poststructuralist thought in general:

> in passing through structuralism, this movement of thought has made transcendental subjectivity disappear *without a trace*, and indeed in such a way that one also loses sight of the system of world relations, speaker perspectives, and validity claims that is inherent in linguistic communication itself. Without this reference system, however, the distinction between levels of reality, between fiction and reality, between everyday practice and extra-ordinary experience, and between the corresponding kinds of texts and genres becomes impossible and even pointless. The house of 'being' is itself sucked into the maelstrom of an undirected linguistic current.
>
> (Habermas 1992b: 210, original italics)

Social relations are manifested in Foucault's work as a continuous battle-ground and given that power has no origin and is seen as the multi-faceted play of social forces, conflict is endemic. The possibility that power might be institutionally stabilized is supplanted by 'the possibility of interpreting the institutionalization of positions of power as a process of the constant use of force' (Honneth 1991: 174). We then become but spectators of discourses that are seen to possess their own constitutive power: that is, they have the ability to define objects in particular ways through warranting some statements and thereby excluding others. Of course, in order not to surrender to structuralism and to retain the role of meaning in the analysis of discourses, Foucault focuses upon the 'serious speech acts' of professionals/experts. His concern being to explain the conditions under which particular speech acts are validated.

Here, again, he runs the danger of removing the realm of human agency for these discourses define 'positions' which any subject might occupy. Given this, it is the rules of the discourse which define these positions and what the subject may, or may not say, as a result. Yet Foucault also speaks of 'strategies' and 'choices'. However, how can such things be spoken of without a theory of human agency? Even in his later work on 'technologies of the self', where he examines how we fashion ourselves, we are not granted much in the way of self-determination (Freundlieb 1994). Instead, it is the structure of discourses which define the conditions of the subject. Despite his attempts to avoid the trap of structuralism, determinism seems to reassert itself.

Summary

In asking the question 'What are we today?' Foucault asks a central question that informs our everyday existences. He does so on grounds that link what we are to the regimes of truth that pronounce on the nature of our being. Here is the rub. Notions of autonomy and transcendence, dear to the liberal position and to our self-conceptions, are analysed by an approach which views the social body as infused with politics. In the process, Foucault shows us that there is critique and life after Cartesianism (Fraser 1989).

It has been argued that to see the operation of power in Foucault's method is problematic. Are our lives so saturated in this way? His own answer to this question suffices. Asked why he was so interested in politics, he replied:

what blindness, what deafness, what density of ideology would have to weigh me down to prevent me from being interested in what is probably the most crucial subject to our existence, that is to say the society in which we live, the economic relations within which it functions, and the system of power which defines the regular forms and the regular permissions and prohibitions of our conduct. The essence of our life consists, after all, of the political functioning of the society in which we find ourselves.

(Foucault in Elders 1974: 168)

Although Foucault was interested in what makes the truth 'true', it does not follow that he denied the concept of validity (Visker 1995), nor does the absence of a normative basis in his work mean that it cannot be used in examining contemporary social relations. His concerns were with the basis of forms of life, or the lifeworld. This did not involve the celebration of relativism, but an investigation of the conditions under which truth is produced. Critical theory with *guarantees* may be abandoned, but it is replaced by a critical research programme with *possibilities*. Therefore, at the end of his life, Foucault could not help but face

> the fact that the understanding of social and historical processes is, if not a component of our self-understanding, at the very least a contribution to our liberation from self-misunderstanding.
>
> (Dews 1989: 40)

Further, his refusal of humanism does not necessarily imply a rejection of the values of modernity (Hoy 1986). However, there are forms of thought which seek to do just that. Here it is argued that we have entered a new epoch. Foucault was sceptical not only regarding there being any solid foundations for modernity, but also over the idea that history possesses such 'breaks'. To that extent at least, his work cannot be subsumed under the subject of the next chapter.

Beyond modernity? Postmodern social theory

The formulation of concepts and theories which may be employed for the purpose of analysing social relations is *the* essential ingredient of an adequate social theory. The attribution of some form of rationality to human conduct, social relations or to social systems as a whole, is the means through which the basis for such an endeavour is often formulated. This tendency is evident in rational action theory, ethnomethodology, through to Habermas's idea of communicative reason and Parsons's and Luhmann's variants of systems theory. Wherever they start and finish, however, they can be viewed as expressing the same underlying characteristic: that is, the desire to move beyond an analysis of the particular in order to derive principles for the understanding and explanation of human relations in general.

For Descartes, the mind was the site of reason which found an order in the world. Then, with Kant, came the tempering of Cartesian certainties. With the external world a less certain place for Kant than it was for Descartes, the ordering powers of the mind were placed at its centre. Then there was the empiricist-minded Hume. For him, it was impressions which gave rise to ideas. The mind is then viewed as more of a reflection of the world, than a coherent entity which sits at its centre. Nevertheless, despite these differences between Kant and Hume, with one stressing reason and the other custom, both held

they could prove that the mind is so constructed that it *must* bring forth from within itself such a tidy, cognizable, Newtonian world. So we were, after all, rationally entitled to believe in it; but the considerations enabling us to do so were henceforth to be based on qualities of our mind alone.

(Gellner 1992: 29, original italics)

In contrast to this route, which laid the basis for society to become an object of study, let us take another route. This route will not seek to uncover something called 'social reality', whether by measuring the external world through 'neutral' instruments, or by generalizing on the basis of rules informing language games that construct the object world. Instead, the task now changes and the role of the social theorist should be to invent

> allusions to the conceivable which cannot be presented. And it is not to be expected that this task will effect the last reconciliation between language-games (which, under the name of faculties, Kant knew to be separated by a chasm), and that only the transcendental illusion (that of Hegel) can hope to totalize them into a real unity . . . We have paid a high enough price for the nostalgia of the whole and the one, for the reconciliation of the concept and the sensible, of the transparent and the communicable experience . . . The answer is: *Let us wage war on totality; let us be witnesses to the unpresentable; let us activate the differences and save the honor of the name.*
>
> (Lyotard 1993: 46, emphasis added)

What is this argument? Why is it invoked? How we get there and the reasons for doing so are the subjects of this chapter. In the process, we will find an argument that we have entered a new epoch and further, that to adequately understand what this consists of requires something called a 'postmodern social theory'. This epoch, called postmodernity, is characterized by heterogeneity, indeterminacy, fragmentation and flexibility. Given this state of affairs, a postmodern social theory necessitates that we relinquish the quest for 'foundations or the search for the one correct or grounded set of premises, conceptual strategy and explanation' (Seidman 1994a: 119).

The emergence and analysis of the postmodern

The rise of the postmodern

Certainty and progress is assumed to characterize the epoch known as modernity. In Part I, an emerging attitude became apparent. This may be called the 'attitude of the modernists'. These were and are the people who celebrate the potentiality which is said to exist in history, art, science and politics and the achievements of the human race. Yet they also

> deplore modernization's betrayal of its own human promise. Modernists demand deeper and more radical renewals: modern men and

women must become the subjects as well as the objects of modernization; they must learn to change the world that is changing them, and to
make it their own.

(Berman 1993: 33)

This attitude, therefore, is one of ambivalence in its viewing of broken
promises and celebrations. We have found those who approached their
analyses of social relations in this manner: for example, Simmel and Weber.
Their writings can be contrasted with the relative optimism of Marx and
Durkheim. Weber regarded Western societies as exhibiting an increased
potential for control in the name of instrumental rationality. A fatalism was
then apparent in his reflections via a recognition that the realm of human
meaning was being trammelled by vast impersonal forces. Weber was not
prepared to overcome such observations through an allusion to the external
by the freezing of time and all of its 'fleeting qualities' (Harvey 1990: 21).
From this point of view, we can read both Weber and Simmel as writers who
were straddling a chasm that was opening up between two epochs.

A recognition of this state of affairs was apparent in the writings of Mills,
who sits within the broad tradition of American pragmatism. He wrote of the
changing ideas of 'reason' and 'freedom' and the collapse of liberalism and
socialism as explanations of ourselves and the relations into which we enter
(there are echoes here of Weber's brittle synthesis of Nietzsche and Marx).
The social sciences are seen to have inherited terms which, although
outdated, are still part of its practices. If generalized to contemporary
situations, they 'become unwieldy, irrelevant, not convincing' (Mills
1970: 184). He thus argues that the Modern Age is being superseded by a
'Fourth Epoch'. He refers to this as the 'postmodern period':

The ending of one epoch and the beginning of another is, to be sure, a
matter of definition. But definitions, like everything social, are historically specific. And now our basic definitions of society and self are being
overtaken by new realities ... I mean that when we try to orient
ourselves – if we do try – we find that many of our old expectations and
images are, after all, tied down historically.

(Mills 1970: 184)

In particular, it is the role of reason and the idea of the free individual which
he argues are the prime legacies that twentieth-century social scientists have
inherited from the Enlightenment (Mills 1970: 186). In the face of change, the
central issues that now face us are concerned with our very nature and our
limits and possibilities. After all, is our destiny to become 'what may be called
The Cheerful Robot?' (Mills 1970: 189).

We may characterize this tension as one which exists between two elements
of the process of modernization: specialization and rationalization. Specialization, as Durkheim noted, necessitates a complex division of labour which,
for the purposes of social cohesion, requires a new form of social integration.

This time, of course, it was with society taking the transcendent role, not the autonomous subject. Authority and freedom, therefore, were not opposites. For Weber, the same process was charted but he then wrote of 'specialists without spirit and sensualist without heart'. This was symptomatic of the process of increasing societal complexity running alongside greater centralization and control.

In the work of Habermas, the process of societal evolution depends upon a normative basis which exists in the lifeworld, but in the forward march of modernity the 'steering media of power and money' evolve which have no basis in the lifeworld. As we have seen, for Habermas there is a way out of this 'iron cage' through a modified Enlightenment project which finds the possibility for a consensus that is not imposed upon the lifeworld, but emerges from within it. However, is this quest for consensus yet another version of the modernists' attitude which is doomed to failure? Do meta-narratives of this type, in their desire to universalize, render violence to heterogeneity? This is clearly the case for Lyotard who, in reference to Habermas, plays on the same themes that the earlier quote indicated:

> Is legitimacy to be found in consensus obtained through discussion, as Jürgen Habermas thinks? Such consensus does violence to the heterogeneity of language games. And invention is always born of dissension. Postmodern knowledge is not simply a tool of the authorities; it refines our sensitivity to differences and reinforces our ability to tolerate the incommensurable. Its principle is not the expert's homology, but the inventor's paralogy.
>
> (Lyotard 1984: xxv)

A recognition of heterogeneity is not the monopoly of postmodernist perspectives (McLennan 1995). That noted, what seems to have changed in socio-theoretical discourse is that those who are the bearers of the dream of universalism now have to defend themselves against the relativists (Bauman 1992). In considering these issues we have to ask if this is symptomatic of a changing set of social conditions such that there can no longer be any unifying principles of co-ordination or communication that are available to us?

In considering this question, we might first recall the arguments of Kroker and Cook that Augustine, whilst signalling the beginning of the modern age, also possessed a discourse on the will that commenced the 'arc of a dead power which will not come fully into light until the nineteenth century in Nietzsche's nightmarish vision of the "will to will"' (Kroker and Cook 1988: 72). In these terms, they can then go on to characterize the postmodern condition as

> a coming home to the 'perfect nihilism' (Nietzsche) which has always been at work in Western consciousness and which only now, in the fully

realized technological society, reveals itself in the fateful meeting of power and the sign.

(Kroker and Cook 1988: 73)

Nihilism may be viewed as the celebration of the relativism of values such that there is no absolute good, or the refusal to create ultimate values, or an absolute subjectivity that accompanies a 'loss of the world' (Glücksmann 1992: 336). Nevertheless, from whatever vantage point it is viewed, if the postmodern condition is that which gives rise to its celebration, then attempts at delineating a new basis for reason are not moving against some trendy intellectual movement, but 'real' historical changes that are taking place in the organization of societies as a whole. If this is the case, then consensus would, as part of the modernists' dream of a better future, indeed become 'a horizon that is never reached' (Lyotard 1984: 61).

As noted, the forward march of modernity came to witness the increasingly complicated nature of the social world being compensated for by mechanisms of communication and control. These functions were taken over by systems which came to represent the need for specialization and co-ordination. These systems are argued to reduce the complexity of the social world. However, does their legitimacy then come to supersede that of the realm of human values? For instance, even matters of risk, as part of both the excitement and tragedy of the human condition, are now open to their calculations:

> In binary coding, modern society possesses a highly specific form for heightening, normalizing and contextualizing risky behaviour. By attributing observations to certain coded systems, we can recognize which risk network we are operating within – and which one we are not operating within. Whenever a matter is dealt with in the context of a binary code, *the implication is that not only the positive value but also the countervalue could be assigned validity*.
>
> (Luhmann 1993: 76, emphasis added)

These systems come to represent the site of reason and it is from these that Habermas seeks to recover its critical capacity in order to restore the power of rational argumentation. Despite these differences, both systemic and critical modernism represent a celebration of the potentiality of reason to achieve regularity and understanding. Yet there is an historical process that might be argued to counter these attempts.

One such process is that of 'de-differentiation' (Lash 1990). The implications of this process being that a differentiation between the aesthetic, cultural, social, economic and political realms, as a characteristic feature of modernity, is no longer a feasible option for analytic purposes. Instead, from a cultural vantage point, we now have a colonization of the moral-political and theoretical spheres by the aesthetic; a collapse of the social into the cultural, accompanied by a breakdown of the barriers between high and low culture and finally, in terms of 'cultural economy', the 'death' of the distinction that was once made between the author and their text and, for instance, the distinction that is made between the production of a play and its reception by its audience who now form part of its cultural production (Lash 1990: 11–12).

If we extend this process, beyond the cultural sphere to which Lash and Urry confine it (Lash and Urry 1987; 1994), it follows that we can no longer divide the social world into autonomous units. In this sense, there are those who are willing to engage in this embrace via the argument that de-differentiation extends to all spheres of social life. Whereas the process of modernization, as series of socio-economic changes, bore witness to the specialization of sub-systems by function such that those systems with similar functions possess similar structures, we are now said to be witnessing 'an extension of this process in which social units are differentiating at the level of structure as well as of function' (Crook, Pakulski and Waters 1992: 33). In these terms:

> Patterns of economic production may be said to be hyperdifferen-tiating, providing a multiplicity of directions in the absence of a unifying structural principle. Such hyperdifferentiation of structure is, we argue, a generalized and widespread pattern.
>
> (Crook, Pakulski and Waters 1992: 33)

Durkheim wrote: 'A discipline may be called a "science" only if it has a definite field to explore. Science is concerned with things, realities' (in Giddens 1972b: 57). The basis upon which this was to proceed is the correspondence between the language of representation (theory) and reality. Yet the process of de-differentiation renders this strategy obsolete. There is no 'reality' to represent, only *realities*. There is no reason to base analysis upon, only *reasons*.

A tension between the forces of centralization and dispersion under postmodernity now manifests itself in various ways. First, the media of control change. Second, as noted above, the ability to control the object world is lessened. Third, there is a collapse of the boundaries between the different spheres of social life: for example, the public and private. In relation to the first aspect, specialization is seen to be superseded by hyperdifferen-tiation whereby control is no longer the province of specific spheres of life, nor specialized disciplines for their study. This all results in the generation of a 'limitless range of media types' within society:

> for example, TV churches can generate money as well as value-commitment and influence, and businesses which professionalize their employees and offer them lifetime security can be a source of value-commitments as well as money. In other words there is no longer an oligopolistic set of sources for money and power and they thus lose their effectivity as sources of control.
>
> (Crook, Pakulski and Waters 1992: 34–35)

Similarly, the breakdown of the correspondence between structure and function, in turn, leads to a breakdown of the potential for prediction and control: 'States become ungovernable, economies unmanageable, and life-worlds anarchistic' (1992: 35). The result being that postmodernization is characterized by unpredictability and chaos, not homogeneity and control. However, not only is system de-differentiation a characteristic of this process, but also when it comes to an analysis of social action, this is seen to be

> divorced from underlying material constraints (or rather these con-
> straints disappear) and enters the voluntaristic realm of taste, choice
> and preference. As it does so the boundaries between determined social
> groups disappear. So class, gender and ethnicity decline in social
> significance and so also do some of their characteristic forms of
> expression, including class-based political action and the distinction
> between high and popular culture.
>
> (Crook, Pakulski and Waters 1992: 35)

With this breakdown of divisions in social space, the cultural realm of signs and symbols comes to penetrate the socio-structural realm of social relations to such an extent that individual and multiple realities come to predominate. Therefore, the potential for individual distinctiveness is heightened. At this point in our journey, it is the ideas of Jean Baudrillard which become of central importance.

Postmodern social theory

Baudrillard argues that we have moved from societies which are character-ized by production, to those of consumption. His ideas have been charted as moving from a development of Marxism, through a transitory phase, before finally becoming a critique of Marxism itself (Gane 1991). For instance, in relation to the object world, Baudrillard was to argue that the things we consume form systems of signs. These systems, to recall our earlier discussions on Saussure, are self-referential and precede the individual. Now, during the earlier stages of his work, whilst seeing consumption as determined by production in a classical Marxist manner, the influences of Barthes and Mauss also provided the basis for a structuralist analysis of symbolic exchange. Ultimately, this was to render Marx's distinction between use and exchange value untenable. Briefly, what form did this transition take?

In Marxist terms, a commodity is seen as having a basis in a reality through the meeting of some specific human need. Adding the insights of French structuralism to this, leads one to see commodities as objects of desire that then enable the individual to relate to the social order via their consumption. In this way, people may be said to be both ordered and differentiated. However, Baudrillard now starts the process of bringing that which is considered to be marginal in Marxist thought, to having analytic primacy. In order to understand this we need to note the distinction that Marx made between exchange and use value in relation to commodities.

Use value is said to relate to the utility that a commodity has in relation to satisfying a human want. Exchange value, on the other hand, possesses value due to its ability to be exchanged for other goods or services. Therefore:

> The use-value and the exchange-value of a commodity are not just two different determinations, or aspects; they are contradictory determinations. A commodity is a use-value only if it is immediately useful to whoever has it. It is an exchange-value only if it is not immediately useful but is used for exchange to get something else.
>
> (Cleaver 1979: 90)

Exchange-value is the opposite of use-value. From a political vantage point, use-value may be related to working-class commodity consumption which is utilized for the satisfaction of needs. Capitalism, on the other hand, is concerned with exchange values for the extraction of surplus value and profit. Despite this, each depends upon the other, for example: 'It is exactly because labor-power is a use-value for capital that it is an exchange-value for labor' (Cleaver 1979: 92). Nevertheless, for Marx, use-value still functions as a basis for the objective assessment of needs that are assumed to exist independently of relations of capital. Yet how can one evaluate and compare in this manner separate from the social context of consumption?

In contrast to this approach Baudrillard argues that use-value should be viewed in terms of structures of symbolic exchange:

> consumption does not arise from an objective need of the consumer, a final intention of the subject towards the object; rather, there is social production, in a system of exchange, of a material of differences, a code of significations and invidious (*statuaire*) values.
>
> (Baudrillard 1981: 75)

This is not a system of consumption whereby the individual subject makes a rational choice, through calculation, in terms of what to consume. Instead, meaning is located within a structure of differences that are conferred upon objects. Take, for example, the consumption of leisure. Is this about the need of the autonomous subject to enjoy 'free time'? No! It is the 'consumption of unproductive time' (Baudrillard 1981: 76). What does this mean? Consider the man [*sic*] of leisure:

> Outside of the competitive sphere there are no autonomous needs. Spontaneous motivation doesn't exist. But for all that, he can't permit himself to do nothing. At a loss for something to do with his free time,

he nevertheless urgently 'needs' to do nothing (or nothing useful), since this has distinctive social value.

(Baudrillard 1981: 77)

Analytic primacy is afforded to the relationship between value and symbolic exchange, not use and exchange value. Use value has now disappeared within a system of sign values: 'This must be recognised today as the truth of the sphere of "consumption" and the cultural system in general' (Baudrillard 1981: 87). Indeed, science, artistic and intellectual work and even 'transgression' and 'innovation' are part of the same process.

Baudrillard could choose to analyse the relationship between the workings of the system and the cultural processes that inform it – as had Marx before him (Gane 1991: 84). However, having asserted primacy to the system of symbolic exchange, he then hovers between seeing the system from the point of view of an oppressed class or group and as a system of signs of consumption which refer only to each other and have no external referent. In arguing for the latter, production is to give way to consumption with its vortex of symbols. As such, any hint of a humanist legacy with respect to a state of 'alienation' is abandoned. At this stage in his thought, he thus exhibits a curious blend of Marx, Durkheim, Nietzsche and Freud in the development of what Mike Gane characterizes as a 'non-humanist idea of alienation' (1991: 95).

All of this was taking place in the era of the 1970s. It was then possible to believe in the theoretical and political possibilities that came with a fusion of Freud and Marx: 'it was in their copulation that things could be saved' (Baudrillard in Gane 1993: 59). This was not to last long with Nietzsche hovering in the background. Here was a thinker who Baudrillard acknowledges is the most influential figure in relation to his thought: 'but not as a point of reference . . . but as a spirit (*esprit*), as a stimulus (*impulsion*), or inspiration' (Baudrillard in Gane 1993: 203).

With Nietzsche in place, Baudrillard will now take us into the condition where models of reality, and not reality itself, predominate. No longer is reality to be measured against the sign, nor are they seen to exist in a dialectical relationship. There is now only the sign:

Now the sign seems to me to posit what I have called the 'principle of hyper-reality'. That is, what we have now is the disappearance of the referent – and it is in relation to this disappearance of the referent that there is a sort of omnipresence of the sign.

(Baudrillard in Gane 1993: 142)

The system now comprises the consumption of signs without an external referent. Critical theory, for example, cannot allude to a dialectic of the Enlightenment to discover the truth with an existing state of affairs. The negation of reality and reality itself are now one: 'In short, what we now have is a principle of non-reality based on "reality" – a principle of hyper-reality as

I call it' (Baudrillard in Gane 1993: 143). This is the era of postmodernity: nothing real exists, but only 'codes' of the original and it is these that enable simulation to predominate over production.

This is Baudrillard's final rejection of Marxism. The real and its representation have become erased to such an extent that everything is either, or has the potential to become, simulacra: that is, we only have models of reality and it is no longer possible to represent things *as they are*. The ability to decide, for example, between ideas, aesthetics and political persuasions, collapses. This is the era in which information is predominant. Computers, the media and information processing systems in general add to a 'politics of seduction' which are part of the signs that are a routine feature of our everyday lives:

> life is conducted in a ceaseless circulation of signs about what is happening in the world (signs about news), about what sort of identity one wishes to project (signs about self), about one's standing (signs of status and esteem), about what purposes buildings serve (architectural signs), about aesthetic preferences (signs on walls, tables, side-boards), and so on.
>
> (Webster 1995: 177)

There is no transcendental position from which one may view this process and pronounce upon its 'truth'. The best we might achieve is to be a spectator in the process of seduction. The sign is no longer to refer to the 'real' as a semiological strategy might seek. The steering media of modernity is now *the* media in postmodernity. What Weber referred to as 'disenchantment' is the irreversible postmodern condition in which meaning has 'imploded'. There is nothing beyond appearance, for appearance is all we have: 'The screen, the image, the sign, the modern message, the media require profusion, proliferation; there must be plenty for everyone' (Baudrillard in Gane 1993: 148). This is the end to history that leaves rationalism in its wake:

> We tend to forget that our reality, including the tragic events of the past, has been swallowed up by the media. That means that it is too late to verify events and understand them historically, for what characterizes our era and our *fin de siècle* is precisely the disappearance of the instruments of this intelligibility. It was necessary to understand history when there was still history.
>
> (Baudrillard in Gane 1993: 160, original italics)

The political realm may no longer be viewed of as autonomous, whilst the social realm is now so saturated with media images that is has become 'anonymous'. It follows that those meaningful referents invoked during the course of social inquiries – class, gender, race, ethnicity, etc. – disappear in the collapse of the 'social'. These concepts are no longer tenable because the real has been overrun by the 'hyperreal'. Allusions to characteristics of the 'masses' are fatally flawed:

> The mass is born short-circuited in 'total circularity'. What seems to occur he argues is a circulation around simulation models, and a collapse of the complex system into itself . . . For no-one, no organisation, as has been the case previously can any longer speak with confidence 'for' the mass.
>
> (Gane 1991: 136)

Baudrillard takes this into America. Here is the postmodern condition where culture and social life are not distinct. Europeans are said to locate themselves in terms of their past and their destiny. However, America is a 'fiction' where the notion of the 'authentic' which accompanies a sense of history disappears in a perpetual simulation in the 'present'. We find cities which are 'exponential', not 'referential'. Las Vegas is Disneyland. This is not a referential city: that is, one with a past, a defined territory and a sense of history. Instead, it is a city whose 'total superficiality . . . is bound up with superficiality of gambling and speculation itself' (Baudrillard 1993: 246). This is the imaginary of the real that is to be found in Disneyland:

> In both Disneyland and Disney World, it is clear that everything that can be derived from the imaginary has been caught, represented, made representable, put on display, made visual. Literally putting on a show for consumption without any metaphors is obviously a radical deterrent to the imaginary. Once again, utopia becomes reality.
>
> (Baudrillard 1993: 246)

With the obliteration of the ability to allude to those processes, products, effects, forms of rational argumentation, rules, or relations of cause and effect which might enable us to explain and decide between truth and falsehood, we have entered the postmodern condition. This is the end of meta-narratives of explanation that accompanies 'an internal erosion of the legitimacy principle of knowledge' (Lyotard 1984: 39). This is yet another vantage point through which we can illuminate Lyotard's antagonism for any search for consensus within social life.

Employing Wittgenstein's idea of language games, Lyotard calls for the abandonment of any search for 'hidden' meanings along the lines, for example, of a depth-hermeneutic approach to the study of social life, in favour of the 'play' of language games about which he makes three observations. First, the rules of such games do not contain their own legitimation, but are part of a contract between players who do not, necessarily, formulate those rules. Second, in the absence of rules, there is no game. In this way, an alteration in rules leads to an alteration in the nature of the game itself. Third, it follows that 'utterances' should be seen as moves within a game.

The third point may be given particular emphasis if we consider it in relation to Habermas's ideas, for 'to speak is to fight, in the sense of playing, and speech acts fall within the domain of a general agonistics' (Lyotard 1984: 10). This is not to suggest that people then 'play to win', simply that there is joy and pleasure to be gained in 'the endless invention of turns of phrase, of words and meanings, the process behind the evolution of language on the level of *parole*' (1984: 10, original italics). This pleasure, however, is still derived from the achievement of success over one's adversary. Underlying this process being the rules of the language game which provide for an 'observable common bond'.

Lyotard divides the normal methodological representation of the 'common bond' into two approaches. First, the functional holism of Parsons, and second, the conflict model of Marxism. The former is seen to chart an optimism in the faith of the system to adjust itself to the demands of stabilization in the age of globalization. The latter, on the other hand, as it evolved over time through the Frankfurt School, came to represent less of a theoretical model of critique based upon an analysis of social divisions, but acquired the status of 'utopia' or 'hope'. In the face of such contrasts we appear to be left with the choice between a technocratic positivism which feeds the system and a critical, hermeneutic or reflexive social theory (Lyotard 1984: 14). The point being, however, that this choice is no longer relevant to the society in which we live. In the postmodern condition, the functions of regulation and reproduction are no longer the province of particular groups or institutions. Instead, it is machines who hold information. Whilst those who have access to that information will continue to make decisions:

> What is new in all of this is that the old poles of attraction represented by nation-states, parties, professions, institutions, and historical traditions are losing their attraction. And it does not look as though they will be replaced, at least not on their former scale.
>
> (Lyotard 1984: 14)

The implication is that if these sources of the social bond are absent from our current social condition, then they should be sought elsewhere: for example, in social origins, or in some authentic history that requires de-coding. However, it cannot be uncovered in a single lifeworld and then used to explain or understand other lifeworlds. Given the necessity for the activation of differences within language games, there is no principle or general rules that enable us to establish meaningful connections. Indeed, the very attempt renders violence to heterogeneity.

In contrast to these strategies, we should understand the ways in which we are part of narratives. It is these language games that position 'the person who asks, as well as the addressee and the referent asked about: it is already the social bond' (Lyotard 1984: 15). In the age of information, these narratives flow through society and participation does not require justification in terms of reference to some grand, legitimizing narrative. As such, any person may occupy the place of the 'speaker'. These narratives are part of a communities relationship to itself and in their transmission we find 'the set of pragmatic rules that constitutes the social bond' (Lyotard 1984: 21).

As Baudrillard said of exponential cities, the meaning of narratives is not derived in relation to a past, but in the immediate act of their telling. This does not require 'science'. Nor does it require legitimation through allusions to humanism: that is, a referent to the autonomy of the will based in reason. The self is now part of the narrative society. As with the systems of rational coordination, the autonomous individual is part of a bygone era that is remembered only in the narratives of utopian radicals. In the dissemination of numerous language games without a common thread: 'The social subject itself seems to dissolve' (Lyotard 1984: 40). Systemic and critical modernism is thereby left in its wake.

As for Baudrillard, Lyotard argues that modernity contained the seeds of its own destruction. The desire for freedom, which is said to come with the greater accumulation of knowledge, is seen as symptomatic of Nietzsche's will to power. Scientific narratives, in the service of reason and progress, are no longer legitimate. Instead, they are part of a self-serving game, symptomatic of the forward march of de-legitimation. What is now at stake is the optimal relationship between inputs and outputs. This is not knowledge in the service of truth, but 'performativity'. Therefore, when it comes to research:

> The State and/or company must abandon the idealist and humanist narratives of legitimation in order to justify the new goal: in the discourse of today's backers of research, the only credible goal is power. Scientists, technicians, and instruments are purchased not to find truth, but to augment power.
>
> (Lyotard 1984: 46)

This system may not be overcome through the allusion to meta-narratives of explanation. It exists alongside narratives whose heterogeneity and dispersion is a cause for celebration. Given this, social theory should tell alternative stories in order to activate these differences and place its 'nostalgia' for 'the whole and the one' finally to rest.

Summary

A new condition requires a new social theory that represent an abrupt disjuncture with its entire history. Therefore, we have entered a new era which stands as the negation of all that went before. In addition, to adequately grasp the implications of this, we also need a radical break from past conceptions of agency and structure and their corresponding relation-ships. Systemic and critical modernism are to be placed in the dustbin of history.

The postmodern condition turns rational systems and the rational subject into fictions. The quest for any sense of consensus amongst peoples is seen to deny the differences upon which society relies for its dynamism via the agonisms that are a fundamental and necessary part of language games. Steering media of co-ordination and control are now part of the information society. Those referents which served as the conceptual monoliths against which the modernist could demarcate the true and the false and the emancipatory and the hegemonic, no longer exist. What we now have are self-serving systems of which the self is a part and not distinct as the discourse of humanism would argue.

Whether or not Mills might have subscribed to the views of Lyotard and Baudrillard, amongst others, is almost an aside, for there are those who have translated his arguments in particular ways. After all, for those in search of a postmodern social theory, he may be employed via a contrast with Parsons's grand theoretical schema that marks out the terrain of social inquiry in the name of conceptual transcendence. This pragmatist-based social theory, recalling Baudrillard's remarks on the United States, is argued to resonate 'deeply with the American emphasis on utility, social consequences and diversity' (Seidman 1994b: 191).

This social theory would not appeal to standards of knowledge as the judge of progress. Knowledge, therefore, is no longer the path to liberation separated from the moral and political realms and the general exercise of power within society. Social theory should now invent new narratives as part of the field of symbolism which now saturates our lives. Groups can then draw upon these: 'in order to define themselves, their social situation, and their possible future' (Seidman 1994a: 130). The ghosts of Descartes, Kant, Hume and Hegel are finally put to rest:

> Today, knowledge – scientific, Western reasons – bears the scars of its many wars. Its dreams are tattered and its confidence irrevocably shaken. In generations past, science and Western reason triumphed grandly by means of a relentless assault on its competitors: religion, myth, narrative, moral philosophy, folk knowledge. Today, it is as if those repressed rivals have returned to take their revenge.
>
> (Seidman 1994b: 327)

Issues in postmodern social theory

To say that postmodernism has met with criticism, as well as embrace, would be an understatement. Critiques have been brought to bear on its presuppo-sitions, insights and consequences for the study of social life (Callinicos 1990;

Harvey 1990; Heller and Fehér 1991; Jameson 1992; Norris 1996; O'Neill 1995). In this section I wish to draw your attention to two issues which are not mutually exclusive. First, whether our current age may be characterized as postmodern, and second, if it does exist, whether its analysis requires a postmodern social theory.

Postmodernism is argued to be a cultural phenomenon. To this extent, in reaction to the ideas associated with social, political and economic conditions as being in some way determinant, it serves as a corrective. However, this has been over-extended in the hands of those cultural theorists for whom the consumption of signs is assumed to be separate from the conditions and relations under which this takes place. In this sense, postmodernism can be read, in its celebration of the fragmentation of the self and social structure, as a form of cultural imperialism.

A number of commentators have noted that this new conservatism heralds an age in which self-consciousness, reflexivity, self-realization – characteristics of the age of modernity – are now part of the reaction of an intelligentsia to the failure of the revolutionary hopes of the late 1960s. Adherents of postmodernism are the very people who have 'turned their backs' on the potential for human emancipation (Callinicos 1990). The idea of a collapse between low and high culture, in a whirlpool of self-referential models of signification, should therefore be resisted in order to maintain a vision. Baudrillard's pronouncements on the death of the social should be subjected to critical scrutiny in order that the postmodernization thesis becomes a topic, not an assumption.

With this in mind, the picture changes. In the process, commodification and reification remain as real today as they have always been. The only difference is that the aesthetic dimension is now utilized in the service of commodity production (Jameson 1992). Postmodernism comes to represent a celebration of the 'freedom to consume' which is nothing more than a sophisticated excuse for the excesses of capitalism. Culture becomes a mask behind which 'old' forces still haunt the social landscape:

> The street scenes of impoverishment, disempowerment, graffiti and decay become grist for the cultural producers' mill, not . . . in the muckraking reformist style of the late nineteenth century, but as a quaint and swirling backdrop (as in *Blade Runner*) upon which no social commentary is to be made. Once the poor become aestheticized, poverty itself moves out of our field of social vision, except as a passive depiction of otherness, alienation and contingency within the human condition.
>
> (Harvey 1990: 336–337, original italics)

For Lyotard, this notion of contingency is placed in postmodern discourse as the celebration of actuality. It is then contrasted with the apparent violence of abstraction reeked by meta-narratives. In Baudrillard's glances into the state of excess, he celebrates the 'masses' recognition of the condition of post-modernity. What form does this take? It is to give ourselves over to fasci-nation and ecstasy in acts of indifference. Indifference is resistance. Again, this is contrasted with the 'intellectuals' strategy who shout in their deserts of nostalgia for the return of a bygone era. In the cultural playground called postmodernism, critics can play with symbolism in the recognition that they have a fatal attraction. The resources for these critiques thus exist in semio-logical minefields. From what place, therefore, can postmodernists claim to speak with any authority?

This issue here may be traced back to Chapter 2. Three of the traditions considered there – hermeneutics, phenomenology and pragmatism – placed in everyday action, speech and forms of life an epistemological status. With the postmodernist abandonment of those insights comes also the absence of a place for everyday practices. They are now consumed by vast impersonal forces. This strategy of rejection should come as no surprise given that the ghost of Nietzsche dances in the lines of their texts. It was Nietzsche who di-rected the attention of his disciples to the extraordinary. However, the result is that 'they contemptuously glide over the practice of everyday life as some-thing derivative or inauthentic' (Habermas 1992a: 339). With the 'edifice of culture' masking everything: 'These lives do not matter – the text does not invite the reader to share their living, nor their dying' (Billig 1994: 164).

Habermas is concerned with the link between theory and practice. This is severed by postmodernist discourses in the assumption that the lifeworld has now disappeared (Baudrillard), or that the heterogeneity of language games necessarily implies a denial of the universal properties of validity claims in speech (Lyotard). On the other hand, we might give some analytic mileage to its arguments in relation to everyday life and cultural consumption. Never-theless, it would be the object of our analysis that changes, not the means of analysis. This strategy entails a qualified acceptance of some of its insights regarding consumer society (Featherstone 1991):

> As far as this strategy is concerned, what matters is that the society (its object) has changed; it does not necessarily admit that its now earlier pursuits were misguided and wasted, and that the crucial novelty in the situation is the dismissal of the old ways of doing sociology and 'dis-covery' of new ways of doing it. Thus to describe a sociology pursuing the strategy under discussion one would speak, say, of a 'post-full-employment' sociology, or a 'sociology of the consumer society', rather than of a 'post-Wittgensteinian' or 'post-Gadamerian' sociology. In other words, this strategy points towards a sociology of postmodernity, rather than a postmodern sociology.
>
> (Bauman 1992: 111)

It is not necessary, as those not always familiar with the history of social theory appear to do, to embrace postmodern social theory as the necessary corollary to postmodernity. Both Harvey and Jameson accept that, to some degree, qualitative changes have taken place in Western societies; although both retain more of a Marxist spirit in their writings than this strategy might imply. From this point of view we can read Baudrillard as one who directs our attention to the ways in which the realities of production are increasingly informed by symbolism. This does not mean accepting the destruction of the lifeworld where anger against injustices remain, together with the desire for change (Best 1994).

We are now in a position to consider the ways in which abstract systems are becoming an increasing part of our everyday lives. In the age of globalization we do not have to follow a path forged by Lyotard (Spybey 1995). Instead, we are recognizing that 'the geo-historicization of social theory is long overdue' (Bhaskar 1993: 146). As Giddens puts it in his analysis of what he calls the state of 'high modernity':

> The globalising tendencies of modernity are simultaneously extensional and intensional – they connect individuals to large-scale systems as part of complex dialectics of change at both local and global poles. . . . Yet this is *not* primarily an expression of cultural fragmentation or of the dissolution of the subject into a 'world of signs' with no centre. It is a process of the simultaneous transformation of subjectivity and global social organisation, against a troubling backdrop of high-consequence risks.
>
> (Giddens 1990: 177, original italics)

Earlier tendencies within modernity are now seen to reach their height and spread through to all parts of social life. The postmodern pill is broken up and only partly swallowed. The transition is not from modern to postmodern societies, but from 'classical' to 'reflexive modernization' or, to express it another way, from 'industrial' to 'risk' societies. This is the place where systems theory meets a 'green consciousness'. Wealth production, distribution and its consequences – the concerns of Marx and Weber – meet a new paradigm, for we are now more aware of those processes which Weber analysed and found only humanity's fate:

> We are therefore concerned no longer exclusively with making nature useful, or with releasing mankind from traditional constraints, but also and essentially with problems resulting from techno-economic development itself. Modernization is becoming *reflexive*; it is becoming its own theme.
>
> (Beck 1992: 19, original italics)

The gloom of postmodernism is replaced by the potential that comes with 'reflexive modernization'. Here, the critical gaze is increasingly turned towards those systems which were once legitimized, but are now undergoing transformation (Beck, Giddens and Lash 1994). With the collapse of abstract systems into daily life comes an increasing awareness of the dual-nature of the forward march of modernity: for example, both empowerment and power-lessness; the fragmentation of identity, together with the possibilities that are created for new identities and the need to act globally, as well as locally (Giddens 1990). In this sense, there is a process of increasing politicization within everyday life as manifested in the growth of new social movements.

We now turn our gaze upon 'disorganized capitalism' (Offe 1985), whose characteristics include those environmental risks which have no sense of national boundaries (Lash and Urry 1994: 323). However, although this is a time in which the reduced potential for co-ordination amongst systems of regulation provides for innovations within the lifeworld, it also has another side in case this sounds too voluntaristic. Baudrillard may be right about the increasing penetration of the cultural into everyday life, but his basis for resistance in consumer society is wrong, for it

> is in fact more often that not its principle of *domination*. That is, that domination in the semiotics of contemporary everyday life is not through the attachment of signifieds, of meanings to images by culture producers, but by the particular strategies of dominant social groups to *refuse* to attach any meanings to such images. That is, the implosion of meaning, subjectivity and the real world or the social is not primarily a way for Baudrillard's 'silent majorities' to resist domination, but instead a way that 'masses' are indeed dominated.
>
> (Lash and Urry 1987: 290, original italics)

The organized and the disorganized thereby coexist and the potential for new ways of life and the development of understanding exists alongside new forms of domination.

Summary

The idea of postmodernization as an epoch and postmodernism as a cultural movement, which includes social theory, has been an attractive one; judging, that is, by the numerous texts that have appeared on the subject. Whether by charting this journey through Baudrillard's modification, critique and subsequent abandonment of the Marxist tradition, or via Lyotard's infor-mation society and the heterogeneity of language games, the message to the modernists has been clear: abandon your dreams. The postmodern condition now celebrates chaos and fragmentation.

The reaction to this state of affairs is often either full embrace or total refutation. However, a third way has been suggested whereby some of the insights are taken to be indicative of real historical trends. From this point of view, we should see Baudrillard as a kind of sounding board against which social theory might be tested. Indeed, he notes that his writings contain 'an element of provocation. . . . It is a sort of challenge to the intellectual and the reader that starts a kind of game' (Baudrillard in Gane 1993: 153–154). Perhaps this, in part, explains why he has refused the label 'postmodernist' (Gane 1990). At the same time, Lyotard's call for the invention of new narratives sounds like a familiar call for resistance in the face of increased commodity fetishism. In this sense, it may be more constructive to see postmodernists as calling upon social theory to awake from any dogmatic slumbers that it may still possess.

Postmodernist writings appear to pick up on the ambivalence that was evident in the works of Simmel and Weber and take it in the direction of fatalism. Another route is available. This is not the route of the assumed complacency of the modernist but, on the contrary, taking the effects of high modernity and applying them to our current malaise. The assumed collapse of the cultural into the social is then tempered, as is the collapse of the aesthetic into the ethical realm whereby moral judgements are simply seen as matters of taste. This strategy is not complacent for it seeks to know and understand the negative, whilst also seeing the potential in new moral discourses that have emerged within lifeworlds in recent times.

Looking back and looking forward

In this final chapter, I wish to do two things. First, to reflect on our journey. Second, to note how social theory is part of the conditions under which it is produced. To that extent, it has to be situated to be understood. In this way it gains its relevance and power of insight by reflecting upon the issues that inform the social milieu of which it is a part. In the process of this discussion, parallels will be drawn between our current age and the end of the nineteenth century.

We started our journey with a brief examination of the work of Descartes, Kant and Hume, for reasons that I drew attention to in subsequent discussions. This discussion also serves to demonstrate the argument that the validation of science, in general, often proceeds to a large degree on grounds informed by philosophical discourse. Take, for example, ideas concerning the capacities and limits of reason. These translated into a series of methodological and theoretical proposals that provided for an examination of the social world. In one direction this was to travel towards an attitude of complacency. This was either represented by assumptions regarding the object world and/or the intrinsic validity of the instruments which are used for its measurement. Its ultimate expression is found within the positivist tradition.

At the same time, we found history becoming of central importance in the study of social life. For Vico, Hume and others, people were viewed as social creatures, not metaphysical entities. Here was a tension between the idea of the autonomous individual 'will' based on reason and the historically situated nature of human activities. These issues, together with the practical/political questions which social theorists faced in their social contexts, provided for a rich history of social thought.

With this background in mind, it was Marx, taking up and criticizing Hegel's historicist critique of Kant, who questioned reason, unmasked it, grounded it materially and then offered a way out of the increased commodification that governs daily life under capitalism. Human potentiality was ultimately stifled by capitalism. Durkheim then socialized reason, located it within the societies of which people were a part and then formulated the idea of moral individualism. This became a prerequisite for social solidarity in the face of the changes he was witnessing in the France of his time. Weber was then to analyse the unintended effects of a particular form of rationality, despite the intentions that provided for its genesis. He then left us in its wake, accompanied by the injunction to act responsibly. In the process, all of them illuminated tensions which, to this day, exist within societies.

Our journey of modification, critique and illumination then continued into the twentieth century. The importance of studying the interpretative lifeworld emerged in the writings of phenomenology, hermeneutics and pragmatism. Whilst possessing differences, a new epistemological self-assurance for the social sciences emerged in the works of both Dilthey and Husserl. Mead and the pragmatists, on the other hand, were to travel in a more anti-Cartesian direction. It was they who provided the conditions for a tradition of sociological thought in which the self and the lifeworld were inseparable. This clearly challenged the ideologically predominant idea of possessive individualism, for the self and community become part of the same, not opposite sides, of the coin.

The analytic power of these approaches came from their prioritization of the lifeworld of meanings, interactions, values and beliefs. It was the future of this world of meaning about which Weber's more Nietzschean-inspired writings were fatalistic. Marx, on the other hand, retained an optimism in terms of *praxis*, whilst Durkheim's holistic structuralism had not focused upon this in any depth given his preoccupations with social solidarity. Yet these were the very attributes of social life which one has to take seriously if wishing to explain why it is that Marx's predictions about the future of capitalism had not come to fruition.

The intellectual armoury for this endeavour did not come from the lifeworld sociologies, for they were seen to reproduce that which was distorted in the first instance. Instead, it was to come from Freud whose work represented yet another critique of the Cartesian tradition. A fusion of the structures of the mind with the process of socialization under capitalism provided for a powerful critique. Nevertheless, whilst the Frankfurt theorists granted Hegelian historicism a place in its formulations, this was not the case when it came to a form of Marxism within the tradition of French structuralism.

Within structuralism the actions of the individual and the role of the historical in social life were both down-played. Saussure held the structure of language to be predominant over its utterances by individuals, whilst Lévi-Strauss was to find in his study of myths, universal features of the human mind. A Marxist expression of this tradition was apparent in the work of Althusser, for whom structures were ideological state apparatuses that provided for self-conceptions, as well as governing relations in general. Returning to Marx and Engels's idea of economic structures as determinant 'in the last instance', he linked psychoanalysis and Marxism in a manner that was assumed to rescue its scientific promise.

We then found Talcott Parsons who, as with Lévi-Strauss, operated within a neo-Kantian framework. Nevertheless, in employing the ideas of Freud, Weber, Durkheim and Pareto, he was more interested in the formulation of a theory of action that linked people to the society of which they were a part. As with Durkheim, he could not conceive of how society would be possible on the basis of utilitarian concepts of action. Moving from this earlier formulation to a theory of interaction within a society of functionally interrelated systems, he provided a model of society which many were to find attractive, despite their criticisms of the absence of an analysis of the lifeworld in his formulations.

Running alongside these developments, women were constructing ideas from the margins of their societies. They had been placed there by a series of unexamined presuppositions and biases within society that social theory itself had drawn upon. Arguing that the role of reason has been attributed along gender lines provided, once again, for the social tempering of what is so often conceived of as an individualistic concept enacted within some kind of social vacuum. These critiques provided the basis for a recovery of women's voices from history.

Armed with this history, the theme with which I proceeded through the book was the conceptualization of the relationship between action and structure against the backdrop of modernity. Our first port of call was then pragmatism and its translation into social theory. The placing of the development of the self within social relations in terms of a dialectical relationship between subject and object was Mead's great achievement. This refusal to countenance a subject–object dualism, however, was thought to be lost in the hands of Blumer. A subjectivist interpretation of Mead, via the attribution of meanings to a social world on the part of the subject, then led to differences within the development of symbolic interactionism.

At this point it was Goffman, influenced by a number of different traditions, who was to situate the self firmly within the lifeworld. His fusion of intentionality, performance and role theory provided the grounds for a fascinating examination of social life within the dramaturgical tradition of social thought. In addition, Goffman recognized the role of power in social life and the constraining nature of the role in relation to its performance. In our journey these aspects in his work were to lead us in two different directions. First, to an examination of the lifeworld through a fusion of

Schutz and linguistic philosophy and second, to a critique of the action–structure dualism in social thought.

Garfinkel knocked rationality from its transcendental status and viewed it as an ongoing accomplishment within the lifeworld. Issues of ontology and epistemology were then constituted as problems with methodological solutions. Nevertheless, having situated it, he and his followers then wavered between relativism and generalization in their desire to find rules of social interaction. This led to a split within this tradition between those who wished to retain the role of meaning within the lifeworld and those who, in the spirit of a new scientism, resorted to conversational analysis. Criticisms of variants of ethnomethodology were then considered in terms of an abandonment of its radical critique of social science through the fusion of endogenous and exogenous reflexivity. Furthermore, in abandoning a hermeneutic dimension to their inquiries, an ontology of the lifeworld was missing from their considerations. Paradoxically, parallels then became evident with structuralism.

Despite these and other criticisms of ethnomethodology, it provided for an important part of the investigation of social life which other socio-theoretical traditions had often overlooked. This much was recognized by Giddens. It is he who employed its insights to construct an ontologically based social theory in which history was not bracketed. History, structure, action and power fuse in the process of an argument that action implies structure and structure implies action. This necessitated yet another critique of Cartesianism, but did not imply a structuralist dissolving of the subject. Issues concerning this hermeneutically inspired social theory, however, revolved around whether social life was actually a dualism between action and structure, rather than a duality. To illuminate this important question, the next chapter was devoted to the ideas of a leading social scientist.

Bourdieu's 'genetic structuralism' represented a rich fusion of ideas, but those gained in the light of a very different history to that of Giddens. With existentialism, phenomenology and structuralism informing the terrain of post-1945 French social thought, Bourdieu formulated an ontological basis for his ideas, but without a refusal to engage in epistemological considerations. In the process, history and social location were examined alongside the strategies of agents in terms of the types of power that inform social relations. We were then left with an understanding of how and why certain types of capital are acquired via human agency, as well as allowing for the concept of ontological security in the matching of habitus to place. However, we found that the role of reason in social life appeared to be left in the wake of the idea that all actions were strategically oriented. Habermas then entered the terrain of modern social theory.

We found Habermas aiming to recover the critical capacities of reason. In so doing, he argued that those such as Marx, the Frankfurt theorists and Weber, amongst others, had built their ideas upon a subject–object dualism.

For those with a critical intent to their writings, this could not be sustained. Instead, what was required was a recovery of the promise of reason from within the linguistic lifeworld itself. For this purpose he constructed an elaborate and highly complicated evolutionary theory of the lifeworld, together with its increasing disjuncture in the unfolding of modernity, from the steering systems of money and power. Social life was then characterized as a dualism, with modernity being an incomplete project, not one in terminal decline.

One of the issues which emerged in our discussions at this point was whether Habermas's use of systems theory was not actually undermining his project. Power, for example, exists within the lifeworld, not simply systems. Here, as throughout our journey, feminist social theory had much to offer. In the case of conceptions of both action and systems, their gendered nature was an important matter. The basis for such a project, however, was often the idea of 'woman'. As a foundation for critique and positive change, the issues of essentialism and determinism were of central importance. Given this, some feminist theorists then found their inspiration in the subjects of our next two chapters.

Michel Foucault's situating of the self within discourses of power and knowledge, provided for conceptions of both the subject and the object. This stood as a highly distinct conceptualization of the action–structure relationship. Foucault's grasp of the history of ideas, combined with his historical excavations, gave us a new perspective on the subject. History makes us what we are. However, when it came to opportunities for positive change, Foucault was silent. Yet his works were also said to provide the basis for critical reflection after the apparent death of Cartesianism; this characteristic could not be so easily applied to the subject of our next chapter.

Postmodernism celebrated the absence of reason within current times and represented an intellectual justification for the end of history. In its denouncements of subject-centred reason, it was said to celebrate difference and diversity and reason itself was held to be totalitarian. The world had become a vortex of symbolism in which the subject was decentred and absorbed into an orgy of consumption. For Baudrillard, indifference then became critique and the weapons of the modernists were turned against themselves. Everything was culture. However, as Bourdieu noted, few ask questions about the conditions under which they are able to pursue their own interests. If postmodernism was reflexive, it was highly limited given that the lifeworld was held to have dissolved into the clutches of culture. Poverty became that which was represented in the cinema. Baudrillard was thus found to work at the extremes of an indulgent commodity fetishism. Whilst refusing the nostalgia of the modernists, it was perhaps for this reason that he did not wish to claim the label 'postmodernist'.

This journey has not been one of progressive linearity. This is often a matter of surprise to those who look to social theory for simple answers and find only a series of questions, often accompanied by a challenge to their assumptions. Once historical flux, as a series of progressions and setbacks, is recognized, social theory will reflect this state of affairs. If its relevance and power of insight is to be maintained, it cannot fix social relations via synchronic representation. It has to be vibrant, it cannot be complacent. It seeks not only to reflect upon the conditions under which social actions take place and their dynamics, but also to transform our understandings of those processes. Without this feature to its practice, we run the risk of complacency in the particularities of our worldviews.

Social theory is a discourse in which ideas and events meet and shape one another. It is for this reason that the arguments of those such as the postmodernists cannot be lightly dismissed. To one degree or another, they represent a call for change which may be derived from changing social landscapes. Here, however, we must make a distinction between the anti-moderns, who simply reverse all that the moderns take-for-granted and in so doing accept their premises and the postmoderns. It is the post-modernists who have picked up on the contradictions inherent in modernity, but then refused the modernists' tools in finding a way out.

From this perspective comes the idea that our world is characterized by an incommensurability of viewpoints. In the face of this we need a clarifying and critical social theory. Clarification takes place through an examination of the presuppositions which are imbedded in particular world views. In the practical-political world, the debates we have considered within social theory are constantly fixed by power relations. In one of my own fields of interest – management and organizations – there are texts which sell hundreds of thousands of copies on topics such as 'quality', 'culture' and 'excellence'. These are sold to those who wish to regain what they think they have, or might, lose: control and profitability. These texts contain presuppositions regarding human actions, motivations, beliefs and values. Their world appears as a complicated place, but one ultimately open to manipulation. Here are the theoretical texts whose claim is to be practical.

The success of these books may be explained by what Weber called 'elective affinity'. We may consider this in terms of the relationship between ideas and interests. In examining such processes, the critical component of social theory comes into play. This has the potential to act as a corrective to the ways in which power is masked behind the screen of what is so often referred to as 'practicality' or the necessities of the 'real world'. Critical social theory can then provide us with new ways of understanding our relations between one another. In terms of our present era, this search has borne witness, once again, to the breaking down of the barriers between science and philosophy. When it comes to the world of theoretical discourse, substantive sociological theory is now argued to have given way to a philosophically preoccupied social theory (Mouzelis 1991). The call is now heard for a return to more 'applied' endeavours, accompanied by suggestions as to how this might proceed (Hage 1994; Mouzelis 1995).

The problem with this debate is that these are not mutually exclusive endeavours. A social theory which develops concepts which are amenable to empirical illuminations is an essential part of the practice of the social sciences. The reasons why gaps have appeared between what we might term empirically oriented and critical-reconstructive social theories is because of the changing times through which we are living. We are seeking not only to illuminate these changes, for which empirical work is indispensable, but also to reach back into the history of social thought to ask if the presuppositions upon which practices are based are still relevant to modern times.

Conflicts such as these were evident in the works of Marx, Durkheim and Weber. Weber's methodology, for example, called for a grounding in the subjective meanings that people attach to their social relations. Yet in his historical writings he was fatalistic about the future of that very sphere of human meaning in the unfolding of modernity. This tension was so beautifully captured in his concepts of substantive and formal rationality. However, these are not simply 'theoretical' ideas, for in the clash between these elements in our current age we can hear the call for freedom.

We have found on our journey that freedom is not simply something which inheres in the 'individual'. In the process of conceptualizing issues such as these, the idea of the individual cannot be held to be separate from the social world of which it is a part. This is not because it is the latest trend in an enclosed universe of theoretical discourse, but because the struggles for new identities and ways of life are a part of our contemporary landscapes. In this sense, Foucault's idea of the agonism between power and freedom hits its mark. As Jon Simons writes of Foucault's ideas in relation to contemporary politics:

> Politics that centres on the identities of social groups converges with issues such as the feminization of poverty and ethnic inequalities. Nor are these by any means merely Western concerns. It is precisely the conjuncture of struggles to control scarce resources with ethnic and national conflicts in Eastern Europe and the former Soviet Union that makes cultural and identity politics all too real.
>
> (J. Simons 1995: 123)

A striving for identity through difference is now a common act. Yet this also provides fertile ground for the seeds of oppression. If one can become something only via a continual contrast with something that one is not, then this seems a probable and perhaps, inevitable, consequence. It is tolerance, not threat, that should be the partner of difference. If we look in this direction, any common grounds upon which we might speak to each other is an essential part of the endeavour. With this in mind, it is the ideas of Habermas which become of central importance. He is concerned, as was Foucault, with what many, in some assumed contrast with the theoretical as somehow indulgent, call 'practical matters'.

Habermas's reconstructive science is abstract. Yet as he notes, we are enabled by this to be sensitive to the ambivalences that characterize our development, whilst he tries, without resorting to a single explanatory framework, to analyse the conditions which are necessary to reach understanding (Habermas 1994: 112). His work, therefore, is part of our changing times:

> One reason why Habermas's work has received so much critical attention is because – despite present fashions – he addresses himself to what many of us still believe, or want to believe: that it is possible to confront honestly the challenges, critiques, the unmasking of illusions; to work through these, and still responsibly reconstruct an informed comprehensive perspective on modernity and its pathologies.
>
> (Bernstein 1985: 25)

It is not only the social sciences, however, which should be reflexive in this manner, but also the natural sciences. In the process, they may come to understand their endeavours in a new light and reconstruct themselves. There are signs that this process is happening. After all, when we approach social theory with this concern in mind, we can see that, for example, both Foucault and Habermas speak to the wishes and struggles of modern times – as had many of their intellectual predecessors. Their differences and the implications of these should, of course, be carefully examined, but it leads us to employ their insights in the service of greater understanding. This is one of the most, if not *the* most, important goals of current times.

Bibliography

Adam, B. (1995) *Timewatch: The Social Analysis of Time*. Cambridge: Polity.

Adorno, T. and Horkheimer, M. (1979) *Dialectic of Enlightenment*. Originally published in 1944. Translated by Cumming, J. London: Verso.

Adorno, T., Frankel-Brunswik, E., Levinson, D. and Sanford, R. (1950) *The Authoritarian Personality*. New York: Harper & Row.

Adorno, T., Albert, H., Dahrendorf, R., Habermas, J., Pilot, H. and Popper, K. R. (1976) *The Positivist Dispute in German Sociology*. Translated by Adey, G. and Frisby, D. London: Heinemann.

Albrow, M. (1987) 'The Application of the Weberian Concept of Rationalization to Contemporary Conditions'. In Lash, S. and Whimster, S. (eds).

Albrow, M. (1990) *Max Weber's Construction of Social Theory*. London: Macmillan.

Alexander, J. C. (1984) 'The Parsons Revival in German Sociology'. *Sociological Theory* 2: 394–412.

Alexander, J. C. (ed.) (1985) *Neofunctionalism*. Beverly Hills, Calif. and London: Sage.

Alexander, J. C. (1990) 'The Centrality of the Classics'. In Giddens, A. and Turner, J. (eds).

Alexander, J. C. (1991) 'Habermas and Critical Theory: Beyond the Marxian Dilemma?' In Honneth, A. and Joas, H. (eds).

Alexander, J. C. (1995) *Fin de Siècle Social Theory: Relativism, Reduction and the Problem of Reason*. London: Verso.

Almquist, E. M. (1979) 'Black Women and the Pursuit of Equality'. In Freeman, J. (ed.).

Althusser, L. (1969) *For Marx*. Translated by Brewster, B. Harmondsworth: Penguin.

Anderson, R., Hughes, J. and Sharrock, W. (1986) *Philosophy and the Human Sciences*. London: Routledge.

Archer, M. S. (1989) *Culture and Agency: The Place of Culture in Social Theory*. Cambridge: Cambridge University Press.

Archer, M. S. (1990) 'Human Agency and Social Structure: A Critique of Giddens'. In Clark, J., Modgil, C. and Modgil, S. (eds).

Armstrong, T. J. (ed.) (1992) *Michel Foucault: Philosopher*. Translated by Armstrong, T. J. London: Harvester Wheatsheaf.

Aronowitz, S. (1992) 'The Tensions of Critical Theory: Is Negative Dialectics All There Is?' In Seidman, S. and Wagner, D. (eds).

Assister, A. (1983) 'Did Man Make Language?' *Radical Philosophy* 34: 25–29.

Atkinson, J. M. (1978) *Discovering Suicide: Studies in the Social Organisation of Sudden Death*. London: Macmillan.

Atkinson, J. M. and Heritage, J. C. (eds) (1984) *Structures of Social Action: Studies in Conversation Analysis*. Cambridge: Cambridge University Press.

Atkinson, P. (1988) 'Ethnomethodology: A Critical Review'. *Annual Review of Sociology* 14: 441–465.

Austin, J. (1976) *How to Do Things with Words*. Oxford: Oxford University Press.

Barber, W. J. (1981) *A History of Economic Thought*. Harmondsworth: Penguin.

Barrett, M. (1988) *Women's Oppression Today: The Marxist/Feminist Encounter*. Revised edn. London: Verso.

Barrett, M. and Phillips, A. (eds) (1992) *Destabilizing Theory: Contemporary Feminist Debates*. Cambridge: Polity.

Baudrillard, J. (1981) *For a Critique of the Political Economy of the Sign*. Originally published in 1972. St Louis, Miss.: Telos.

Baudrillard, J. (1983) *Simulations*. New York: Semiotext(e).

Baudrillard, J. (1993) 'Hyperreal America'. Translated by Macey, D. *Economy and Society* 22(2): 243–252.

Bauman, Z. (1978) *Hermeneutics and Social Science: Approaches to Understanding*. London: Hutchinson.

Bauman, Z. (1987) *Legislators and Interpreters: On Modernity, Post-Modernity and Intellectuals*. Cambridge: Polity.

Bauman, Z. (1989) *Modernity and the Holocaust*. Cambridge: Polity.

Bauman, Z. (1991) *Modernity and Ambivalence*. Cambridge: Polity.

Bauman, Z. (1992) *Intimations of Postmodernity*. London: Routledge.

Beck, U. (1992) *Risk Society: Towards a New Modernity*. London: Sage.

Beck, U., Giddens, A. and Lash, S. (1994) *Reflexive Modernization: Politics, Tradition and Aesthetics in the Modern Social Order*. Cambridge: Polity.

Becker, H. (1963) *Outsiders: Studies in the Sociology of Deviance*. New York: Free Press.

Beechey, V. (1986) 'Women and Employment in Contemporary Britain'. In Beechey, V. and Whitelegg, E. (eds).

Beechey, V. and Whitelegg, E. (eds) (1986) *Women in Britain Today*. Milton Keynes: Open University Press.

Beetham, D. (1974) *Max Weber and the Theory of Modern Politics*. London: Allen & Unwin.

Bell, D. (1960) *The End of Idelogy*. New York: Collier.

Beloff, M. (1954) *The Age of Absolutism: 1660–1815*. London: Hutchinson.

Bendix, R. (1977) *Max Weber: An Intellectual Portrait*. Berkeley, Calif.: University of California Press.

Benhabib, S. (1992) *Situating the Self: Gender, Community and Postmodernism in Contemporary Ethics*. Cambridge: Polity.

Benjamin, A. (ed.) (1991) *The Problems of Modernity: Adorno and Benjamin*. London: Routledge.

Benson, D. (1974) 'Critical Note: A Revolution in Sociology'. *Sociology* 8: 125–129.

Benton, T. (1977) *Philosophical Foundations of the Three Sociologies*. London: Routledge & Kegan Paul.

Berger, P. L. and Luckmann, T. (1967) *The Social Construction of Reality: A Treatise in the Sociology of Knowledge*. New York: Anchor.

Berman, M. (1988) *All That is Solid Melts into Air: The Experience of Modernity*. 2nd edn. London: Verso.

Berman, M. (1993) 'Why Modernism Still Matters'. In Lash, S. and Friedman, J. (eds).

Bernauer, J. and Rasmussen, D. (eds) (1991) *The Final Foucault*. Cambridge, Mass.: MIT Press.

Bernstein, R. (1983) *Beyond Objectivism and Relativism: Science, Hermeneutics and Praxis*. Oxford: Basil Blackwell.

Bernstein, R. (1985a) 'Introduction'. In Bernstein, R. (ed.).

Bernstein, R. (ed.) (1985b) *Habermas and Modernity*. Cambridge: Polity.

Bershady, H. J. (1991) 'Practice against Theory in American Sociology: An Exercise in the Sociology of Knowledge'. In Robertson, R. and Turner, B. S. (eds)

Best, S. (1994) 'The Commodification of Reality and the Reality of Commodification: Baudrillard, Debord, and Postmodern Theory'. In Kellner, D. (ed.).

Bhaskar, R. (1993) *Dialectic: The Pulse of Freedom*. London: Verso.

Bierstedt, R. (1979) 'Sociological Thought in the Eighteenth Century'. In Bottomore, T. and Nisbet, R. (eds).

Billig, M. (1994) 'Sod Baudrillard! Or Ideology Critique in Disney World'. In Simons, H. W. and Billig, M. (eds).

Bittner, E. (1974) 'The Concept of Organization'. Originally published in 1965. Reprinted in Turner, R. (ed.).

Blackman, H. J. (ed.) (1967) *Objections to Humanism*. Harmondsworth: Penguin.

Blackman, H. J. (1968) *Humanism*. Harmondsworth: Penguin.

Bloor, D. (1983) *Wittgenstein: A Social Theory of Knowledge*. London: Macmillan.

Blumer, H. (1937) 'Social Psychology'. In Schmidt, E. P. (ed.).

Blumer, H. (1969) *Symbolic Interactionism: Perspective and Method*. Englewood Cliffs, NJ: Prentice-Hall.

Blumer, H. (1972) 'Society as Symbolic Interaction'. In Rose, A. (ed.).

Blumer, H. (1983) 'Going Astray with a Logical Scheme'. Reprinted in Plummer, K. (ed.) (1991a).

Boden, D. and Zimmerman, D. H. (eds) (1993) *Talk and Social Structure: Studies in Ethnomethodology and Conversation Analysis*. Cambridge: Polity.

Bosanquet, T. (1967) 'Auguste Comte and the Positive Philosophers'. In Hearnshaw, F. J. C. (ed.).

Bottomore, T. (1979) 'Marxism and Sociology'. In Bottomore, T. and Nisbet, R. (eds).

Bottomore, T. and Nisbet, R. (1979a) 'Structuralism'. In Bottomore, T. and Nisbet, R. (eds).

Bottomore, T. and Nisbet, R. (eds) (1979b) *A History of Sociological Analysis*. London: Heinemann.

Bourdieu, P. (1962) *The Algerians*. Boston, Mass.: Beacon.

Bourdieu, P. (1977) *Outline of a Theory of Practice*. Translated by Nice, R. Cambridge: Cambridge University Press.

Bourdieu, P. (1981) 'Men and Machines'. In Knorr-Cetina, K. and Cicourel, A. (eds).

Bourdieu, P. (1984) *Distinction: A Social Critique of the Judgement of Taste*. Translated by Nice, R. London: Routledge & Kegan Paul.

Bourdieu, P. (1988) *Homo Academicus*. Translated by Collier, P. Cambridge: Polity.

Bourdieu, P. (1989) 'Social Space and Symbolic Power'. *Sociological Theory* 7(1): 14–25.

Bourdieu, P. (1990) *In Other Words: Essays Towards a Reflexive Sociology*. Translated by Adamson, M. Cambridge: Polity.

Bourdieu, P. (1991a) 'Meanwhile, I Have Come to Know All the Diseases of Sociological Understanding: An Interview'. Conducted by Krais, B. In Bourdieu, P., Chamboredon, J.-C. and Passeron, J.-C.

Bourdieu, P. (1991b) *The Political Ontology of Martin Heidegger*. Translated by Collier, P. Cambridge: Polity.

Bourdieu, P. (1992a) *The Logic of Practice*. Translated by Nice, R. Originally published in 1980 as *Le Sens pratique*. Cambridge: Polity.

Bourdieu, P. (1992b) *Language and Symbolic Power*. Edited and introduced by Thompson, J. B. Translated by Raymond, G. and Adamson, M. Cambridge: Polity.

Bourdieu, P. (1993a) 'Concluding Remarks: For a Sociogenetic Understanding of Intellectual Works'. In Calhoun, C., LiPuma, E. and Postone, M. (eds).

Bourdieu, P. (1993b) *Sociology in Question*. Translated by Nice, R. London: Sage.

Bourdieu, P. (1995) *The Rules of Art: Genesis and Structure of the Literary Field*. Translated by Emanuel, S. Cambridge: Polity.

Bourdieu, P. and Passeron, J.-C. (1990) *Reproduction in Education, Society and Culture*. 2nd edn. London: Sage.

Bourdieu, P., Chamboredon, J.-C. and Passeron, J.-C. (1991) *The Craft of Sociology: Epistemological Preliminaries*. Edited by Krais, B. Translated by Nice, R. New York: Walter de Gruyter.

Bourdieu, P. and Wacquant, L. J. (1992) *An Invitation to Reflexive Sociology*. Cambridge: Polity.

Bourdieu, P, Passeron, J.-C. and de Saint Martin, M., with contributions by Baudelot, C. and Vincent, G. (1994) *Academic Discourse: Linguistic Misunderstanding and Professorial Power*. Translated by Teese, R. Cambridge: Polity.

Boyne, R. (1991) 'Power-Knowledge and Social Theory: The Systematic Misrepresentation of Contemporary French Social Theory in the Work of Anthony Giddens'. In Bryant, C. and Jary, D. (eds).

Brenner, J. and Ramas, M. (1990) 'Rethinking Women's Oppression'. In Lovell, T. (ed.).

Bronner, S. (1994) *Of Critical Theory and its Theorists*. Oxford: Blackwell.

Bronner, S. and Kellner, D. (eds) (1989) *Critical Theory and Society: A Reader*. London: Routledge.

Bronowski, J. and Mazlish, B. (1970) *The Western Intellectual Tradition*. Harmondsworth: Penguin.

Brown, P. and Jordanova, L. J. (1981) 'Oppressive Dichotomies: The Nature/Culture Debate'. In Cambridge Women's Studies Group (eds).

Brubaker, R. (1985) 'Rethinking Classical Theory: The Sociological Vision of Pierre Bourdieu'. *Theory and Society* 14(6): 745–775.

Brunkhorst, H. (1992) 'Culture and Bourgeois Society: The Unity of Reason in a Divided Society'. In Honneth, A., McCarthy, M., Offe, C. and Wellmer, A. (eds) (1992)

Brunt, R. and Rowan, C. (eds) (1982) *Feminism, Culture and Politics*. London: Lawrence & Wishart.

Bryant, C. and Jary, D. (eds) (1991) *Giddens Theory of Structuration: A Critical Appreciation*. London: Routledge.

Bulmer, M. (1984) *The Chicago School of Sociology: Institutionalization, Diversity, and the Rise of Sociological Research*. Chicago: University of Chicago Press.

Burchell, G., Gordon, C. and Miller, P. (eds) (1991) *The Foucault Effect: Studies in Govermentality*. London: Harvester Wheatsheaf.

Burke, K. (1969) *A Grammar of Motives*. Originally published in 1945. Berkeley, Calif.: University of California Press.

Burke, P. (1980) *Sociology and History*. London: Allen & Unwin.

Burns, T. (1992) *Erving Goffman*. London: Routledge.

Button, G. (1991a) 'Introduction: Ethnomethodology and the Foundational Respecification of the Human Sciences'. In Button, G. (ed.).

Button, G. (ed) (1991b) *Ethnomethodology and the Human Sciences*. Cambridge: Cambridge University Press.

Button, G. and Casey, N. (1984) 'Generating Topic: The Use of Topic Initial Elicitors'. In Atkinson, J. M. and Heritage, J. (eds).

Bynner, J. and Stribley, K. (eds) (1979) *Social Research: Principles and Procedures*. Milton Keynes: Open University Press.

Calhoun, C. (ed.) (1994) *Social Theory and the Politics of Identity*. Oxford: Blackwell.

Calhoun, C. (1995) *Critical Social Theory: Culture, History, and the Challenge of Difference*. Oxford: Blackwell.

Calhoun, C., LiPuma, E. and Postone, M. (eds) (1993) *Bourdieu: Critical Perspectives*. Cambridge: Polity.

Callinicos, A. (1990) *Against Postmodernism: A Marxist Critique*. Cambridge: Polity.

Callinicos, A. (1993) 'What is Living and What is Dead in the Philosophy of Althusser?' In Kaplan, E. and Sprinker, M. (eds).

Cambridge Women's Studies Group (eds) (1981) *Women in Society: Interdisciplinary Essays*. London: Virago.

Chappell, V. C. (ed.) (1968) *Hume*. London: Macmillan.

Chodorow, N. J. (1978) *The Reproduction of Mothering: Psychoanalysis and the Sociology of Gender*. Berkeley, Calif.: University of California Press.

Chodorow, N. J. (1986) 'Towards a Relational Individualism: The Mediation of Self through Psychoanalysis'. In Heller, T., Sosna, M. and Wellbery, D. with Davidson, A., Swidler, A. and Watt, I. (eds).

Chomsky, N. (1980) *Rules and Representation*. Oxford: Blackwell.

Cicourel, A. V. (1964) *Method and Measurement in Sociology*. London: Macmillan.

Cicourel, A. V. (1973) *Cognitive Sociology: Language and Meaning in Social Interaction*. Harmondsworth: Penguin.

Cicourel, A. V. (1976) *The Social Organisation of Juvenile Justice*. 2nd edn. London: Heinemann.

Cicourel, A. V. (1981) 'Notes on the Integration of Micro- and Macro-Levels of Analysis'. In Knorr-Cetina, K. and Cicourel, A. (eds).

Cicourel, A. V. (1993) 'Aspects of Structural and Processual Theories of Knowledge'. In Calhoun, C., LiPuma, E. and Postone, M. (eds).

Clammer, J. (1976) 'Wittgensteinianism and the Social Sciences'. *Sociological Review* 24(4): 775–791.

Clark, J., Modgil, C. and Modgil, S. (eds) (1990) *Anthony Giddens: Consensus and Controversy*. Brighton: Falmer.

Clark, S. (1991) 'The *Annales* Historians'. In Skinner, Q. (ed.).

Cleaver, H. (1979) *Reading 'Capital' Politically*. Brighton: Harvester.

Cockburn, C. (1990) 'The Material of Male Power'. In Lovell, T. (ed.).

Cohen, G. A. (1984) *Karl Marx's Theory of History: A Defence*. Oxford: Oxford University Press.

Cohen, I. (1989) *Structuration Theory: Anthony Giddens and the Constitution of Social Life*. London: Macmillan.

Coleman, J. S. (1990) *Foundations of Social Theory*. Cambridge, Mass.: Belknap.

Collins, R. (1981) 'Micro-Translation as a Theory Building Strategy'. In Knorr-Cetina, K. and Cicourel, A. (eds).

Collins, R. (ed.) (1984) *Sociological Theory*. San Francisco: Josey Bass.

Cooke, M. (1994) *Language and Reason: A Study of Habermas's Pragmatics*. Cambridge, Mass.: MIT Press.

Cooley, C. H. (1902) *Human Nature and the Social Order*. New York: Free Press.

Coser, L. (1979) 'American Trends'. In Bottomore, T. and Nisbet, R. (eds).

Coulter, J. (1979) *The Social Construction of Mind: Studies in Ethnomethodology and Linguistic Philosophy*. London: Macmillan.

Coulter, J. (1983) *Rethinking Cognitive Theory*. London: Macmillan.

Coulter, J. (ed.) (1990) *Ethnomethodological Sociology*. Aldershot: Edward Elgar.

Coward, R. (1982) 'Sexual Politics and Psychoanalysis'. In Brunt, R. and Rowan, C. (eds).

Craib, I. (1992) *Anthony Giddens*. London: Routledge.

Crook, S., Pakulski, J. and Waters, M. (1992) *Postmodernization: Change in Advanced Society*. London: Sage.

Crosland, M. (1992) *Simone de Beauvoir: The Woman and her Work*. London: Heinemann.

Crowley, H. and Himmelweit, S. (eds) (1992) *Knowing Women: Feminism and Knowledge*. Cambridge: Polity.

Dahrendorf, R. (1959) *Class and Class Conflict in Industrial Society*. London: Routledge & Kegan Paul.

Davis, K., Leijenaar, M. and Oldersma, J. (eds) (1991) *The Gender of Power*. London: Sage.

Dawe, A. (1970) 'The Two Sociologies'. *British Journal of Sociology*. 21: 207–218.

Dean, M. (1994) *Critical and Effective Histories: Foucault's Methods and Historical Sociology*. London: Routledge.

de Beauvoir, S. (1972) *The Second Sex*. Originally published in 1949. Harmondsworth: Penguin.

de Lauretis, T. (1990) 'Upping the Anti [*sic*] in Feminist Theory'. In Hirsch, M. and Fox Keller, E. (eds).

Delmar, R. (1976) 'Looking Again at Engels' "Origin of the Family, Private Property and the State"'. In Oakley, A. and Mitchell, J. (eds).

Delphy, C. and Leonard, D. (1992) *Familiar Exploitation: A New Analysis of Marriage in Contemporary Western Society*. Cambridge: Polity.

Denzin, N. K. (1974) 'Symbolic Interactionism and Ethnomethodology'. In Douglas, J. D. (ed.).

Denzin, N. K. (1992) *Symbolic Interactionism and Cultural Studies: The Politics of Interpretation*. Oxford: Blackwell.

Derrida, J. (1978) *Writing and Difference*. London: Routledge.

Dewey, J. (1896) 'The Reflexive Arc Concept in Psychology'. *Psychological Review* 3: 357–370.

Dews, P. (1989) 'The Return of the Subject in the Late Foucault'. *Radical Philosophy* 51: 37–41.

Dews, P. (ed.) (1992) *Autonomy and Solidarity: Interviews with Jürgen Habermas*. Revised edn. London: Verso.

Diamond, I. and Quinby, L. (eds) (1988) *Feminism and Foucault: Reflections on Resistance*. Boston, Mass.: Northeastern University Press.

Ditton, J. (ed.) (1980) *The View from Goffman*. London: Macmillan.

Docherty, T. (ed.) (1993) *Postmodernism: A Reader*. London: Harvester Wheatsheaf.

Doney, W. (ed.) (1967) *Descartes: A Collection of Critical Essays*. London: Macmillan.

Dore, R. P. (1973) 'Function and Cause'. In Ryan, A. (ed.).

Douglas, J. D. (ed.) (1974) *Understanding Everyday Life: Towards the Reconstruction of Sociological Knowledge*. London: Routledge & Kegan Paul.

Douglas, M. (1970) *Purity and Danger: An Analysis of the Concepts of Pollution and Taboo*. New York: Pantheon.

Douglas, M. (1978) *Implicit Meanings: Essays in Anthropology*. London: Routledge & Kegan Paul.

Drew, P. and Wootton, A. (eds) (1988) *Erving Goffman: Exploring the Interaction Order*. Cambridge: Polity.

Dreyfus, H. and Rabinow, P. (1982) *Michel Foucault: Beyond Structuralism and Hermeneutics*. Chicago: University of Chicago Press.

Dreyfus, H. and Rabinow, P. (1993) 'Can There be a Science of Existential Structure and Social Meaning?' In Calhoun, C., LiPuma, E. and Postone, M. (eds).

Du Bois, W. (1989) *The Souls of Black Folk*. Originally published in 1903. New York: Bantam.

Durkheim, E. (1964) *The Division of Labour in Society*. Originally published in 1893. Translated by Simpson, G. New York: Free Press.

Durkheim, E. (1983) *Pragmatism and Sociology*. Originally published in 1955. Edited by Allcock, J. B. Translated by Whitehouse, J. C. Cambridge: Cambridge University Press.

Durkheim, E. (1992) 'Review Article on F. S. Merlino's "Formes et essences du socialisme"'. Originally published in 1899. In Gane, M. (ed.).

Dworkin, A. (1987) *Intercourse*. London: Secker & Warburg.

Easthope, A. and McGowan, K. (eds) (1992) *A Critical and Cultural Theory Reader*. Milton Keynes: Open University Press.

Eco, U. (1993) 'The City of Robots'. In Docherty, T. (ed.).

Elders, F. (ed.) (1974) *Reflexive Waters: The Basic Concerns of Mankind*. London: Souvenir.

Elias, N. (1991) *The Symbol Theory*. London: Sage.

Elliott, A. (1992) *Social Theory and Psychoanalysis in Transition: Self and Society from Freud to Kristeva*. Oxford: Blackwell.

Engels, F. (1942) *The Origin of the Family, Private Property and the State*. Originally published in 1884. New York: International Publishers.

Evans, M. (ed.) (1982) *The Woman Question: Readings on the Subordination of Women*. London: Fontana.

Faberman, H. A. (1985) 'The Foundations of Symbolic Interactionism: James, Cooley and Mead'. Reprinted in Plummer, K. (ed.) (1991a).

Fairclough, N. (1989) *Language and Power*. London: Longman.

Farganis, S. (1994) *Situating Feminism: From Thought to Action*. London: Sage.

Featherstone, M. (ed.) (1991) *Consumer Culture and Postmodernism*. London: Sage.

Featherstone, M. and Turner, B. (1995) 'Body and Society: An Introduction'. *Body and Society* 1(1): 1–12.

Figes, E. (1978) *Patriarchal Attitudes: Women in Society*. Originally published in 1970. London: Virago.

Firestone, S. (1988) *The Dialectic of Sex: The Case for Feminist Revolution*. Originally published 1970. London: Women's Press.

Fisher, B. M. and Strauss, A. L. (1978) 'The Chicago Tradition and Social Change: Thomas, Park and their Successors'. Reprinted in Plummer, K. (ed.) (1991a).

Fisher, B. M. and Strauss, A. L. (1979) 'Interactionism'. In Bottomore, T. and Nisbet, R. (eds).

Foucault, M. (1979) *The History of Sexuality, Volume 1: An Introduction*. Translated by Hurley, R. Harmondsworth: Penguin.

Foucault, M. (1980) *Power/Knowledge, Selected Interviews and Other Writings 1972–1977*. Edited by Gordon, C. Brighton: Harvester.

Foucault, M. (1982) 'The Subject and Power'. In Dreyfus, H. and Rabinow, P. (eds).

Foucault, M. (1984) *The Foucault Reader*. Edited by Rabinow, P. Harmondsworth: Penguin.

Foucault, M. (1988a) 'The Political Technology of Individuals'. In Martin, L. H., Gutman, H. and Hutton, P. H. (eds).

Foucault, M. (1988b) 'Technologies of the Self'. In Martin, L. H., Gutman, H. and Hutton, P. H. (eds).

Foucault, M. (1988c) 'Truth, Power, Self: An Interview'. In Martin, L. H., Gutman, H. and Hutton, P. H. (eds).

Foucault, M. (1989) *The Archaeology of Knowledge*. Originally published in 1969. London: Routledge.

Foucault, M. (1991a) *Remarks on Marx: Conversations with Duccio Trombadori*. Translated by Goldstein, R. J. and Cascaito, J. New York: Semiotext(e).

Foucault, M. (1991b) 'The Ethic of Care for the Self as a Practice of Freedom: An interview with Fornet-Betancourt, R., Becker, H. and Gomez-Müller, A. Translated by Gauthier Snr, J. D. In Bernauer, J. and Rasmussen, D. (eds).

Foucault, M. (1991c) 'Questions of Method'. In Burchell, G., Gordon, C. and Miller, P. (eds).

Foucault, M. (1991d) *Discipline and Punish: The Birth of the Prison*. Originally published in 1977. Translated by Sheridan, A. Harmondsworth: Penguin.

Foucault, M. (1992) *The Order of Things: An Archaeology of the Human Sciences*. Originally published in 1970. London: Routledge.

Fraser, N. (1989) *Unruly Practices: Power, Discourse and Gender in Contemporary Social Theory*. Cambridge: Polity.

Freeman, J. (ed.) (1979) *Women: A Feminist Perspective*. 2nd edn. Palo Alto, Calif.: Mayfield.

Freud, S. (1938) *Psychopathology of Everday Life*. Harmondsworth: Penguin.

Freud, S. (1969) *Civilization and its Discontents*. Translated by Riviere, J. Edited by Strachey, J. London: Hogarth.

Freund, J. (1979) 'German Sociology in the Time of Max Weber'. In Bottomore, T. and Nisbet, R. (eds).

Freundlieb, D. (1994) 'Foucault's Theory of Discourse and Human Agency'. In Jones, C. and Porter, R. (eds).

Friedan, B. (1965) *The Feminine Mystique*. Harmondsworth: Penguin.

Frisby, D. (1991) 'The Aesthetics of Modern Life: Simmel's Interpretation'. In Featherstone, M. (ed.).

Frisby, D. (1992a) *Sociological Impressionism: A Reassessment of Georg Simmel's Social Theory*. 2nd edn. London: Routledge.

Frisby, D. (1992b) *Simmel and Since: Essays on Georg Simmel's Social Theory*. London: Routledge.

Fromm, E. (1969) *Escape from Freedom*. Originally published in 1941. New York: Avon.

Gadamer, H. G. (1975) *Truth and Method*. Originally published in 1960. London: Sheed & Ward.

Gane, M. (1990) 'Ironies of Postmodernism: Fate of Baudrillard's Fatalism'. *Economy and Society* 19(3): 314–334.

Gane, M. (1991) *Baudrillard: Critical and Fatal Theory*. London: Routledge.

Gane, M. (ed.) (1992) *The Radical Sociology of Durkheim and Mauss*. London: Routledge.

Gane, M. (ed.) (1993) *Baudrillard Live: Selected Interviews*. London: Routledge.

Garfinkel, H. (1967) *Studies in Ethnomethodology*. Englewood Cliffs, NJ: Prentice-Hall.

Garfinkel, H. (1974) 'The Origins of the Term "Ethnomethodology"'. Originally published in 1968. Reprinted in Turner, R. (ed.).

Garfinkel, H. (ed.) (1986) *Ethnomethodological Studies of Work*. London: Routledge & Kegan Paul.

Garfinkel, H. (1991) 'Respecification: Evidence for Locally Produced, Naturally Accountable Phenomena of Order, Logic, Reason, Meaning, Method, etc. In and as of the Essential Haecceity of Immortal Ordinary Society, (1) – An Announcement of Studies'. In Button, G. (ed.).

Garfinkel, H. and Sacks, H. (1986) 'On Formal Structures of Practical Actions'. In Garfinkel, H. (ed.).

Gartman, D. (1991) 'Culture as Class Symbolization or Mass Reification? A Critique of Bourdieu's *Distinction*'. *American Journal of Sociology* 97(2): 421–447.

Gellner, E. (1968) *Words and Things*. Penguin: Harmondsworth.

Gellner, E. (1974) 'The New Idealism: Cause and Meaning in the Social Sciences'. In Giddens, A. (ed.).

Gellner, E. (1988) *Culture, Identity and Politics*. Cambridge: Cambridge University Press.

Gellner, E. (1992) *Reason and Culture: The Historic Role of Rationality and Rationalism.* Oxford: Blackwell.

Gerth, H. and Mills, C. W. (eds) (1970) *From Max Weber: Essays in Sociology.* Originally published in 1948. London: Routledge & Kegan Paul.

Giddens, A. (1971) *Capitalism and Modern Social Theory: An Analysis of the Writings of Marx, Durkheim and Max Weber.* Cambridge: Cambridge University Press.

Giddens, A. (1972a) *Politics and Sociology in the Thought of Max Weber.* London: Macmillan.

Giddens, A. (ed.) (1972b) *Emile Durkheim: Selected Writings.* Cambridge: Cambridge University Press.

Giddens, A. (ed.) (1974) *Positivism and Sociology.* London: Heinemann.

Giddens, A. (1976) *New Rules of Sociological Method: A Positive Critique of Interpretive Sociologies.* London: Hutchinson.

Giddens, A. (1977) *Studies in Social and Political Theory.* London: Hutchinson.

Giddens, A. (1979) *Central Problems in Social Theory: Action, Structure and Contradiction in Social Analysis.* London: Macmillan.

Giddens, A. (1981a) *A Contemporary Critique of Historical Materialism: Volume 1: Power, Property and the State.* London: Macmillan.

Giddens, A. (1981b) 'Agency, Institution, and Time-Space Analysis'. In Knorr-Cetina, K. and Cicourel, A. (eds).

Giddens, A. (1982) *Profiles and Critiques in Social Theory.* Berkeley, Calif.: University of California Press.

Giddens, A. (1984) *The Constitution of Society: Outline of the Theory of Structuration.* Cambridge: Polity.

Giddens, A. (1985) *The Nation-State and Violence: Volume 2 of A Contemporary Critique of Historical Materialism.* Cambridge: Polity.

Giddens, A. (1987) *Social Theory and Modern Sociology.* Cambridge: Polity.

Giddens, A. (1989) 'A Reply to my Critics'. In Held, D. and Thompson, J. B. (eds).

Giddens, A. (1990) *The Consequences of Modernity.* Cambridge: Polity.

Giddens, A. (1991a) 'Structuration Theory: Past, Present and Future'. In Bryant, C. and Jary, D. (eds).

Giddens, A. (1991b) *Modernity and Self-Identity.* Cambridge: Polity.

Giddens, A. (1992) *The Transformation of Intimacy: Sexuality, Love and Eroticism in Modern Societies.* Cambridge: Polity.

Giddens, A. (1993) *New Rules of Sociological Method: A Positive Critique of Interpretive Sociologies.* 2nd edn. Cambridge: Polity.

Giddens, A. (1994) *Beyond Left and Right: The Future of Radical Politics.* Cambridge: Polity.

Giddens, A. and Turner, J. (eds) (1990) *Social Theory Today.* Cambridge: Polity.

Gjertsen, D. (1992) *Science and Philosophy: Past and Present.* Harmondsworth: Penguin.

Glücksmann, A. (1992) 'Michel Foucault's Nihilism'. In Armstrong, T. (ed.).

Goffman, E. (1961) *Encounters: Two Studies in the Sociology of Interaction.* Harmondsworth: Penguin.

Goffman, E. (1968) *Asylums: Essays on the Social Situation of Mental Patients and Other Inmates.* Originally published in 1961. Harmondsworth: Penguin.

Goffman, E. (1971) *Relations in Public: Microstudies of the Public Order.* Harmondsworth: Penguin.

Goffman, E. (1972) *Interaction Ritual: Essays on Face-to-Face Behaviour.* Harmondsworth: Penguin.

Goffman, E. (1974) *Frame Analysis: An Essay on the Organization of Experience.* New York: Harper & Row.

Goffman, E. (1979) *Gender Advertisements.* London: Macmillan.

Goffman, E. (1981) *Forms of Talk.* Philadelphia, Pa: University of Pennsylvania Press.

Goffman, E. (1983) 'The Interaction Order'. The 1982 American Sociological Association Presidential Address. Reprinted in Plummer, K. (ed.) (1991b).

Goffman, E. (1984) *The Presentation of Self in Everyday Life.* Originally published in 1959. Harmondsworth: Penguin.

Goldthorpe, J. H. (1973) 'A Revolution in Sociology?' *Sociology* 7: 449–462.

Goldthorpe, J. H. and Marshall, G. (1992) 'The Promising Future of Class Analysis'. *Sociology* 26(3): 381–400.

Gordon, C. (1987) 'The Soul of the Citizen: Max Weber and Michel Foucault on Rationality and Government'. In Lash, S. and Whimster, S. (eds).

Gouldner, A. (1971) *The Coming Crisis in Western Sociology.* London: Heinemann.

Gramsci, A. (1971) *Prison Notebooks: Selections.* Translated by Hoare, Q. and Smith, G. N. New York: International Publishers.

Greer, G. (1970) *The Female Eunuch.* London: MacGibbon & Kee.

Gregson, N. (1989) 'On the (Ir)relevance of Structuration Theory to Empirical Research'. In Held, D. and Thompson, J. B. (eds).

Griffiths, M. (1988) 'Feminism, Feelings and Philosophy'. In Griffiths, M. and Whitford, M. (eds).

Griffiths, M. and Whitford, M. (eds) (1988) *Feminist Perspectives in Philosophy.* London: Macmillan.

Grimshaw, J. (1989) 'Mary Wollstonecraft and the Tensions in Feminist Philosophy'. *Radical Philosophy* 52: 11–17.

Gross, E. (1992) 'What is Feminist Theory?' In Crowley, H. and Himmelweit, S. (eds).

Grosz, E. (1990) 'A Note on Essentialism and Difference'. In Gunew, S. (ed.).

Gunew, S. (ed.) (1990) *Feminist Knowledge: Critique and Construct.* London: Routledge.

Habermas, J. (1975) *Legitimation Crisis.* Translated by McCarthy, T. Boston, Mass.: Beacon.

Habermas, J. (1981) 'Towards a Reconstruction of Historical Materialism'. In Knorr-Cetina, K. and Cicourel, A. (eds).

Habermas, J. (1984) *Theory of Communicative Action. Volume 1: Reason and the Rationalization of Society.* Translated by McCarthy, T. London: Heinemann.

Habermas, J. (1986) 'Taking Aim at the Heart of the Present'. In Hoy, D. C. (ed.).

Habermas, J. (1987) *Theory of Communicative Action. Volume 2: Lifeworld and System: A Critique of Functionalist Reason.* Translated by McCarthy, T. Cambridge: Polity.

Habermas, J. (1989a) *Knowledge and Human Interests.* Originally published in 1968. Translated by Shapiro, J. J. Cambridge: Polity.

Habermas, J. (1989b) *The Structural Transformation of the Public Sphere.* Translated by Berger, T. and Lawrence, F. Cambridge, Mass.: MIT Press.

Habermas, J. (1990) *On the Logic of the Social Sciences.* Originally published in 1970. Translated by Nicholsen, S. W. and Stark, J. A. Cambridge: Polity.

Habermas, J. (1991) 'A Reply'. In Honneth, A. and Joas, H. (eds).

Habermas, J. (1992a) *The Philosophical Discourse of Modernity: Twelve Lectures.* Cambridge: Polity.

Habermas, J. (1992b) *Postmetaphysical Thinking: Philosophical Essays.* Translated by Hohengarten, W. M. Cambridge, Mass.: MIT Press.

Habermas, J. (1992c) *Moral Consciousness and Communicative Action.* Translated by Lenhardt, C. and Nicholsen, S. Introduction by McCarthy, T. Cambridge: Polity.

Habermas, J. (1993) *Justification and Application: Remarks on Discourse Ethics.* Translated by Cronin, C. Cambridge: Polity.

Habermas, J. (1994) *The Past as Future.* Interviewed by Haller, M. Translated and edited by Pensky, M. Cambridge: Polity.

Habermas, J. (1996) *Between Facts and Norms: Contributions to a Discourse Theory of Law and Democracy.* Cambridge: Polity.

Hage, J. (ed.) (1994) *Formal Theory in Sociology: Opportunity or Pitfall?* Albany, NY: State University of New York Press.

Hall, P. M. (1987) 'Interactionism and the Study of Social Organization'. Reprinted in Plummer, K. (ed.) (1991b).

Hall, S. and Gieben, B. (eds) (1992) *Formations of Modernity.* Polity Press in association with the Open University. Cambridge: Polity.

Hamilton, P. (1983) *Talcott Parsons.* London: Tavistock.

Hamilton, P. (ed.) (1985) *Readings from Talcott Parsons.* London: Tavistock.

Hamilton, P. (1992) 'The Enlightenment and the Birth of Social Science'. In Hall, S. and Gieben, B. (eds).

Haraway, D. (1991) *Simians, Cyborgs, and Women: The Reinvention of Nature.* New York: Routledge.

Harding, S. (1986) *The Science Question in Feminism.* Milton Keynes: Open University Press.

Harding, S. (1991) *Whose Science? Whose Knowledge? Thinking from Women's Lives.* Milton Keynes: Open University Press.

Harding, S. and Hintikka, M. B. (1983a) 'Introduction'. In Harding, S. and Hintikka, M. B. (eds).

Harding, S. and Hintikka, M. B. (eds) (1983b) *Discovering Reality: Feminist Perspectives on Epistemology, Metaphysics, Methodology, and Philosophy of Science.* London: D. Reidel.

Hartsock, N. (1983) 'The Feminist Standpoint: Developing the Ground for a Specifically Feminist Historical Materialism'. In Harding, S. and Hintikka, M. B. (eds).

Harvey, D. (1990) *The Condition of Postmodernity: An Enquiry into the Origins of Cultural Change.* Oxford: Blackwell.

Hawthorn, G. (1976) *Enlightenment and Despair: A History of Sociology.* Cambridge: Cambridge University Press.

Hearn, J. and Morgan, D. (eds) (1990) *Men, Masculinities and Social Theory.* London: Unwin Hyman.

Hearnshaw, F. J. C. (ed.) (1967) *The Social and Political Ideas of Some Representative Thinkers of the Age of Reaction and Reconstruction: 1815–1865.* Originally published in 1932. London: Dawsons.

Hegel, G. W. F. (1967a) *The Phenomenology of Mind.* Translated by Baillie, J. B. Oxford: Oxford University Press.

Hegel, G. W. F. (1967b) *Hegel's Philosophy of Right*. Translated by Knox, T. M. Oxford: Oxford University Press.

Heilbron, J. (1995) *The Rise of Social Theory*. Translated by Gogol, S. Cambridge: Polity.

Hekman, S. (1990a) 'Hermeneutics and the Crisis of Social Theory: A Critique of Giddens's Epistemology'. In Clark, J., Modgil, C. and Modgil, S. (eds).

Hekman, S. (1990b) *Gender and Knowledge: Elements of a Postmodern Feminism*. Cambridge: Polity.

Held, D. (1990) *Introduction to Critical Theory: Horkheimer to Habermas*. Cambridge: Polity.

Held, D. and Thompson, J. (eds) (1989) *Social Theory of Modern Societies: Anthony Giddens and his Critics*. Cambridge: Cambridge University Press.

Heller, A. (1984) *Everyday Life*. Translated by Campbell, G. London: Routledge & Kegan Paul.

Heller, A. and Fehér, F. (1991) *The Postmodern Political Condition*. Cambridge: Polity.

Heller, T., Sosna, M. and Wellbery, D. with Davidson, A., Swidler, A. and Watt, I. (eds) (1986) *Reconstructing Individualism: Autonomy, Individuality, and the Self in Western Thought*. Stanford, Calif.: Stanford University Press.

Heritage, J. (1984) *Garfinkel and Ethnomethodology*. Cambridge: Polity.

Heritage, J. (1990) 'Ethnomethodology'. In Giddens, A. and Turner, J. (eds).

Hill, R. J. and Stones Crittenden, K. (eds) (1968) 'Proceedings of the Purdue Symposium on Ethnomethodology'. Purdue University: Institute for the Study of Social Change, Department of Sociology.

Hindness, B. (1996) *Discourses of Power: From Hobbes to Foucault*. Oxford: Blackwell.

Hirsch, M. and Fox Keller, E. (eds) (1990) *Conflicts in Feminism*. London: Routledge.

Hole, J. and Levine, E. (1979) 'The First Feminists'. In Freeman, J. (ed.).

Hollingdale, R. J. (ed.) (1977) *A Nietzsche Reader*. Translated by Hollingdale, R. J. Harmondsworth: Penguin.

Hollis, M. and Lukes, S. (eds) (1982) *Rationality and Relativism*. Oxford: Blackwell.

Holton, R. and Turner, B. (1990) *Max Weber on Economy and Society*. London: Routledge.

Holtzman, S. and Leich, C. (eds) (1981) *Wittgenstein: To Follow a Rule*. London: Routledge & Kegan Paul.

Holub, R. C. (1991) *Jürgen Habermas: Critic in the Public Sphere*. London: Routledge.

Homans, G. (1961) *Social Behaviour: Its Elementary Forms*. New York: Harcourt Brace Jovanovich.

Homans, G. (1973) 'Bringing Men Back In'. In Ryan, A. (ed.).

Honneth, A. (1991) *The Critique of Power: Reflective Stages in a Critical Social Theory*. Translated by Baynes, K. Cambridge, Mass.: MIT Press.

Honneth, A. (1993) 'Critical Theory in Germany Today: An Interview'. *Radical Philosophy* 65: 33–41.

Honneth, A. and Joas, H. (1988) *Social Action and Human Nature*. Cambridge: Cambridge University Press.

Honneth, A. and Joas, H. (eds) (1991) *Communicative Action: Essays on Jürgen Habermas's 'The Theory of Communicative Action'*. Translated by Gains, J. and Jones, D. L. Cambridge, Mass.: MIT Press.

Honneth, A., McCarthy, M., Offe, C. and Wellmer, A. (eds) (1992) *Cultural-Political Interventions in the Unfinished Project of Enlightenment*. Cambridge, Mass.: MIT Press.

Horkheimer, M. (1993) *Between Philosophy and Social Science: Selected Early Writings*. Translated by Hunter, G. F., Kramer, M. S. and Torpey, J. Cambridge, Mass.: MIT Press.

Houtkoop-Steenstra, H. (1993) 'Opening Sequences in Dutch Telephone Conversations'. In Boden, D. and Zimmerman, D. H. (eds).

Hoy, D. C. (1986a) 'Power, Repression, Progress: Foucault, Lukes, and the Frankfurt School'. In Hoy, D. C. (ed.).

Hoy, D. C. (ed.) (1986b) *Foucault: A Critical Reader*. Oxford: Blackwell.

Hoy, D. C. and McCarthy, T. (1994) *Critical Theory*. Oxford: Blackwell.

Hughes, E. (1971) *The Sociological Eye: Selected Papers*. Chicago: Aldine-Atherton.

Hughes, S. H. (1979) *Consciousness and Society: The Reorientation of European Social Thought 1890–1930*. Brighton: Harvester.

Humm, M. (ed.) (1992) *Feminisms: A Reader*. London: Harvester Wheatsheaf.

Jaggar, A. (1983) *Feminist Politics and Human Nature*. London: Harvester.

James, W. (1890) *Principles of Psychology*. 2 volumes. New York: Holt.

Jameson, F. (1992) *Postmodernism, or, The Cultural Logic of Late Capitalism*. London: Verso.

Jay, M. (1973) *The Dialectical Imagination: A History of the Frankfurt School and the Institute of Social Research 1923–1950*. London: Heinemann.

Joas, H. (1985) *G. H. Mead: A Contemporary Re-Examination of his Thought*. Translated by Meyer, R. Cambridge: Polity.

Joas, H. (1993) *Pragmatism and Social Theory*. Chicago: University of Chicago Press.

Johnson, L. C. (1990) 'Socialist Feminisms'. In Gunew, S. (ed.).

Johnson, P. (1993) 'Feminism and the Enlightenment'. *Radical Philosophy* 63: 3–12.

Johnson, T., Dandeker, C. and Ashworth, C. (1984) *The Structure of Social Theory: Dilemmas and Strategies*. London: Macmillan.

Jones, C. (1992) 'Reason without Emotion'. *Radical Philosophy* 61: 32–33.

Jones, C. and Porter, R. (eds) (1994) *Reassessing Foucault: Power, Medicine and the Body*. London: Routledge.

Kamuf, P. (ed.) (1991) *A Derrida Reader: Between the Blinds*. London: Harvester Wheatsheaf.

Kaplan, E. A. and Sprinker, M. (eds) (1993) *The Althusserian Legacy*. London: Verso.

Keat, R. and Urry, J. (1975) *Social Theory as Science*. London: Routledge & Kegan Paul.

Kellner, D. (1993) 'Popular Culture and the Construction of Postmodern Identities'. In Lash, S. and Friedman, J. (eds).

Kellner, D. (ed.) (1994) *Baudrillard: A Critical Reader*. Oxford: Blackwell.

Kelly, M. (ed.) (1994) *Critique and Power: Recasting the Foucault/Habermas Debate*. Cambridge, Mass.: MIT Press.

Kinnaird, J. K. (1983) 'Mary Astell: Inspired by Ideas'. In Spender, D. (ed.).

Knorr-Cetina, K. (1981) 'The Micro-Sociological Challenge of Macro-Sociology: Towards a Reconstruction of Social Theory and Methodology'. In Knorr-Cetina, K. and Cicourel, A. (eds).

Knorr-Cetina, K. and Cicourel, A. (eds) (1981) *Advances in Social Theory and Methodology: Towards an Integration of Micro and Macro Theories*. London: Routledge & Kegan Paul.

Kolakowski, L. (1978a) *Main Currents of Marxism, Volume 1*. Oxford: Oxford University Press.

Kolakowski, L. (1978b) *Main Currents of Marxism, Volume 2*. Oxford: Oxford University Press.

Kortian, G. (1980) *Metacritique: The Philosophical Argument of Jürgen Habermas*. Translated by Raffan, J. Cambridge: Cambridge University Press.

Kroker, A. and Cook, D. (1988) *The Postmodern Scene: Excremental Culture and Hyper-Aesthetics*. London: Macmillan.

Kurtz, L. (1984) *Evaluating Chicago Sociology: A Guide to the Literature with an Annotated Bibliography*. Chicago: Chicago University Press.

Laclau, E. and Mouffe, C. (1990) *Hegemony and Socialist Strategy: Towards a Radical Democratic Politics*. Third impression. London: Verso.

Landry, D. and MacLean, G. (1993) *Materialist Feminisms*. Oxford: Blackwell.

Larrabee, M. J. (ed.) (1993) *An Ethic of Care: Feminist and Interdisciplinary Perspectives*. London: Routledge.

Lash, S. (1990) *The Sociology of Postmodernism*. London: Routledge.

Lash, S. (1993) 'Pierre Bourdieu: Cultural Economy and Social Change'. In Calhoun, C., LiPuma, E. and Postone, M. (eds).

Lash, S. and Friedman, J. (eds) (1993) *Modernity and Identity*. Oxford: Blackwell.

Lash, S. and Urry, J. (1987) *The End of Organized Capitalism*. Cambridge: Polity.

Lash, S. and Urry, J. (1994) *Economies of Signs and Space*. London: Sage.

Lash, S. and Whimster, S. (eds) (1987) *Max Weber, Rationality and Modernity*. London: Allen & Unwin.

Laslett, P. and Runciman, W. G. (eds) (1967) *Philosophy, Politics and Society*. Oxford: Oxford University Press.

Lawler, S. (1995) 'Mothering the Self: A Study of the Mother–Daughter Relationship'. Unpublished Ph.D. Centre for Women's Studies, Department of Sociology, University of Lancaster.

Layder, D. (1987) 'Key Issues in Structuration Theory: Some Critical Remarks'. *Current Perspectives in Social Theory* 8: 25–46.

Leeds Revolutionary Feminist Group (1982) 'Political Lesbianism: The Case against Heterosexuality'. In Evans, M. (ed.).

Lemert, C. (1979) 'De-Centred Analysis: Ethnomethodology and Structuralism'. *Theory and Society* 7: 289–306.

Lemert, C. (ed.) (1993) *Social Theory: The Multicultural and Classic Readings*. Oxford: Westview.

Lévi-Strauss, C. (1963) *Structural Anthropology*. New York: Basic Books.

Lewis, J. D. and Smith, R. L. (1980) *American Sociology and Pragmatism: Mead, Chicago Sociology and Symbolic Interactionism*. Chicago: University of Chicago Press.

Lincourt, J. M. and Hare, P. H. (1973) 'Neglected American Philosophers in the History of Symbolic Interactionism'. Reprinted in Plummer, K. (ed.) (1991a).

Lindsay, A. D. (1967) 'Hegel the German Idealist'. In Hearnshaw, F. J. C. (ed.).

Lockwood, D. (1976) 'Social Integration and System Integration'. In Zollschan, G. K. and Hirsch, W. (eds).

Lofland, J. (1976) *Doing Social Life*. New York: Wiley.

Lovell, T. (ed.) (1990) *British Feminist Thought: A Reader*. Oxford: Blackwell.

Löwith, K. (1993) *Max Weber and Karl Marx*. New edn. Preface by Turner, B. S. Edited with an introduction by Bottomore, T. and Outhwaite, W. London: Routledge.

Luhmann, N. (1982) *The Differentiation of Society*. Translated by Holmes, S. and Larmore, C. New York: Columbia University Press.

Luhmann, N. (1986) 'The Individuality of the Individual'. In Heller, T., Sosna, M. and Wellbery, D. with Davidson, A., Swidler, A. and Watt, I. (eds).

Luhmann, N. (1993) *Risk: A Sociological Theory*. Translated by Barrett, R. New York: Walter de Gruyter.

Lukács, G. (1971) *History and Class Consciousness: Studies in Marxist Dialectics*. Originally published in 1923. London: Merlin.

Lukes, S. (1967) 'Alienation and Anomie'. In Laslett, P. and Runciman, W. G. (eds).

Lukes, S. (1973) 'Methodological Individualism Reconsidered'. In Ryan, A. (ed.).

Lukes, S. (1981) *Emile Durkheim: His Life and Work: A Historical and Critical Study*. Harmondsworth: Penguin.

Lukes, S. (1985) *Marxism and Morality*. Oxford: Oxford University Press.

Lyman, S. (1991) *Militarism, Imperialism and Racial Accommodation: An Analysis and Interpretation of the Early Writings of Robert E. Park*. Fayetteville, Ark.: University of Arkansas Press.

Lyon, D. (1994) *The Electronic Eye: The Rise of Surveillance Society*. Cambridge: Polity.

Lyotard, J. F. (1984) *The Postmodern Condition: A Report on Knowledge*. Translated by Bennington, G. and Massumi, B. Foreword by Jameson, F. Manchester: Manchester University Press.

Lyotard, J. F. (1993) 'Answering the Question: What is Postmodernism?' In Docherty, T. (ed.).

McCarthy, T. (1984) *The Critical Theory of Jürgen Habermas*. Cambridge: Polity.

McCarthy, T. (1991) 'Complexity and Democracy: Or the Seducements of Systems Theory'. In Honneth, A. and Joas, H. (eds).

McHugh, P. (1974) 'On the Failure of Positivism'. In Douglas, J. D. (ed.).

McHugh, P., Raffel, S., Foss, D. C. and Blum, A. F. (1974) *On the Beginning of Social Inquiry*. London: Routledge & Kegan Paul.

MacIntyre, A. (1973) 'The Idea of a Social Science'. In Ryan, A. (ed.)

MacIntyre, A. (1985) *After Virtue: A Study in Moral Theory*. 2nd edn. London: Duckworth.

MacKinnon, C. (1988) 'Desire and Power: A Feminist Perspective'. In Nelson, C. and Grossberg, L. (eds).

McLellan, D. and Sayers, S. (eds) (1990) *Socialism and Morality*. London: Macmillan.

McLennan, G. (1995) *Pluralism*. Buckingham: Open University Press.

McNay, L. (1994) *Foucault: A Critical Introduction*. Cambridge: Polity.

McPhail, C. and Rexroat, C. (1979) 'Mead vs. Blumer: The Divergent Methodological Perspectives of Social Behaviourism and Symbolic Interactionism'. Reprinted in Plummer, K. (ed.) (1991a).

Mannheim, K. (1952) *Essays on the Sociology of Knowledge*. Translated and edited by Kecskemeti, P. New York: Oxford University Press.

Manning, P. (1992) *Erving Goffman and Modern Sociology*. Cambridge: Polity.

Marcuse, H. (1966) *Eros and Civilization: A Philosophical Inquiry into Freud*. 2nd edn. Boston, Mass.: Beacon.

Marcuse, H. (1968a) *One Dimensional Man: The Ideology of Industrial Society*. London: Sphere.

Marcuse, H. (1968b) *Negations: Essays in Critical Theory*. Boston, Mass.: Beacon.

Marcuse, H. (1969) *Reason and Revolution: Hegel and the Rise of Social Theory*. London: Routledge & Kegan Paul.

Marshall, B. L. (1994) *Engendering Modernity: Feminism, Social Theory and Social Change*. Cambridge: Polity.

Martin, J. R. (1994) 'Methodological Essentialism, False Difference, and Other Dangerous Traps'. *Signs* 19(3): 630–657.

Martin, L. H., Gutman, H. and Hutton, P. H. (eds) (1988) *Technologies of the Self: A Seminar with Michel Foucault*. London: Tavistock.

Marx, K. (1961) *The Poverty of Philosophy*. Originally published in 1847. Edited by Arthur, C. J. London: Lawrence & Wishart.

Marx, K. (1964) *The German Ideology*. London: Lawrence & Wishart.

Marx, K. (1980) 'The Eighteenth Brumaire of Louis Bonaparte'. In Marx, K. and Engels, F.

Marx, K. (1981) *Economic and Philosophical Manuscripts of 1844*. London: Lawrence & Wishart.

Marx, K. (1983) *Capital: A Critique of Political Economy. Volume 1: The Process of Production of Capital*. Edited by Engels, F. Translated by Moore, S. and Aveling, E. English edition first published in 1887. London: Lawrence & Wishart.

Marx, K. and Engels, F. (1953) *Selected Correspondence: 1843–1895*. London: Lawrence & Wishart.

Marx, K. and Engels, F. (1970) *The German Ideology*. London: Lawrence & Wishart.

Marx, K. and Engels, F. (1980) *Selected Works in One Volume*. London: Lawrence & Wishart.

Mayer, T. (1994) *Analytical Marxism*. London: Sage.

Maynard, D. W. and Clayman, S. E. (1991) 'The Diversity of Ethnomethodology'. *Annual Review of Sociology* 17: 385–418.

Mead, G. H. (1910) 'What Social Objects Must Psychology Presuppose?' Reprinted in Reck, A. J. (ed.).

Mead, G. H. (1930) 'Cooley's Contribution to American Social Thought'. Reprinted in Plummer, K. (ed.) (1991a).

Meltzer, B. N. and Petras, J. W. (1973) 'The Chicago and Iowa Schools of Symbolic Interactionism'. In Shibutani, T. (ed.).

Meltzer, B. N., Petras, J. W. and Reynolds, L. T. (1975) *Symbolic Interactionism: Genesis, Varieties and Criticism*. London: Routledge & Kegan Paul.

Mennell, S. (1975) 'Ethnomethodology and the New *Methodenstreit*'. *Acta Sociologica* 18(4): 287–302.

Mennell, S. (1992) *Norbert Elias: An Introduction*. Oxford: Blackwell.

Merton, R. (1968) *Social Theory and Social Structure*. New York: Free Press.

Meštrović, S. (1992) *The Coming Fin de Siècle: An Application of Durkheim's Sociology to Modernity and Postmodernity*. London: Routledge.

Meštrović, S. (1993) *The Barbarian Temperament: Towards a Critical Postmodern Theory*. London: Routledge.

Milband, R. (1990) 'Class Analysis'. In Giddens, A. and Turner, J. (eds).

Millett, K. (1969) *Sexual Politics*. New York: Avon.

Millett, K. (1992) 'Beyond Politics? Children and Sexuality'. In Vance, C. S. (ed.).

Mills, C. W. (1970) *The Sociological Imagination*. Originally published in 1959. Harmondsworth: Penguin.

Mitchell, J. (1966) 'Women: The Longest Revolution'. *New Left Review* 40: 11–37.

Mitchell, J. (1974) *Woman's Estate*. Harmondsworth: Penguin.

Mitchell, J. (1986) 'Reflections on Twenty Years of Feminism'. In Mitchell, J. and Oakley, A. (eds).

Mitchell, J. and Oakley, A. (eds) (1986) *What is Feminism?* Oxford: Blackwell.

Moi, T. (1991) 'Appropriating Bourdieu: Feminist Theory and Pierre Bourdieu's Sociology of Culture'. *New Literary History* 22: 1017–1049.

Mommsen, W. J. (1992) *The Political and Social Theory of Max Weber: Collected Essays*. Cambridge: Polity.

Monk, R. (1990) *Ludwig Wittgenstein: The Duty of Genius*. London: Vintage.

Mouzelis, N. (1991) *Back to Sociological Theory: The Construction of Social Orders*. London: Macmillan.

Mouzelis, N. (1995) *Sociological Theory: What Went Wrong? Diagnoses and Remedies*. London: Routledge.

Mullan, B. (1987) *Sociologists on Sociology: Interviews with Contemporary Sociologists*. London: Croom Helm.

Murgatroyd, L. (1989) 'Only Half the Story: Some Blinkering Effects of 'Malestream" Sociology'. In Held, D. and Thompson, J. B. (eds).

Nelson, C. and Grossberg, L. (eds) (1988) *Marxism and the Interpretation of Culture*. London: Macmillan.

Nisbet, R. (1970) *The Sociological Tradition*. London: Heinemann.

Norris, C. (1987) *Derrida*. London: Fontana.

Norris, C. (1996) *Reclaiming Truth: Contribution to a Critique of Cultural Relativism*. London: Lawrence & Wishart.

Nuyen, A. T. (1990) 'Truth, Method, and Objectivity: Husserl and Gadamer on Scientific Method'. *Philosophy of the Social Sciences* 20(4): 437–452.

Oakley, A. (1972) *Sex, Gender and Society*. London: Maurice Temple Smith.

Oakley, A. (1974) *The Sociology of Housework*. Oxford: Martin Robertson.

Oakley, A. and Mitchell, J. (eds) (1976) *The Rights and Wrongs of Women*. Harmondsworth: Penguin.

O'Connor, J. (1987) *The Meaning of Crisis: A Theoretical Introduction*. Oxford: Blackwell.

Offe, C. (1985) *Disorganized Capitalism*. Edited by Keane, J. Cambridge: Polity.

Okin, S, M. (1980) *Women in Western Political Thought*. London: Virago.

Ollman, B. (1979) *Social and Sexual Revolution: Essays on Marx and Reich*. London: Pluto.

O'Neill, J. (1995) *The Poverty of Postmodernism*. London: Routledge.

Ortner, S. B. (1982) 'Is Female to Male as Nature is to Culture?' In Evans, M. (ed.).

Osborn, R. (1937) *Freud and Marx: A Dialectical Study*. Introduction by Strachey, J. London: Gollancz.

Outhwaite, W. (1975) *Understanding Social Life: The Method Called 'Verstehen'*. London: Allen & Unwin.

Outhwaite, W. (1994) *Habermas*. Cambridge: Polity.

Paci, E. (1972) *The Function of the Sciences and the Meanings of Man*. Translated by Piccone, P. and Hansen, J. Evanston, Ill.: Northwestern University Press.

Park, R. E. (1936) 'Human Ecology'. *American Journal of Sociology* 42: 1–15.

Park, R. E. (1972) *The Crowd and the Public and Other Essays*. Edited by Elsner, H. Translated by Elsner, C. Chicago: University of Chicago Press.

Parsons, T. (1937) *The Structure of Social Action*. New York: McGraw-Hill.

Parsons, T. (1951) *The Social System*. New York: Free Press.

Parsons, T. (1965) 'An Outline of the Social System'. In Parsons, T., Shils, E., Naegele, K. D. and Pitts, J. R. (eds).

Parsons, T., Shils, E., Naegele, K. D. and Pitts, J. R. (eds) (1965) *Theories of Society: Foundations of Modern Sociological Theory*. New York: Free Press.

Pearce, F. (1989) *The Radical Durkheim*. London: Unwin Hyman.

Petras, J. W. (1968) 'Psychological Antecedents of Sociological Theory in America: Williams James and James Mark Baldwin'. Reprinted in Plummer, K. (ed.) (1991a).

Plamenatz, J. (1963) *Man and Society: Volume 1: A Critical Examination of Some Important Social and Political Theories from Machiavelli to Marx*. London: Longman.

Plummer, K. (ed.) (1991a) *Symbolic Interactionism, Volume 1: Foundations and History*. Aldershot: Edward Elgar.

Plummer, K. (ed.) (1991b) *Symbolic Interactionism, Volume 2: Contemporary Issues*. Aldershot: Edward Elgar.

Pollner, M. (1991) 'Left of Ethnomethodology: The Rise and Decline of Radical Reflexivity'. *American Sociological Review* 56(3): 370–380.

Poulantzas, N. (1978) *State, Power, Socialism*. Translated by Camiller, P. London: New Left Books.

Ramazanoglu, C. (1990) *Feminism and the Contradictions of Oppression*. London: Routledge.

Ramazanoglu, C. (ed.) (1993) *Up against Foucault: Explorations of some Tensions between Foucault and Feminism*. London: Routledge.

Rattansi, A. (1994) ' "Western" Racisms, Ethnicities and Identities in a "Postmodern" Frame'. In Rattansi, A. and Westwood, S. (eds).

Rattansi, A. and Westwood, S. (1994a) 'Modern Racisms, Racialized Identities'. In Rattansi, A. and Westwood, S. (eds).

Rattansi, A. and Westwood, S. (eds) (1994b) *Racism, Modernity and Identity on the Western Front*. Cambridge: Polity.

Rawls, A. W. (1987) 'The Interaction Order *Sui Generis*: Goffman's Contribution to Social Theory. *Sociological Theory* 5(2): 136–149.

Ray, L. and Reed, M. (eds) (1994) *Organizing Modernity: New Weberian Perspectives on Work, Organization and Society*. London: Routledge.

Reck, A. J. (ed.) (1964) *Selected Writings: George Herbert Mead*. Chicago: University of Chicago Press.

Rex, J. (1961) *Key Problems of Sociological Theory*. London: Routledge & Kegan Paul.

Rich, A. (1980) 'Compulsory Heterosexuality and Lesbian Existence'. *Signs: Journal of Women in Culture and Society* 5(4): 631–660.

Ricoeur, P. (1982) *Hermeneutics and the Human Sciences*. Edited and translated by Thompson, J. B. Cambridge: Cambridge University Press.

Risseeuw, C. (1991) 'Bourdieu, Power and Resistance: Gender Transformation in Sri Lanka'. In Davis, K., Leijenaar, M. and Oldersma, J. (eds).

Robbins, D. (1991) *The Work of Pierre Bourdieu: Recognizing Society*. Milton Keynes: Open University Press.

Robertson, R. and Turner, B. S. (eds) (1991) *Talcott Parsons: Theorist of Modernity*. London: Sage.

Rocher, G. (1974) *Talcott Parsons and American Sociology*. Translated by Mennell, B. and Mennell, S. London: Thomas Nelson.

Rock, P. (1979) *The Making of Symbolic Interactionism*. London: Macmillan.

Rogers, K. M. (ed.) (1979) *Before Their Time: Six Women Writers of the Eighteenth Century*. New York: Frederick Unger.

Rogers, M. F. (1977) 'Goffman on Power'. *American Sociologist* 12(April): 88–95.

Rogers, M. F. (1983) *Sociology, Ethnomethodology, and Experience: A Phenomenological Critique*. Cambridge: Cambridge University Press.

Rogers, M. F. (1984) 'Everyday Life as Text'. In Collins, R. (ed.).

Rorty, R. (1982) *Consequences of Pragmatism: Essays 1972–1980*. Minneapolis, Minn.: University of Minneapolis Press.

Rorty, R. (1989) *Contingency, Irony and Solidarity*. Cambridge: Cambridge University Press.

Rorty, R. (1993) 'Cosmopolitanism without Emancipation: A Response to Lyotard'. In Lash, S. and Friedman, J. (eds).

Rose, A. (ed.) (1972) *Human Behaviour and Social Processes: An Interactionist Approach*. London: Routledge & Kegan Paul.

Rose, J. (1990) 'Femininity and its Discontents'. In Lovell, T. (ed.).

Ross, D. (1991) *The Origins of American Social Science*. Cambridge: Cambridge University Press.

Rowbotham, S. (1973) *Woman's Consciousness, Man's World*. Harmondsworth: Penguin.

Rowland, R. and Klein, R. D. (1990) 'Radical Feminism: Critique and Construct'. In Gunew, S. (ed.).

Rubinstein, D. (1981) *Marx and Wittgenstein: Social Praxis and Social Explanation*. London: Routledge & Kegan Paul.

Runciman, W. G. (1973) 'What is Structuralism?' In Ryan, A. (ed.).

Russell, B. (1955) *History of Western Philosophy and its Connection with Political and Social Circumstances from the Earliest Times to the Present Day*. Fifth impression. London: Allen & Unwin.

Ryan, A. (ed.) (1973) *The Philosophy of Social Explanation*. Oxford: Oxford University Press.

Ryan, A. (1986) *Property and Political Theory*. Oxford: Blackwell.

Sacks, H. (1963) 'Sociological Description'. *Berkeley Journal of Sociology* 8: 1–16.

Sacks, H. (1972) 'An Initial Investigation of the Usability of Conversational Data for Doing Sociology'. In Sudnow, D. (ed.).

Sartre, J.-P. (1960) *Critique of Dialectic Reason*. London: New Left Books.

Sarup, M. (1993) *An Introductory Guide to Post-Structuralism and Postmodernism*. 2nd edn. London: Harvester Wheatsheaf.

Sayer, A. (1992) *Method in Social Science: A Realist Approach*. 2nd edn. London: Routledge.

Sayer, D. (1991) *Capitalism and Modernity: An Excursus on Marx and Weber*. London: Routledge.

Sayers, S. (1989) 'Knowledge as Social Phenomenon'. *Radical Philosophy* 52: 34–37.

Schmidt, E. P. (ed.) (1937) *Man and Society*. New York: Prentice Hall.

Schroeder, R. (1992) *Max Weber and the Sociology of Culture*. London: Sage.

Schutz, A. (1972) *The Phenomenology of the Social World*. Originally published in 1932. Translated by Walsh, G. and Lehnert, F. Introduction by Walsh, G. London: Heinemann.

Schutz, A. (1979) 'Concept and Theory Formation in the Social Sciences'. In Bynner, J. and Stribley, K. (eds).

Schwartz, J. (1990) 'Antihumanism in the Humanities'. *Public Interest* 99: 29–44.

Sciulli, D. (1985) 'The Practical Groundwork of Critical Theory: Bringing Parsons to Habermas (and vice versa)'. In Alexander, J. (ed.).

Segal, L. (1987) *Is the Future Female? Troubled Thoughts on Contemporary Feminism*. London: Virago.

Seidman, S. (1994a) 'The End of Sociological Theory'. In Seidman, S. (ed.) (1994c).

Seidman, S. (1994b) *Contested Knowledge: Social Theory in the Postmodern Era*. Oxford: Blackwell.

Seidman, S. (ed.) (1994c) *The Postmodern Turn: New Perspectives on Social Theory*. Cambridge: Cambridge University Press.

Seidman, S. and Wagner, D. (eds) (1992) *Postmodernism and Social Theory*. Oxford: Blackwell.

Sharrock, W. and Anderson, B. (1986) *The Ethnomethodologists*. London: Tavistock.

Sharrock, W. and Anderson, B. (1991) 'Epistemology: Professional Scepticism'. In Button, G. (ed.).

Shibutani, T. (ed.) (1973) *Human Nature and Collective Behaviour: Papers in Honor of Herbert Blumer*. New Brunswick, NJ: Transaction.

Shilling, C. (1993) *The Body and Social Theory*. London: Sage.

Shott, S. (1987) 'Emotion and Social Life: A Symbolic Interactionist Analysis'. Reprinted in Plummer, K. (ed.) (1991b).

Shotter, J. (1993) *Cultural Politics of Everyday Life: Social Constructionism, Rhetoric and Knowing of the Third Kind*. Buckingham: Open University Press.

Simons, H. W. and Billig, M. (eds) (1994) *After Postmodernism: Reconstructing Ideology Critique*. London: Sage.

Simons, J. (1995) *Foucault and the Political*. London: Routledge.

Singer, P. (1983) *Hegel*. Oxford: Oxford University Press.

Skinner, Q. (ed.) (1991) *The Return of Grand Theory in the Human Sciences*. Cambridge: Cambridge University Press.

Slater, D. (1994) 'Exploring Other Zones of the Postmodern: Problems of Ethnocentrism and Difference across the North–South Divide'. In Rattansi, A. and Westwood, S. (eds).

Smart, B. (1990) 'Modernity, Postmodernity and the Present'. In Turner, B. S. (ed.).

Smith, C. W. (1983) 'A Case Study of Structuration: The Pure-Bred Beef Business'. *Journal for the Theory of Social Behaviour* 13: 4–18.

Smith, D. E. (1974) 'Theorizing as Ideology'. In Turner, R. (ed.).

Smith, D. E. (1987) *The Everyday World as Problematic: A Feminist Sociology*. Milton Keynes: Open University Press.

Smith, D. E. (1993) *Texts, Facts and Femininity: Exploring the Relations of Ruling*. London: Routledge.

Smith, N. (1993) 'Putting Practice into Theory: A Review Essay'. *Radical Philosophy* 63: 42–44.

Soper, K. (1993) 'Productive Contradictions'. In Ramazanoglu, C. (ed.).

Spencer, H. (1969) *Herbert Spencer*. Edited with an introduction by Low-Beer, A. London: Macmillan.

Spender, D. (1980) *Man-Made Language*. London: Routledge & Kegan Paul.

Spender, D. (ed.) (1983) *Feminist Theorists: Three Centuries of Women's Intellectual Traditions*. London: Women's Press.

Spender, D. (1983) *Women of Ideas (and what men have done to them)*. London: Ark.

Spybey, T. (1995) *Globalization and World Society*. Cambridge: Polity.

Stinchcombe, A. L. (1990) 'Milieu and Structure Updated: A Critique of the Theory of Structuration'. In Clark, J., Modgil, C. and Modgil, S. (eds).

Strasser, S. (1985) *Understanding and Explanation: Basic Ideas Concerning the Humanity of the Human Sciences*. Pittsburgh, Pa: Duquesne University Press.

Strauss, A. (1978) *Negotiations, Varieties, Contexts, Processes and Social Order*. San Francisco: Jossey Bass.

Strauss, A. (1982) 'Interorganizational Negotiation'. Reprinted in Plummer, K. (ed.) (1991b).

Stryker, S. (1980) *Symbolic Interactionism: A Social Structural Version*. Menlo Park, Calif.: Benjamin/Cummings.

Sudnow, D. (ed.) (1972) *Studies in Social Interaction*. New York: Free Press.

Sydie, R. (1987) *Natural Women, Cultured Men: A Feminist Perspective on Sociological Theory*. Milton Keynes: Open University Press.

Tannen, D. (ed.) (1993) *Gender and Conversational Interaction*. New York: Oxford University Press.

Taylor, C. (1981) 'Understanding in Human Science'. *Review of Metaphysics* 34: 25–38.

Taylor, C. and Montefiore, A. (1980) 'From an Analytical Perspective'. An introductory essay in Kortian, G.

Thomas, W. I. and Thomas, D. S. (1928) *The Child in America: Behavior Problems and Programs*. New York: Knopf.

Thomas, W. I. and Znaniecki, F. (1918–19) *The Polish Peasant in Europe and America*. 5 volumes. Boston, Mass.: Badger.

Thompson, J. B. (1981) *Critical Hermeneutics: A Study in the Thought of Paul Ricoeur and Jürgen Habermas*. Cambridge: Cambridge University Press.

Thompson, J. B. (1984) *Studies in the Theory of Ideology*. Cambridge: Polity.

Thorne, B., Kramerae, C. and Henley, N. (eds) (1983) *Language, Gender and Society*. Rowley, Mass.: Newbury House.

Tiryakian, E. A. (1979) 'Emile Durkheim'. In Bottomore, T. and Nisbet, R. (eds).

Tong, R. (1989) *Feminist Thought: A Comprehensive Introduction*. London: Unwin Hyman.

Toynbee, A. (1954) *A Study of History: Volume 9*. London: Oxford University Press.

Turner, B. S. (1981) *For Weber: Essays on the Sociology of Fate*. London: Routledge & Kegan Paul.

Turner, B. S. (ed.) (1990) *Theories of Modernity and Postmodernity*. London: Sage.

Turner, B. S. and Robertson, R. (1991) 'How to Read Parsons'. In Robertson, R. and Turner, B. S. (eds).

Turner, J. H. (1974) 'Parsons as a Symbolic Interactionist: A Comparison of Action and Interaction Theory'. Reprinted in Plummer, K. (ed.) (1991a).

Turner, R. (1974a) 'Words, Utterances and Activities'. In Turner, R. (ed.).

Turner, R. (ed.) (1974b) *Ethnomethodology*. Harmondsworth: Penguin.

Vance, C. S. (ed.) (1992) *Pleasure and Danger: Exploring Female Sexuality*. London: Pandora.

Visker, R. (1995) *Michel Foucault: Genealogy as Critique*. Translated by Turner, C. London: Verso.

Wacquant, L. (1992) 'The Structure and Logic of Bourdieu's Sociology'. In Bourdieu, P. and Wacquant, L.

Wacquant, L. (1993) 'Bourdieu in America: Notes on the Transatlantic Importation of Social Theory'. In Calhoun, C., LiPuma, E. and Postone, M. (eds).

Walby, S. (1986) *Patriarchy at Work: Patriarchal and Capitalist Relations in Employment*. Cambridge: Polity.

Walby, S. (1990) *Theorizing Patriarchy*. Cambridge: Polity.

Wallerstein, I. (1990) 'World-Systems Analysis'. In Giddens, A. and Turner, J. (eds).

Warren, M. (1992) 'Max Weber's Nietzschean Conception of Power'. *History of the Human Sciences* 5(3): 19–37.

Weber, M. (1949) *The Methodology of the Social Sciences*. Edited by Shils, E. and Finch, H. Glencoe, Ill.: Free Press.

Weber, M. (1985) *The Protestant Ethic and the Spirit of Capitalism*. Originally published in 1930. London: Unwin.

Webster, F. (1995) *Theories of the Information Society*. London: Routledge.

Weedon, C. (1987) *Feminist Practice and Poststructuralist Theory*. Oxford: Blackwell.

Weinbaum, B. (1978) *The Curious Courtship of Women's Liberation and Socialism*. Boston, Mass.: South End Press.

Weinstein, D. and Weinstein, M. (1991) 'Georg Simmel: Sociological Flâneur Bricoleur'. In Featherstone, M. (ed.).

West, C. and Zimmerman, D. H. (1983) 'Small Insults: A Study of Interruptions in Cross-Sex Conversations with Unacquainted Persons'. In Thorne, B., Kramerae, C. and Henley, N. (eds).

White, S. (1990) *The Recent Work of Jürgen Habermas: Reason, Justice and Modernity*. Cambridge: Cambridge University Press.

Wieder, D. L. (1974) 'On Meaning by Rule'. In Douglas, J. D. (ed.).

Wiggershaus, R. (1995) *The Frankfurt School: Its History, Theories and Political Significance*. Translated by Robertson, M. Cambridge: Polity.

Williams, M. and May, T. (1996) *Introduction to the Philosophy of Social Research*. London: UCL Press.

Williams, Raymond (1961) *Culture and Society: 1780–1950*. Harmondsworth: Penguin.

Williams, Robin (1980) 'Goffman's Sociology of Talk'. In Ditton, J. (ed.).

Williams, Robin (1988) 'Understanding Goffman's Methods'. In Drew, P. and Wootton, A. (eds).

Wilson, B. (ed.) (1970) *Rationality*. Oxford: Blackwell.

Wilson, E. (1990) 'Psychoanalysis: Psychic Law and Order?' In Lovell, T. (ed.).

Winch, P. (1990) *The Idea of a Social Science and its Relation to Philosophy*. 2nd edn. Originally published in 1958. London: Routledge.

Wolff, K. H. (1979) 'Phenomenology and Sociology'. In Bottomore, T. and Nisbet, R. (eds).

Wolffensperger, J. (1991) 'Engendered Structure: Giddens and the Conceptualisation of Gender'. In Davis, K., Leijenaar, M. and Oldersma, J. (eds).

Wollstonecraft, M. (1989) *A Vindication of the Rights of Women*. Originally published in 1792. Buffalo, NY: Prometheus.

Wright, E. O. (1989) 'Models of Historical Trajectory: An Assessment of Giddens's Critique of Marxism'. In Held, D. and Thompson, J. B. (eds).

Zimmerman, D. H. and Wieder, D. L. (1974) 'Ethnomethodology and the Problem of Order: Comments on Denzin'. In Douglas, J. D. (ed.).

Zollschan, G. K. and Hirsch, W. (eds) (1976) *Social Change: Explorations, Diagnoses and Conjectures*. New York: Wiley.

Index

SOCIAL RESEARCH
ISSUES, METHODS AND PROCESS

Tim May

... a wide ranging introductory text ... provides a thorough coverage of official statistics, questionnaires, interviewing, documentary research and comparative research.

Journal of Social Policy

The book provides a good theoretical and practical grounding.

Journal of the Institute of Health Education

The aim of this book is to bridge the gap between theory and methods in social research. It is written in a clear, accessible style and will equip students with an in-depth understanding of the subject. The book has been carefully designed with the reader in mind and is divided into two parts. Part 1 examines the issues and Part 2, the methods used in social research. The topics covered in Part 1 include:

- perspectives which help students understand the aims and practice of social research – positivism, idealism, critical research and feminisms
- the relationship between theory and data
- the place of values and ethics in the research process

These important issues are then directly linked to Part 2 of the book which includes chapters on:

- official statistics
- the use and design of questionnaires
- the method of participant observation
- successful documentary research
- methods and process of interviewing
- comparative research

Each of the methods chapters follows a common structure to promote an understanding of the place, process and analysis of social research methods. Complete with questions at the end of chapters, it will enable the reader not just to engage in empirical work, but to have the confidence and ability to reflect upon research practice and be aware of the various methods available for data analysis. Whilst it is specifically designed as a complete course of study for sociology and social policy students, it will also be of value to those who wish to reconsider or clarify the relationship between current social, political and theoretical issues in general and the practice of research in particular.

Contents
Introduction – Part I: Issues in social research – Perspectives on research – Social theory and social research – Values and ethics in the research process – Part II: Methods of social research – Official statistics as a research source – The use and design of questionnaires – Interviewing: methods and process – The method of participant observation – Documentary research – Comparative research: potential and problems – Bibliography – Indexes.

208pp   0 335 19054 5 (Paperback)

PROBATION: POLITICS, POLICY AND PRACTICE
Tim May

This book is about change. It is about the effect of changes in the criminal justice system and society in general upon the organization and everyday work of the probation service in England and Wales. These changes include a collapse of confidence in the treatment or rehabilitation model of probation work, and the actions of a Conservative Government determined to create a punitive correctional service in the community.

Tim May traces paradigm, political and organizational changes; explores how they are interpreted and implemented in probation service policy; and analyzes the effects of policy shifts and how they are perceived by probation staff. He moves from the general to the specific: from the nature of these changes to an examination of their consequences within one probation service which, for the purposes of anonymity, is called 'Treen'. He also analyzes the work of probation personnel in different work settings; and considers the appropriateness of the recent administrative changes in relation to the everyday realities of probation work. He weaves the political and theoretical issues into a substantial and fascinating empirical study, and provides us with a well-grounded overview of the probation service today.

Contents
Introduction – Part I: The historical and political context – An evolving organization and occupation – Change and conflict – Part II: Policy and practice – Implementing policy change – Accountability, autonomy and changing roles – At the front line – In prisons – Looking back: conflicts in modes of working – Postscript: looking forward – Appendix: research design – Notes – Bibliography – Index.

224pp   0 335 09377 9 (Paperback)